Le paysan parvenu: or, the fortunate peasant. Being memoirs of the life of Mr. -- Translated from the French of M. de Marivaux.

Pierre Carlet de Chamblain de Marivaux

ECCO
PRINT EDITIONS

Eighteenth Century
Collections Online
Print Editions

Gale ECCO Print Editions

Relive history with *Eighteenth Century Collections Online*, now available in print for the independent historian and collector. This series includes the most significant English-language and foreign-language works printed in Great Britain during the eighteenth century, and is organized in seven different subject areas including literature and language; medicine, science, and technology; and religion and philosophy. The collection also includes thousands of important works from the Americas.

The eighteenth century has been called "The Age of Enlightenment." It was a period of rapid advance in print culture and publishing, in world exploration, and in the rapid growth of science and technology – all of which had a profound impact on the political and cultural landscape. At the end of the century the American Revolution, French Revolution and Industrial Revolution, perhaps three of the most significant events in modern history, set in motion developments that eventually dominated world political, economic, and social life.

In a groundbreaking effort, Gale initiated a revolution of its own: digitization of epic proportions to preserve these invaluable works in the largest online archive of its kind. Contributions from major world libraries constitute over 175,000 original printed works. Scanned images of the actual pages, rather than transcriptions, recreate the works *as they first appeared.*

Now for the first time, these high-quality digital scans of original works are available via print-on-demand, making them readily accessible to libraries, students, independent scholars, and readers of all ages.

For our initial release we have created seven robust collections to form one the world's most comprehensive catalogs of 18th century works.

Initial Gale ECCO Print Editions collections include:

History and Geography
Rich in titles on English life and social history, this collection spans the world as it was known to eighteenth-century historians and explorers. Titles include a wealth of travel accounts and diaries, histories of nations from throughout the world, and maps and charts of a world that was still being discovered. Students of the War of American Independence will find fascinating accounts from the British side of conflict.

Social Science

Delve into what it was like to live during the eighteenth century by reading the first-hand accounts of everyday people, including city dwellers and farmers, businessmen and bankers, artisans and merchants, artists and their patrons, politicians and their constituents. Original texts make the American, French, and Industrial revolutions vividly contemporary.

Medicine, Science and Technology

Medical theory and practice of the 1700s developed rapidly, as is evidenced by the extensive collection, which includes descriptions of diseases, their conditions, and treatments. Books on science and technology, agriculture, military technology, natural philosophy, even cookbooks, are all contained here.

Literature and Language

Western literary study flows out of eighteenth-century works by Alexander Pope, Daniel Defoe, Henry Fielding, Frances Burney, Denis Diderot, Johann Gottfried Herder, Johann Wolfgang von Goethe, and others. Experience the birth of the modern novel, or compare the development of language using dictionaries and grammar discourses.

Religion and Philosophy

The Age of Enlightenment profoundly enriched religious and philosophical understanding and continues to influence present-day thinking. Works collected here include masterpieces by David Hume, Immanuel Kant, and Jean-Jacques Rousseau, as well as religious sermons and moral debates on the issues of the day, such as the slave trade. The Age of Reason saw conflict between Protestantism and Catholicism transformed into one between faith and logic -- a debate that continues in the twenty-first century.

Law and Reference

This collection reveals the history of English common law and Empire law in a vastly changing world of British expansion. Dominating the legal field is the *Commentaries of the Law of England* by Sir William Blackstone, which first appeared in 1765. Reference works such as almanacs and catalogues continue to educate us by revealing the day-to-day workings of society.

Fine Arts

The eighteenth-century fascination with Greek and Roman antiquity followed the systematic excavation of the ruins at Pompeii and Herculaneum in southern Italy; and after 1750 a neoclassical style dominated all artistic fields. The titles here trace developments in mostly English-language works on painting, sculpture, architecture, music, theater, and other disciplines. Instructional works on musical instruments, catalogs of art objects, comic operas, and more are also included.

biblioLife
old books. new life.

The BiblioLife Network

This project was made possible in part by the BiblioLife Network (BLN), a project aimed at addressing some of the huge challenges facing book preservationists around the world. The BLN includes libraries, library networks, archives, subject matter experts, online communities and library service providers. We believe every book ever published should be available as a high-quality print reproduction; printed on-demand anywhere in the world. This insures the ongoing accessibility of the content and helps generate sustainable revenue for the libraries and organizations that work to preserve these important materials.

The following book is in the "public domain" and represents an authentic reproduction of the text as printed by the original publisher. While we have attempted to accurately maintain the integrity of the original work, there are sometimes problems with the original work or the micro-film from which the books were digitized. This can result in minor errors in reproduction. Possible imperfections include missing and blurred pages, poor pictures, markings and other reproduction issues beyond our control. Because this work is culturally important, we have made it available as part of our commitment to protecting, preserving, and promoting the world's literature.

GUIDE TO FOLD-OUTS MAPS and OVERSIZED IMAGES

The book you are reading was digitized from microfilm captured over the past thirty to forty years. Years after the creation of the original microfilm, the book was converted to digital files and made available in an online database.

In an online database, page images do not need to conform to the size restrictions found in a printed book. When converting these images back into a printed bound book, the page sizes are standardized in ways that maintain the detail of the original. For large images, such as fold-out maps, the original page image is split into two or more pages

Guidelines used to determine how to split the page image follows:

- Some images are split vertically; large images require vertical and horizontal splits.
- For horizontal splits, the content is split left to right.
- For vertical splits, the content is split from top to bottom.
- For both vertical and horizontal splits, the image is processed from top left to bottom right.

Le Payſan Parvenu:

OR, THE

FORTUNATE

PEASANT.

BEING

MEMOIRS

OF

The LIFE of Mr. ——

Tranſlated from

The *French* of M. DE MARIVAUX.

LONDON:

Printed for JOHN BRINDLEY, at the *King's-Arms* in *New Bond-ſtreet*; CHARLES CORBETT, at *Addiſon*'s Head, and RICHARD WELLINGTON, at the *Dolphin* and *Crown*, both without *Temple-Bar*.

M.DCC.XXXV.

THE

Fortunate PEASANT.

THE Title which I have prefixed to my Memoirs, acquaints you with my Birth; it's a Truth which I never dif-sembled to any who ask'd me the Queſtion, and Heaven feems to have taken a pleaſure in recompencing my Sincerity; for I never obferv'd on any Occaſion, that I was either leſs regarded, or leſs eſteem'd on that Account.

Notwithſtanding I have met with a great many impertinent People, who neither poffefs'd, nor would acknowledge any other Merit in the World, than that of being born Noble, or of a genteel Stock, and have often heard them defpife Men incomparably their Superiors in Worth, only becauſe they were not Gentlemen; the Reafon of which is, becauſe thofe whom they thus infulted, and who were otherwife to be refpeſted for a thouſand good Qualities, had themfelves the weakneſs to bluſh at their Extraction, to hide it, and by a mean Diffimulation to endeavour to fcreen themfelves, from the Contempt of the World.

B

But

But this Artifice feldom or never fucceeds; they may conceal a truth of this Nature which way they pleafe, fooner or later it's certain to rife up in Judgment againft them, and to revenge itfelf of the Falfities in which they difguis'd it. A Man is betray'd by an infinite Number of little concurring Accidents, which it's impoffible either to avoid, or forefee: I never obferv'd a Vanity of this kind come to a good End.

Befides it's an Error to imagine that an obfcure Birth debafes us, when we ourfelves avow it, and are the firft who proclaim it. The Malice of Mankind drops you there, you rob it of its Reward, its fole Aim was to humble you, you fupplant its Pretenfions; you humble yourfelf, it has nothing left to fay.

Men have fomething of Modefty in fpite of themfelves; a Retort to an undeferv'd Scorn will always pleafe, Reafon compels them to approve it; it's a Fortitude which filences them, by fhewing them the very Root of Nobility; in fhort, it's a fenfible Pride, which can never fail putting to Shame an impertinent Vanity.

But enough has been faid on this Subject; thofe whom my Reflection concerns will find it their Advantage to believe me.

It's cuftomary in writing a Book, to begin with a little Preamble, I have comply'd with the Mode, and now return to my felf.

The Story of my Adventures won't be unufeful to thofe who love to inform themfelves, which is one Reafon why I make them publick; the other is I love to amufe my felf.

I live in a Country Place, to which I've made my Retreat, and where the leifure I enjoy infpires

fpires me with that Spirit of Reflection which I'm going to exercife upon the Events of my own Life. I fhall give a detail of them in the beft Manner I can ; every Man has his peculiar turn of Expreffion, which proceeds from his peculiar Way of Thinking.

Among the Adventures which I'm about to relate, I believe fome will be thought curious ; and in Favour of them, I hope my Stile will find Excufe this I dare affure the Reader, that the Facts are all really true, it's not a Hiftory forg'd for Diverfion, which I imagine will eafily be difcern'd.

As for my Name, I fupprefs it : Nor can my concealing it be thought amifs ; fince my telling it would only lay a Reftraint upon my Narrations.

There are fome Perfons who I'm fenfible will know me, but I've too good an Opinion of their Difcretions, to think them capable of making a wrong Ufe of the Difcovery. To begin.

I was born at a Village in the Country, and be it remember'd by the Way, it's to the Wine of my Country that I owe the rife of my Fortune.

My Father was Farmer to his Patron, a Man extreamly rich, (I fpeak of the Patron) and one who wanted nothing but a Title to make him a Gentleman.

His Poffeffions he deriv'd from his Bufinefs, and had ally'd himfelf to feveral Noble Families, by the Marriages of two of his Sons, one of which had betaken himfelf to the Gown, and the other to the Sword.

Both Father and Sons liv'd in a very grand Manner ; they had affum'd the Name of *Terres* ;

and

and to ſpeak Truth, I believe had hardly any Remembrance of their own, or themſelves either.

Their Original was bury'd under a heap of immenſe Riches, tho' every body knew it, yet nobody ſpoke of it; for the Greatneſs of their Alliances had ſo entirely dazzel'd the Imaginations of People, that they now paſs'd undiſtinguiſh'd among the moſt honourable both in Court and City. The Pride of Men is nothing at the bottom but an odd Compoſition of Prejudice: it ſeems ſenſible itſelf of the Weakneſs of its own Foundation.

This was their Situation when I came into the World. The Manner which my Father farm'd, and which was purchas'd by them, was chiefly conſiderable for the Wine which it produc'd in large Quantities

This Wine was the moſt exquiſite in the Country, and it was my eldeſt Brother who convey'd it to our Maſter at *Paris*; for there were three Children of us, two Boys and a Girl, but I was the youngeſt of all.

My Brother, in one of his Journeys to *Paris*, fell in Love with a Victualler's Widow, who was pretty rich, her Heart prov'd no difficult Conqueſt: in ſhort, ſhe marry'd him with his Inheritance, that is to ſay with nothing.

But his Children have had great Occaſion ſince that I ſhould own them for my Nephews; for their Father, who is ſtill living, and at preſent actually with me, having carry'd on the Buſineſs of a Victualler, had the Mortification in ten Years time, to ſee his Family entirely ruin'd by the Extravagance of his Wife.

As

As for his Sons, my Affiftance has plac'd them in a genteel Situation, and they are now happily eftablifh'd ; but for all that, I have made them ungrateful, and by nothing but only reproaching them with a little two much Pride.

In fhort, they have chang'd their Names, and hold no farther Correfpondence with their Father, whom before they had us'd to vifit pretty often.

But I muft beg leave to enlarge a Word or two more concerning them.

I took notice of their Foppery the laft time they came to fee him ; for in their Difcourfe they call'd him Sir ; at which the good Man turn'd fhort, imagining they were fpeaking to fomebody, who was coming in, that he did not fee.

No, no, Brother, cry'd I, there's nobody coming in ; it's to you they addrefs themfelves : to me ! faid he, and why in that manner ? What my Sons, don't you know me ? An't I your Father ? Oh, yes ! faid I, you are their Father as much as you pleafe, but it will be unmannerly to call you fo. What ! reply'd he, is it ill Manners then for a Man to be the Father of his own Children ? The deuce ! What kind of a Fafhion is this pray ?

Becaufe, anfwer'd I, the Word Father is too ungenteel and too grofs; it's a Term made ufe of by none but your little underling fort of People ; but amongft Perfons of Diftinction, fuch as the young Gentlemen your Sons, they always fupprefs in their Difcourfe thefe trifling Relations of Nature, and inftead of clownifhly crying, Father ! like your Boors and Mechanicks, they fay, Sir ! which founds more like Quality.

My

My Nephews colour'd, and were very much out of Countenance at my Criticifms upon their Impertinence, but their Father was in a downright Paffion, not fuch a one indeed as became a Sir; for his was the Anger of a real Father, and a real Victualler.

Here if you pleafe we'll difmifs my Nephews, they have made me wander a little from my Story; and fo much the better; for it's proper I fhould accuftom my Readers betimes to my Digreffions; I am not very pofitive whether I fhall be guilty of many, perhaps I may, and perhaps I may not; I can anfwer for neither; only this I am refolv'd, not to confine my felf: I am to give you a Relation of my Life, and if I intermix any thing elfe, it fhall be nothing but what naturally prefents itfelf without my feeking.

I have already inform'd you that it was my eldeft Brother who us'd to convoy to our Mafters, the Wine of the Mannor committed to my Father's Care.

But his marrying having engaged him to fettle at *Paris*, I fucceeded him in his Poft of being Convoy to the Wine.

I was then between eig'teen and nineteen Years of Age; People were pleafed to tell me I was a handfome Youth, I mean by it, fuch a fort of Handfomenefs as a Peafant can be imagined to have, whofe Face is continually expos'd to the Mercy of the Weather, and the Fatigues of Husbandry. But fetting that afide, I believe I really had a pretty good Afpect; you may alfo add, that I had fomething I don't know what, of Franknefs in my Countenance, and withal a

brisk

brisk Eye, which befpoke a little Wit, and perhaps was not altogether miftaken.

It was therefore the Year after my Brother's
Wedding, that I arriv'd at *Paris*, with my
Convoy, and honeft ruftick Behaviour.

I was tranfported to find my felf in fuch a po-
pulous City; but whatever I faw, rather diverted
than furpriz'd me; and what they call'd the great
World, feem'd very engaging to me.

I met with a very welcome Reception at our
Mafter's Houfe, and was a Favourite with all
the Servants in a trice; for I delivered my Opinion bluntly upon every thing which offer'd itfelf; and my Sentiments being generally accompany'd with a good Country Meaning, made
them take a Pleafure in asking me Queftions.

Nothing but *Jacob* was talk'd of, for the firft
five or fix Days that I was amongft them. My
Miftrefs had alfo a defire to fee me, upon the Report which her Women had given of me.

She was a Woman who pafs'd her Life in all
the Gaieties of the *Beau Monde*, fhe went to
every fine Show, fupp'd abroad, retired to Bed
at four a Clock in the Morning, rofe again at
one in the Afternoon, had her Levy of Lovers,
whom fhe receiv'd at her Toilette, read over their
Billet-Doux, and then let them be draggled all
the Houfe over, read them who would; but
there was no body took notice of this, for her
Women found nothing at all ftrange in it, nor
was her Husband at all fcandaliz'd at it. They
feem'd to look upon it as one of the unavoidable
Appendages of Matrimony. As for Madam,
fhe was not reckon'd a Coquet at home, nor indeed was fhe; for fhe was one without Reflecti-

on,

on, or without knowing that she was so ; and a Woman will never own that she is a Coquet, when she herself is ignorant that she is one, and lives in her Coquetry with the same Ease and Unconcern, as if she led the most decent and regular Life imaginable.

Such was our Mistress, and this kind of Life was as familiar to her as eating and drinking ; in short it was a little Libertinism, but the most harmless in the World.

In calling it a little Libertinism, I think I have given it its proper Title ; for though it was entirely free from Design on her Part, and attended with no Reflection, yet it was nevertheless what I have call'd it.

As to the remaining Part of her Character, I never set my Eyes upon a better Woman ; her Behaviour exactly resembled her Countenance, which was a beautiful round.

She was good humour'd and generous, and piqued herself so little upon Formalities, that she was rather familiar with her Servants than otherwise, abridging the Respects of some, and the Reverences of others ; for plain Dealing with her supply'd the Place of Politeness. In short, she was a Character averse to Ceremony. In regard to herself, nobody committed a capital Crime, nor was there any room to dread a Reprimand ; for she would rather endure any thing ill done, than bear the Fatigue of telling you how to do it better. Virtue she lov'd at her Heart, but had no Antipathy to Vice ; for nothing with her was blame-worthy, not even the Malice of those whom she heard slander her Acquaintance. It was impossible to visit her without

Commendations

Commendations or Favours; and I could never obferve that fhe hated any thing, but the Sin, which perhaps fhe detefted as devoutly as any body. As to the reft, fhe was a Friend to all the World, and efpecially to all the Foibles fhe could difcover in it.

Good morrow! my Lad, cry'd fhe, when I addreffed her. Well, and how do'ft like *Paris?* Then turning herfelf to her Women, pofitively, added fhe, this Peafant has a very promifing Mein.

Truly, Madam, anfwer'd I, I have only the very worft in our Village. Go, go, faid fhe, you neither feem to want Wit, nor a good Shape; I would advife you to ftay at *Paris,* you'll come to fomething in time.

As God pleafes, Madam return'd I; but if I have any Merit, I have no Money. Poverty and Merit are but forry Companions.

You are in the right, faid fhe, and laugh'd, but time will remedy that Inconvenience; you fhall ftay here, I intend to place you with my Nephew, who is juft come out of *Provence.* They are going to fend him to the College, and you fhall wait on him.

May God be your recompence, Madam, reply'd I: only pleafe to tell me whether you are refolv'd, that I may write to my Father: I fhall grow fo wife by feeing my young Mafter ftudy, that I dare promife you one Day or other, to have Learning enough to read Mafs to you. Why who knows, Madam? As Chance governs the World, it's often a Man finds himfelf a Bifhop, or a good fat Vicar, without being able to divine how it happen'd.

She

She was mightily diverted with my Difcourfe, and her Gaiety ferv'd only to embolden me; fo that I was not afham'd of any Impertinencies I faid to her, provided they were but pleafant; for notwithftanding my Inexperience, I could remark that they never hurt a Perfon who is not oblig'd to underftand better; on the contrary they do him a fervice, and it's accounted fome Merit, that he has Courage enough to anfwer at all.

This Lad is very diverting, faid fhe, and I am refolv'd to take Care of him; and pray do you take Care of yourfelves, added fhe, turning to her Women; his pleafantry is Matter of Mirth to you now, and you are only taken with his Country Talk; but this Peafant will foon become dangerous. Remember I have forewarn'd you.

Oh, Madam, anfwer'd I, there's no room to wait the Accomplifhment of that; I never can become dangerous, for I am already fo. Thefe are all very handfome Damfels; and nothing polifhes a Man fo much, or makes him fo foon fhake off the Village. I find myfelf a Native of *Paris* the moment I fee them.

How's this, cry'd fhe? Why thou art a perfect Gallant already; and pray for which of them do you declare yourfelf? *Favote's* an agreeable white, added fhe: and Mrs. *Genevieve* a very agreeable brown, cry'd I immediately.

Genevieve blufhed a little at my Expreffion; but it was the Blufh of a tickled Vanity: She alfo hid her Satisfaction at the preference I gave her under a Smile, which however feemed to fay I thank thee, tho' at the fame time it declared, I laugh at nothing but his buffoon Bluntnefs.

It's

It's certain I was not miftaken in my Aim, as you'll find by the Sequel ; my Excurfion had made a fhrewd Wound in her Heart, nor was I backward in following the Advantage : I made no queftion but fhe ought to be pleafed with what I faid ; and from that moment refolved to ob-ferve her narrowly, to know whether I was right or wrong in my Judgment.

We were going to continue the Converfation, which began to fall upon the third of Madam's Women, who was neither brown, nor white, nor of any Colour, but one of thofe indifferent Faces which we fee every where, and take notice of no where.

I was juft endeavouring to avoid giving my Opinion of her, but with fuch an awkard undiffembled Confufion, as fhow'd I meant no Panegyrick, when one of Madam's Admirers entered the Room, and obliged us to retire.

I was mightily pleafed with the Step I had ta-ken in concluding to ftay at *Paris* ; for the few Days I had been there had fet my Heart in a blaze, fo that in an inftant my Head run of no-thing but making my Fortune.

It was neceffary to fend my Father an Ac-count of the Pofture of my Affairs ; but for my part I could not write a Word : However, at laft I bethought myfelf of Mrs. *Genevieve* ; and with-out any farther Deliberation, away I went, to beg the Favour of her to write my Letter.

She was alone when I fpoke to her ; and not only wrote it for me, but did it in the prettieft manner in the World.

What I dictated, fhe found lively and full of Senfe ; fo that fhe only corrected my Phrafe.

Take

Take Care and improve the favourable Opinion my Miſtreſs has conceiv'd of you, ſaid ſhe; I foreſee your Advancement. Oh! Mrs. *Genevieve*, return'd I, if you aſſiſt my Fortune with your Friendſhip, there's not a Man in the World I would change Places with; nor can you doubt it, when I tell you, I love you. How! reply'd ſhe, you love me! pray, what do you mean by that, *Jacob?*

What ſhould I mean, anſwered I, but an honeſt and hearty Affection? Such a one as a young Fellow like me, can't help entertaining for a Damſel ſo charming as you are : I know very well, that I've little to recommend me, being nothing but a poor Peaſant as I am; but, by *Jupiter!* was I a King, you ſhould ſoon ſee which of us two ſhould be a Queen, it could not be me that's certain, therefore it muſt be you : nothing can refute what I have ſaid.

I am very much obliged to thee for harbouring ſuch Thoughts of me, reply'd ſhe in a bantering Manner, and if you was a King indeed, it would deſerve ſome Conſideration. But Mrs. *Genevieve*, ſaid I, there's a great many Men belov'd by handſome Laſſes, though they are not Kings; is there no hopes that one Day or other I may become like one of them?

Why really, anſwer'd ſhe, you are very preſſing Where was it you learn'd to make Love? Troth! ſaid I, you ſhould aſk that Queſtion of your own Merit; I never had any other Schoolmaſter, I only repeat what that has taught me

Juſt then, *Genevieve* being call'd by her Miſtreſs, left me, but with a very pleaſant look, ſaying as ſhe went out, go, *Jacob*, you'll certainly

make

make your Fortune, and I wifh with all my Heart you may.

Many thanks, faid I, paying her at the fame time a Compliment with my Hat, which had more of Affection than Politenefs in it. I recommend my felf to you, Mrs. *Genevieve*, pray don't forget me ! The beft way of making my Fortune will be to compleat my Happinefs. After which I took the Letter, and carry'd it to the Poft-Houfe.

This Conference which came from *Genevieve* had put my Spirits in fuch a gay Situation, that I was grown more diverting than ever.

For an Improvement of which good Humour, I was call'd that very Evening for the Taylor who work'd for the Family, to take my Meafure, and it's impoffible to defcribe how much this little Accident contributed to encourage my Hopes, and enliven my Imagination.

It was to the Goodnefs of my Miftrefs, that I ow'd this Indulgence

Two Days afterwards, I had a compleat Suit brought me, with Linnen, and a Hat, and all the reft of the Appurtenances. A Footman who belong'd to the Family, and had taken a liking to me, curl'd my Hair, which was naturally pretty good ; my Complexion was alfo fomething mended by my ftay at *Paris*, fo that when I was beau'd out, troth ! *Jacob* made a very promifing Figure.

The pleafure which I conceiv'd in feeing my felf fo well garb'd, made my Countenance more lively, and animated it with fomething which look'd like the Dawn of a future good Fortune; at leaft every body foretold one for me, and I made no Queftion of the Truth of their Predictions.

I

I had a great many Compliments paid me upon my good Mein, and whilst I was waiting for my Miſtreſs's becoming viſible, I went to make a trial of my new Attractions upon Mrs. *Genevieve*, whom I really thought very agreeable.

She ſeem'd perfectly ſurpriz'd at the Appearrance I made in my new Array; and for my part I imagin'd my ſelf poſſeſſed with more Wit than uſual; but we had ſcarce began to ſpeak, before I receiv'd on Order from my Miſtreſs to wait upon her.

This obliging Command redoubled my Gratitude; I rather flew than went.

I'm here, Madam! ſaid I, as I entered the Door; I only wiſh I had Wit enough to thank you as I would; but I'll die for your Service if you'll give me leave. It's my Reſolution to be your Slave all the Days of my Life.

It's very well, reply'd ſhe, thou haſt both Senſe and Gratitude, and I'm glad to obſerve them in thee: thy Suit fits the mighty well; thou haſt no longer the Air of a Peaſant. Madam, cry'd I, I have the Air of your eternal humble Servant; and there is nothing I'm ſo proud of.

She then bid me draw nearer to her, that ſhe might examine my Dreſs; it was a plain Suit without Livery. She ask'd me who had curl'd my Hair, and charg'd me to take particular care of it, adding that it was very becoming, and that ſhe would fain have me be a Credit to her Service. As much as you pleaſe, Madam, reply'd I, you don't want Credit; but no Matter, the more the better. It muſt not be forgot, that Madam had juſt plac'd herſelf at her Toilette, and

her

her Diſhabille had ſomething ſo provoking in the Negligence of it, that I could not help ſtanding at full Gaze.

My Temper was not naturally indifferent, it was far from it; and my Miſtreſs had ſuch a bloom in her Features, and ſuch an agreeable Perſon withal, that in ſpight of me my Eyes would run away with my Senſes.

She was immediately aware of it, and burſt out a laughing at the Diſtraction ſhe obſerv'd me in; for my part, when I perceiv'd I was catch'd, I burſt out a laughing too, which the Shame of being detected, and the Pleaſure of ſeeing her, made me half ſilly, and half tender; thus I continued looking at her with a Mixture of both, but ſaid not a word.

In this Manner we had a ſilent Interview of ſome Minutes, which compos'd one of the pleaſanteſt Scenes in the World; when recollecting herſelf, with a careleſs Air, *Jacob*, ſays ſhe, what are you thinking of? why Madam anſwered I, I was thinking that it does me good to ſee you, and that my Maſter has a very fine Lady.

I don't know what Effect this had upon her, but ſhe ſeem'd to me not at all diſpleas'd with the Freedom of my Humour.

The *Dœux Yeux* of a Man of the *Beau Monde*, have nothing of Novelty for a polite Woman; ſhe is us'd to their Expreſſions, which have all the ſame caſt, and are ſo familiar to her, that her Pride conſiders them only as things of courſe, and which are generally nothing but meer Civilities.

But this was not my Caſe; for my Looks had nothing of Gallantry in them, nor had they any

Notion

Notion of a Compliment. I was a Peasant,
Young and pretty Handsome withall, and the
Homage I paid her Charms, proceeded from nothing but the pure Pleasure I took in seeing
them. My Rusticity was void of Dissimulation,
and was only the greatest Flatterer by its not
knowing how to flatter at all.

I had other Eyes, other Looks, and another
sort of Countenance, which all put together gave
me very singular Attractions. I could perceive
my Mistress was a little touch'd with them.

You are very bold for staring at me in this
Manner, said she, laughing all the while; truly
Madam, answer'd I, it's none of my Fault; why
are you so handsome? Get you gone! cry'd she,
with a peremptory tone, but not an angry one,
indeed I believe you'd tell me so, if you durst.
After which she sat down again to her Toilette,
and I went about my Business, still turning my
Head to look at her. Nor was my Action un-
observ'd; for she follow'd me with her Eyes
quite to the Door.

The same Evening she presented me to her
Nephew, and install'd me in his Service. I still
kept up my Interest with *Genevieve*; but the
very Moment I perceiv'd that my Mistress was not
displeas'd with me, my Inclination for *Genevieve*
began to abate of its Fervor, her Heart seem'd no
more a Conquest of Importance, and I no longer thought it an Honour to be in her Favour.

Genevieve's Behaviour was quite different; for
she took a downright liking to me, not only from
the Hopes she had of my future Advancement,
but from a real Prepossession which she had entertain'd for me; and as I was less assiduous in
seeking

feeking after her, fhe was more fo in feeking after me She had not been long come into the Family, and my Mafter had hardly feen her yet.

My Mafter and Miftrefs had each of them their feparate Apartment, whence they would fend in a Morning to enquire after one another's Health, (which was almoft the only Communication they had together) it happen'd one Morning, that my Miftrefs hearing my Mafter was flightly indifpos'd, fent *Genevieve* to know how he did

She met me upon the Stair-cafe as fhe was going, and defir'd me to wait her coming back She ftay'd a long time, but at laft return'd with Eyes full of Coquettery.

You're very merry, Mrs. *Genevieve*, faid I, as foon as I faw her. Oh! reply'd fhe, you can't guefs the Reafon; if I had a Mind, I could make my Fortune.

You muft be very difficult, anfwer'd I, if you have it in your Power, and won't. Oh! faid fhe, but there's a little Stumbling-block in the way, which I can't fo well get over; the Condition of the Obligation is, that I fhould be rather too much at my Mafter's Command, who has juft now been making a Declaration of Love to me.

That's worth juft nothing, faid I, it's in bad Money this Fortune of your's; don't meddle with fuch Merchandife, but e'en keep your own: remember, when a Maid is once fold, I would not give the Buyer a Farthing for his Bargain.

I talked to her in this manner, becaufe I really lov'd her a little at the bottom; and befides I had naturally a Principle of Honour.

You

You are in the right, faid fhe, a little confufed at the Notions I difcovered ; and for the fame
reafon I turned it all into jeft ; why I would not
have any thing to fay to him, if he would give
me all he's worth.

You defended yourfelf like a perfect Heroine,
faid I ; for I did not obferve your Temper much
ruffled when you came from him ; that was, replied
fhe, becaufe I made a jeft of every thing he faid.
But it would not be amifs another time, anfwered
I, to put yourfelf in a little Paffion ; that's a much
fafer way than making a jeft of him, for fear at
laft he fhould make a jeft of you. We don't
always win at play, fometimes we lofe ; and
when we have once loft all, why then all's gone.

As we were upon the Stair-cafe, we thought
proper to drop the Converfation. She returned
to her Miftrefs, and I to my young Mafter, who
was making a Theme, or rather his Tutor was
making it for him, that the Proficience of his
Scholar might turn to his Credit, and that Credit
continue him in his Tutorfhip, which was a
very gainful one.

Genevieve had received her Mafter's Declaration with more Complaifance than fhe told me.

This Mafter of mine was not at all a generous
Man ; but the Wealth which he poffeffed, and
never was born to, had made him vain ; and that
Vanity had made him profufe ; fo that he was
fometimes liberal to an Extravagance, and efpecially in any thing where his Pleafure was con-
cerned.

He had made *Genevieve* a very advantageous
Offer, on Condition fhe would entertain him as a
Gallant, and fhe herfelf own'd to me two Days
                                                    afterwards,

afterwards, that he had carry'd it fo far, as to offer her a Purfe full of Gold; which is certainly the moft dangerous Shape the Devil can take to tempt a young Girl who is a little upon the Coquette, and a little mercenary into the bargain.

Now *Genevieve* had a natural Foible to both thefe venal Picadilles: fo that it was not at all probable, fhe would in earneft make a Jeft of the Courtfhip in Queftion. I never faw her after but fhe was upon the Mufe; the fight of that Gold, and the eafe of making it her own, had entirely turn'd her Head; her Modefty could ftand its ground no longer, but bled like a Coward.

Her Spark (its my Mafter I fpeak of) was not in the leaft difcouraged at receiving a firft Repulfe; he had obferved how much her Virtue was ftaggered: and therefore took care to return to the Attack better armed than he was before; for which purpofe he affembled a Re-inforcement of a thoufand little Fineries, which he forced her to accept without naming why; and let me tell you, Fineries ready bought, and thrown into a Girl's Lap, are to the full as feducing as the Money itfelf which paid for them.

Thus Prefents upon Prefents being given and received, without faying wherefore, at laft it was propofed, that fhe fhould have an Annuity fettled upon her, to which was to be added a pretty private Lodging, which he promifed to take for her, provided fhe would quit her Miftrefs.

I difcovered all the particulars of this ungodly Treaty, by a Letter which *Genevieve* dropped, and which fhe had wrote to one of her Coufins;

who,

who, by what I could learn, had nothing to subsist on but what she got by a Treaty of the same nature, which she had concluded with a rich old Man, who was mentioned in the Letter.

But *Genevieve* had another very singular Temptation, besides the mercenary Spirit which possessed her; and that Temptation was me.

I have already told you, that she had taken a downright liking to me; and for her part she took it for granted that I was deeply smitten by her; though not without frequent Complaints of the Indifference I show'd, in neglecting to see her when I had Opportunities to do it: but that I made ample amends for by the Satisfaction I expressed when I was with her; so that the Result of the whole was, that I really lov'd her, as indeed I did; but then it was in such a manner, as gave me no Disturbance.

This Certainty, and the Fear she was in of losing me, (for neither she nor I had any thing) made her bethink herself, that her Master's Offers, his Money, and the great things he promis'd her, would be a certain means of hastening our Marriage; and that this Fortune, when she was possessed of it, would make me eager in my turn, and cure me of those Qualms of Conscience which I shew'd at first.

In this thought *Genevieve* answered her Master's Caresses with less Rigour than usual, and opened her Hand to receive the Money which he was continually palming upon her.

In such a Juncture, when the first Step is made, the other Foot is already up to second it, and then away at a venture.

The

The poor Girl took all in good part ; she was loaded with Gifts, and had soon enough to buy her a Husband. therefore when she found herself in this comfortable Situation, one Day as we were walking together in the Garden which belong'd to the Houfe : My Mafter still continues to follow me, faid she, flyly, but in fuch an honourable manner, that I can't tell how to be affronted at it As to my felf, I can depend upon my own Difcretion ; but with fubmiffion to thy better Judgment, I really think it might not be amifs, if I was to take the Advantage of his liberal Humour towards me, he knows well enough that his Love fignifies nothing ; for I've told him plainly that he fhan't have his Ends. Why, no matter for that faid he, I only defire you would take fomething to remember me by. Pray accept what I offer you, there fhall be no Obligation on your Side. But hitherto I have always refus'd his Kindnefs, added she, though I believe it was a wrong way of arguing. What fay you ? He's my Mafter, he has taken a Friendfhip for me ; for Friendfhip or Love, you know its all the fame thing, confidering how I return it. He's rich too: Why look you ! it's juft as. if my Miftrefs fhould give me any thing, and I fhould refufe it. Is it not fo ? Prithee fpeak !

Me ! reply'd I, quite fhock'd at the Difpofition I perceiv'd her in, and refolv'd to leave her to the Devil and herfelf; if things are as you fay, why then they're wondrous well. It's certainly ill Manners to refufe what a Miftrefs gives you; fince my Mafter's like a Miftrefs, and fince his Love is nothing but Friendfhip, why that's

ex-

extraordinary well too: For my part, I never had any Notion of this sort of Friendſhip, not I: I thought he lov'd you, as one commonly loves a pretty Wench; but ſince he's ſo modeſt and ſo diſcreet, why you may ev'n venture boldly; only take care you don't ſtumble when he ſtumbles, for Men are waggiſh and apt to be uppermoſt.

Oh! reply'd ſhe, let me alone, I warrant I know how to manage him; and indeed ſhe was in the right on't, for ſhe had not that Leſſon to learn; what ſhe told me was only deſign'd to reconcile me to it by little and little.

I am tranſported, ſaid ſhe, as ſhe was going, that we jump ſo in our Opinions: Farewel, *Jacob.* Your humble Servant, Mrs. *Genevieve,* return'd I, I congratulate you upon the Friend-ſhip of your Lover; he is a mighty honeſt Gen-tleman to be ſo ſmitten with your Perſon, and to hanker ſo little after it: good morrow, till I ſee you again; may Heaven direct you!

I ſaid all this with ſuch a gay Air, as I parted from her, that ſhe was not aware I banter'd her.

Mean time my Maſter's Intrigue with *Gene-vieve* began to take Air in the Family; the waiting Women her Companions murmur'd at it, though more perhaps through Envy than real Reſentment.

Is it not a moſt wicked and audacious thing? ſaid *Toinete* to me, who was the handſome white Girl I ſpoke of. Huſh! anſwer'd I, let's have no Diſturbance, Mrs. *Toinete:* Who knows how things may come round? You have a provoking Face as well as ſhe, and my Maſter has a Hawk's Eye. To Day it is *Genevieve's* turn to be a

Favourite;

Favourite ; perhaps it may be your's to Morrow :
then what fignifies your railing at her at this
rate ? truft me ; a little charitable for your own
fake, if you have none for her.

Toinete was fo nettled at my Anfwer, that fhe
went crying to complain of me to her Miftrefs ;
but fhe apply'd herfelf to the wrong Perfon to
meet with Redrefs. My Miftrefs burft out a laughing at the comical Repetition fhe made of our
Difcourfe ; the turn I had given it was exactly
in her Tafte, nothing could be better adapted to
her Humour.

However fhe learn'd the Infidelity of her Hufband by it ; but that was fo far from being any
Concern to her, that it was merely a Matter of
pleafantry : And art thou pofitive my Husband's
in Love with the Creature ? faid fhe to *Toinete*,
with the Air of a Perfon who wanted to be refolv'd, whether fhe fhould laugh outright or not.
It's very pleafant ; but, *Toinete*, thou art really
handfomer than her, which was all *Toinete* could
get from her, as I guefs'd before hand ; for I was
no ftranger to my Miftrefs's Temper.

Genevieve, who had been deceiv'd by the Air
with which I anfwer'd her Difcourfe concerning
my Mafter's Prefents, and who had already a
plentiful Hoard of them, came now, to fhew
me a part, to accuftom me by degrees to fee the
whole.

At firft fhe conceal'd her Money from me, and
I was only admitted to a fight of fome fine Silks
to make all forts of Habits, with variety of Cam-
bricks for Head-dreffes, and a load of Ribbans of
all Colours ; and that Ribban itfelf is a terrible De-
coyer of pretty young Maids, efpecially waiting Women.   Can

Can any thing be imagin'd more generous?
cry'd she, than his giving me all these and for
no other Reason but because he likes me.

Oh! said I, that's no wonder at all; a Man's
Friendship for a pretty Girl will run much greater
Lengths, he won't stop here depend on't: indeed
reply'd she, I'm inclin'd to think so; for he often asks me if I have not occasion for Money. Aye,
to be sure, said I, you have occasion for it You
want a great many little Toys besides these. Take
all, refuse none, if you can't make use on't, I can;
I'll engage to find a way of laying it out. With
all my heart, cry'd she, quite charm'd with the
Humour she saw me in, and the favourable Pro-
spect it gave her of succeeding in her Designs; I
assure thee, I shall accept it purely upon thy account, and thou shalt certainly have some, perhaps to Morrow; for there's never a day passes
over my head, but he presses it upon me.

She was as good as her Word, and the next
day I had six *Louis d'Ors* at my command, which
with three my Mistress had given me to pay my
writing Master, amounted to nine mighty immense
Pistoles; which I may venture to say was a Trea-
sure to a Man who before had never any thing
better than a few crooked Sous in his Pocket.

I was perhaps to blame for taking *Genevieve*'s
Money, and I think, it was not acting according
to the strict Rules of Honour; for in short, I
amus'd the Girl with a Notion of my loving
her, in which I grosly deceiv'd her. for I had
no longer any Value for her; it's true I still
thought her agreeable, but then it was only the
Opinion of my Eyes, my Heart had no share in
it.

.Besides,

Befides the Money which fhe offer'd me, was Antichriftian, and I knew it was, which made me a kind of Accomplice in all the little Irregularities in Point of Virtue which procur'd it ; at leaft it was encouraging *Genevieve* to trade on at the fame Rate : But I had no fuch refin'd Reflexions at that time of Day, and my principles of honefty were confin'd in a much narrower compafs . However I am in hopes God has forgiven me the unrighteous Gain on't, becaufe I made a very good Ufe of it, and it did me admirable Service ; for I learn'd to write and caft Accounts by the help on't, which was one great ftep towards my Advancement where I am.

The pleafure with which I received this Money, ferv'd only to forward *Genevieve* in pufhing her Defigns ; fhe made no queftion but I would facrifice every thing to the Satisfaction of having a great Deal; and in this perfuafion threw off the mask, and herfelf entirely off her guard.

Follow me, faid fhe, one Morning, I want to fhew you fomething.

I follow'd her accordingly, and fhe led me into her Chamber, where we were no fooner enter'd, but fhe open'd a little trunk quite full of the rewards of her complaifance : In a word, it was top-full of Gold, and undoubtedly the Sum muft have been very confiderable. None but a favourite of the Devil's could have contriv'd to damn herfelf at fuch an expence. Many Women who hold their Heads a vaft deal higher, would jump for joy to make half fo good a Market as this *Abigail.*

I had fome difficulty to conceal the aftonifhment I was in at the fight of this fcandalous

C   Wealth ;

Wealth; but still keeping up the same air of gaiety I had before affected and is all this for me too ? said I , my Chamber is not so well furnish'd as your's and this little trunk will become it to a Miracle.

Oh ! as for this Money, reply'd she, you won't think it amiss if I never dispose of it except in favour of a Husband when I get one. Consider of that a little.

Troth! said I, I can't tell where to get you one at present. I'm acquainted with nobody that wants a Wife. And what do'st mean by giving me such an Answer? reply'd she . what are thy wits gone a Wool-gathering? do'st not understand me then ? I don't ask thee to get me a Husband ; thou may'st be one thyself if thou will; ben't you a branch of the same wood as they're made of ? Pray ! said I, no more of the Wood, nor the Branches neither, they're Words of ill Omen. But as to the rest, continu'd I, not willing to come to a Quarrel, if it stuck at nothing but my being your Husband, I would become so this Instant ; nor should I be afraid of any thing but dying for Joy . Can you make a doubt on't ? is there never a looking Glass here ? Look at yourself, and then tell me your Opinion. See, if you think I should require much time to resolve whether I'd say I will, or I will not, to Mrs. *Génevieve*, you yourself can't imagine it, with your Considers and you. That's not the Difficulty.

Well; and what is it then ? replyed she with an eager and contented Look : Oh ! nothing but a little trifle said I, it's only my Master's Friendship for you, which perhaps may oblige me with

the

the baſtinadoe, if I am too great with his Friend;
I have ſeen ſuch Friendſhips before now, they
have no notion of raillery; and after all, pray
what would you do with a black and blue Husband?

Why, what Maggot has bit you by the Brain
now, cry'd, ſhe? I'll hold a Wager, if my Maſter knew I lik'd you, that he'd be overjoy'd you
ſhould marry me, and that he'd be at the charge
of the Wedding.

That's the leaſt of my Care, ſaid I, for that's
an expence which I can eaſily bear without thank-
ing any body. But in ſhort, I dare not venture
a ſtep father; this Friendly of your's is a perfect
Bug-bear. It's very ſuſpicious that his honourable Affection is nothing but Grimace, and I'm
deſperately afraid that he's no better than a fox in
lamb's Cloathing, who only watches his opportunity to ſnap up the Pullet, and when he
ſees ſuch a little animal as me noſe after her, I
leave you to judge whether he won't baulk the
Scent, and if this hypocrite of a Fox will ſuffer
me ſo much as to touch a Feather!

And is that the only block you ſtumble at, reply'd ſhe? Is that all? You may depend upon't,
ſaid I, Well, well, anſwer'd ſhe, I'll ſet thee eaſy
upon that Saddle, and will convince thee that nobody watches to ſnap the Pullet. But I ſhould
be aſhamed to have any body catch thee here,
we'll part for the preſent; but I'll warrant our
buſineſs done.

Upon this I left her, a little uneaſy how our
adventure might end, and with ſome regret for
having taken any of her Money, for I immediately
gueſſed what biaſs ſhe'd take to come round me:

I expected my Mafter to interfere in the Affair, nor was I miftaken.

The next Day a Footman came with a Meffage, that my Mafter wanted to fpeak with me; accordingly I waited on him, but was very much embaraffed about the Manner of my Appearance. Well, Mr. *Jacob*, fays he, pray how does your young Mafter? Does he ftudy hard? He's feldom idle, S'r, faid I; well, and how does *Paris* agree with you? faid he.

Troth! S'r, anfwer'd I, I eat and drink with as good an Appetite here as any where

I underftand, faid he, that thy Miftrefs has taken thee under her Protection, and I'm very glad of it; but you don't tell me all; I can hear news of you, you're a brisk Spark I affure you, why here you have not been amongft us above two or three Months, and yet you have made a Conqueft already · No fooner in the Warren, than after the pretty Girls, faith, *Genevieve* perfectly doats on thee, I fuppofe there's no love loft between you.

Alas! S'r, faid I, what can the poor Girl have done to deferve my hatred? Oh! faid he, fpeak boldly, you may open your Mind to me. Your Father has been many Years in my Service, and I have always found him fo faithful, that it o'erjoys me to think I've an occafion of fhewing kindnefs to the Son. it's happy for thee, that thou'rt a Favourite with *Genevieve*, and I approve her Choice. Thou'rt young and well-made, and as I'm told, prudent and active; as for her Part, *Genevieve* is a very agreeable Girl. I have a particular value for her Parents, and took her into the Houfe for no other reafon than to have her

near

near me, when any thing offer'd for her Service. Her prepoſſeſſion for thee a little diſconcerts my Meaſures ; for thou haſt nothing, and I intended to have match'd her mo e to her advantage ; but in ſhort ſhe loves thee, and will hear of nobody elſe , why let it be ſo, I think my good Offices may amply ſupply thy deficience, and ſtand thee inſtead of a Patrimony. I have already preſented her with a conſiderable Sum of Money, and will inſtruct thee how to lay it out ; but I'll do more, I'll furniſh you a little Houſe, of which I'll pay the Rent myſelf, and eaſe you of that Burthen, till it better ſuits your convenience to bear it. As to any thing elſe you need not trouble your ſelf, for I dare promiſe to procure you ſome very profitable Poſts. Live well with the Wife I give thee, ſhe's of a very tractable diſpoſition and very modeſt ; but above all, remember that at leaſt one half of what I do in this Affair, muſt be plac'd to thy own Account ; for notwithſtanding the kindneſs which I have for *Genevieve*'s Parents, I ſhould not have went ſo far, if I had not ſtill greater for thee and thine. Before ſpeak nothing of it, thy Miſtreſs's Companions would never let me reſt, but would continually teaze me, to get them Husbands as well as her. I'd have you take leave without much ceremony ; you may ſay you're offer'd a Place of more advantage, and one that ſuits you better. *Genevieve* for her part ſhall pretend the neceſſity of a journey to ſee her Mother, who is very ancient. As ſoon as you're out of the Houſe, you may get married directly. Farewell ; don't ſtay for thanks, I'm a little buſy at preſent, but go and acquaint *Genevieve*

with

with what I've faid to you, and take that little Purfe of Money which lies upon the Table ; it will ferve to bear your Expence at the Tavern, whilft you wait there till *Genevieve* comes to you

I ftood like a Statue during this Difcourfe ; for on one hand the Advantages which he offer'd me were very confiderable.

I faw at my very firft fetting out, that I who had neither any Acquirement, nor any Preferment to recommend me, but was only a poor Peafant, who had no profpect but working all my Days for a livelihood (and even that livelihood in my moft diftant Hopes was nothing in comparifon of the propofal made me) I faw I fay a pretty Settlement juft ready to drop into my Mouth.

And what a fort of Settlement : Why, a Houfe compleatly furnifh'd from top to bottom, a great deal of ready Money, with profitable Pofts which I could infift upon being provided with upon the Spot. In fhort, the protection of a Man in Power, with fuch a Situation as would make me eafy the firft Day, and enrich me after.

Was not this *Adam*'s Apple in a literal Senfe?

I can't fay but I relifh'd the Propofition, the fuddennefs of this Fortune put my Spirits in a flutter ; my Heart beat, and my Eyes fparkled.

To have no trouble but the bare giving one's Hand to be happy, what flattering Temptation ! was it not enough to make a Perfon paffive in point of Honour ?

But on the other fide, this Honour pleaded his Caufe in my Heart, which was in a perfect Uproar, whilft Ambition pleaded his. In Favour

of

of which shall I decide, thought I? I hardly know which to hear.

Said Honour to me, stand your Ground firm, despise the scandalous Advantages they offer thee, they'll all lose their Charms when you have once marry'd *Genevieve*; the remembrance of her Fault will make her insupportable to thee, and though thou art but a poor Peasant, yet since I have got a footing in thy Breast, I shall turn Tyrant, I shall persecute thee all the Days of thy Life; thy Infamy will be spread abroad every where, thy House will become thy Purgatory, and thou and thy Wife will live but a hellish sort of Life; every thing will go to Rack, and depend upon it her Gallant will revenge her Quarrel; for she will always have it in her Power to ruin thee, you won't be the first that has been serv'd so; think well upon that, *Jacob*! the Fortune of thy intended is a Gift of the Devil's, and the Devil was a deceiver from the beginning; he will certainly hook it from thee one Day or other, for the meer pleasure of damning thee by Despair, after having gall'd thee by such a Merchandize.

The Representations of Honour may perhaps be thought a little tedious; but there is a Necessity he should speak a good while; in order to make an Impression, he has more difficulty to persuade than the Passions.

As for Example, Ambition answer'd all this by only a Word or two; but though his Eloquence was so laconick, yet it was very forcible

What the plague Business of thine is it, said he, to concern thy self about that Chimera call'd Honour? Does it not become thee wonderfully to pique thy self about such Punctillioes, wretched

Clown

Clown as thou art? Aye, aye, away with thee and thy Honour to the Hofpital, you will both make an admirable Figure there to be fure.

Not fuch an admirable Figure neither, reply'd I to my felf, its burying Honour to put it in an Hofpital ; I can't fancy it can fhine much there.

But does Honour always bring one thither? Yes, faith, very often ; or if not there, at leaft thereabouts.

But can a Perfon be call'd happy, when he is afham'd of being fo ? or can there be any Satif-faction in living well againft the Grain ? What a Labyrinth I am in !

This was the whole of what crowded itfelf into my Mind in an Inftant, and for an Addition to my Confufion, I could not help now and then cafting an Eye towards the Purfe which lay on the Table, it feem'd exceeding well lin'd, what pity to lofe it !

In the mean time, my Mafter being furpriz'd that I neither gave him any Anfwer, nor made the leaft offer to take the Purfe, which he had laid there to enforce his Difcourfe, ask'd me, what I was thinking on? What have you never a Word to fay, added he ?

Truly, Sir, return'd I, was thinking, and thinking a great deal ; you fhall know what if you pleafe: But you muft excufe my Franknefs: Suppofe I was you, and you me, why then do you fee you would be a poor Man ; but do poor Men love to be Cuckolds ? Yet perhaps you'd be one if I fhould marry you to *Genevieve*. That's all, Sir, this is the Subject I was ruminating on.

How

How is this! cry'd he immediately, is not *Genevieve* a modeſt Girl? very modeſt, reply'd I, as to what concerns the carrying a how d'ye, or dropping a Courteſy; but as to making a Man a good Wife, I muſt acknowledge I have no very ſuperlative Notions of the Modeſty ſhe has for that Purpoſe.

And pray what haſt thou to reproach her with, ſaid he; ha, ha, ha, Sir reply'd I, you know beſt the long and the ſhort of that Affair, you was by, and I was not, but I hope there is no offence in gueſſing. Pardon me, Sir, I only beg to be reſolv'd one Queſtion, which is, whether a Gentleman has any Occaſion for a Chamber-maid? or if he has one, whether ſhe is the proper Perſon to undreſs him? for my part, I always thought otherwiſe.

Oh! upon my Word ſaid he, *Jacob*, you ſpeak very ingenuouſly, I underſtand you; though you are but a Peaſant, I find you don't want Wit. Therefore pray afford me your Attention, to what I am going to ſay in my turn.

All you imagine about *Genevieve* is entirely falſe; but ſuppoſing it true, you have ſeen thoſe Gentlemen who come here to viſit me, they are all Perſons of Conſideration, are very rich, and have great Attendance.

But let me tell you, that there is ſome amongſt them whom it is not neceſſary to name, who owe the riſe of their Grandeur to nothing but their marrying with your *Genevieve*'s.

Now, do you conceit yourſelf a better Man than any of them? or is it the fear of being laugh'd at, which frights you? and who muſt laugh at you? who knows you? or are you a Creature of any

Conſequence

Confequence in Life? Pray, who will trouble
their Heads about your Honour? or will any
body fo much as imagine you have any belonging
to you, wretch as you are? you hazard nothing
but one thing, and that's this, the having as
many envy your Circumftances, as there are
People of your Station acquainted with you. Go,
go my Lad, the Honour of fuch as you, is to
have wherewithal to fubfift, and wherewith to
raife themfelves out of their original Obfcurity.
Do you underftand me? the meaneft of Men in
this World, is he that has nothing in it.

No matter for that, Sir, return'd I, with an
Air half Sorrow and half Mutiny; I had rather
be the meaneft of Men, than the moft unhappy.
The pooreft Beggar can always eat his Bread
with a guft when it is given him, but an unhappy Man has never an Appetite to any thing;
the moft delicate Morfel can yield him no
Comfort, though it was even the Wing of a Par-
tridge. And truly I think a good Appetite worth
keeping, yet I fhould lofe mine for all my good
Cheer, if I fhould marry your Chamber-maid.

Your refolution is taken then? cry'd my Mafter: Troth! yes, Sir, anfwer'd I, I am forry for
it, but what would you have me do? In our
Village we have a Cuftom of marrying none but
Maids, and if there happens to be any Girl who
has been Chamber-maid to a Gentleman, why
fhe muft ev'n content her felf with a Sweet-Heart;
for as for the chance of a Husband, there's no
fuch thing; if it rain'd Husbands, not one would
drop for her; it's a rule amongft us, and efpecially in our Family. My mother was marry'd
a Maid, her Grandmother the fame; and fo
from

from Grandmothers, to great Grandmothers; I am come into the World directly as I tell you, and am oblig'd to make no Alteration in that particular.

I had scarce explain'd my self in this decisive Manner, when frowning upon me with a Countenance full of Fury and Indignation; You are a Rascal, said he, here you have openly pretended Love to *Genevieve* in my House; at first you was ambitious of nothing but the Happiness of marrying her, as she has told me, and the others of my Wife's Women can testify; but now you have the Impudence to accuse her of not being a Girl of Honour: It seems you have got that impertinent Notion in your Head; and consequently I do not question but your Tongue runs accordingly, when you talk of her; you are a Person who have no conduct in your Discourse; and it's me, nothing but my pure good will towards her, that is the Occasion of all your Injustice to her. No, no, Master *Jacob*, I shall take another Course; and since I have troubled my self so far as the being concern'd at all in the Affair, and since you have had Money of her, upon the footing of a Person who was to be her Husband; I shan't allow you to make a Fool of her. I won't leave you at liberty to hurt her, and if you do not marry her, I declare to you, that your next Business shall be with me. Determine your self, I give you four and twenty Hours, chuse either her Hand or a Jail; that is all I have to say to you. Away, be gone you Villian!

This Order and the Epithet which back'd it, frighten'd me so, that I made but one Step to the Door.

Genevieve,

Genevieve, who had been inform'd of the Hour when her Mafter would fend for me, waited my return upon the Stair-cafe.

So, fo, faid fhe, as if our Meeting was accidental, what have you been with my Mafter? what does he want with you?

Softly, Mrs. *Genevieve*, faid I; I have four and twenty Hours before me, to give you an Anfwer, and I fhan't fay a word what I think till the laft Minute.

Upon which, I brufh'd forwards with an Air very grum and a little brutifh, leaving *Genevieve* quite ftupify'd, and with her Eyes upon the full Stretch, as if they feem'd difpos'd for crying; but that ne'er concern'd me; for the alternate of her Hand, or a Jail, had fo effectually rooted out the little kindnefs I had remaining for her, that my Heart was as clean and as trim, as if fhe had never been there; without reckoning the fright I was feiz'd with, and which of itfelf was antidote enough againft Tendernefs.

She call'd me back feveral times with a plaintive Voice: Why *Jacob*? Pray fpeak to me *Jacob!* Four and twenty Hours hence, Mrs. *Genevieve*, cry'd I; and immediately to my Heels, without knowing where I was running; for I was like one loft in a wood.

But at laft I found myfelf in the Garden, with an aking Heart, regretting the honeft brown Bread in the Country, and curfing the Girls at *Paris*, whom they force you to marry with a Piftol at you breaft. I had rather, faid I, to myfelf, buy a Wife at the Broker's. What an unfortunate wretch I am!

The

The Circumſtance I was in made me ſo com-
paſſionate of my ſelf, that I burſt out a crying,
and was juſt turning into a little Grove to vent
my doleful Exclamations, when I met my Miſtreſs coming out with a Book in her Hand.

And what is the Matter with thee, my poor *Jacob!* ſaid ſhe, with thy Eyes bath'd in Tears thus?

Oh Madam, return'd I, throwing my ſelf
at her Feet, oh my good Miſtreſs, your poor
Jacob muſt be haul'd away to Priſon, when the
Clock ſtrikes four and twenty Hours hence.

To Priſon! cry'd ſhe, haſt thou committed
any baſe Crime then? Quite the contrary, anſwer'd
I, it is becauſe I won't commit one. You order'd me to be a Credit to you, you may remember you did, Madam! but how is it poſſible?
How can I get any Credit for you? when they
won't ſo much as let me keep the little I have
for my ſelf. My Maſter ſays he won't ſuffer
me to give my ſelf the Air of having any.
What a deplorable Place is this, Madam! here a
Man muſt be laid by the Heels for ſtanding upon
his Credit; but he that has none to ſtand on,
muſt be entertain'd in the beſt Parlour. Marry a
Gentleman's Chamber-maid, and you ſhall have
Purſes of Money; but take an honeſt Girl, and
they will clap you on a Stone Doublet. This is
my Maſter's notion of the Matter, Madam, who
begging your Pardon, would have me marry his
Chamber-maid.

Prithee explain thy ſelf a little better, ſaid my
Miſtreſs, biting her Lips to contain laughing;
I do not underſtand thee. What is this thou art
raving about a Chamber-maid? Has my Huſband
one then? Yes, he has Madam, ſaid I, he has
your's;

-your's; it is Mrs. *Genevieve* I mean, who haunts me like a Ghoſt, and whom they command me to take to Wife.

Harkee! *Jacob*, ſaid ſhe, I adviſe thee to lay thy Hand upon thy Heart, and conſult that. Why, Madam, anſwer'd I, my Heart and I have been arguing it over already till we are both tir'd, and my Heart abſolutely refuſes to hear a Word more about it.

However it is certain, ſaid ſhe, it would make thy Fortune; my Husband would ſtick cloſe by you, I know he would.

But pray! Madam, ſaid I, for Charity's ſake! conſider a little, how you'd like to have Child'ren call you Father, when you knew in your own Conſcience they ly'd? It's a terrible Story! and yet if I marry *Genevieve*, I'm in danger of having no other ſort of Children than ſuch. I ſhall be oblig'd to provide them Nurſes too, which will break my Heart, and you'll ſoon ſee an End of poor *Jacob*! I have a natural averſion, Madam, to Children that come in at Window, and yet I've only four and twenty Hours to reſolve whether I ſhan't have perhaps a Dozen to my own ſhare. Pity me, Madam! and lend me your Aſſiſtance. This jail they threaten me with diſtracts me, and I fancy it will be moſt adviſable to run away.

No, no, reply'd ſhe, I forbid thy attempting it. I'll ſpeak to my Husband myſelf, and will engage no harm ſhall come to thee. Go, return to thy Buſineſs, and make thyſelf eaſy.

After this diſcourſe ſhe left me, to purſue her Reading; and I went to attend my young Maſter who was not very well.

In

In going back it was impossible for me to avoid passing by *Genevieve*'s room, the door of which I found open, and she herself all in Tears sitting there, and watching for me.

Art thou there then? ungrateful Traytor! cry'd she, as soon as she saw me, thou Villain! Who not content with refusing my Hand, loadest me with Shame and Disgrace. (She had hold of my Sleeve, whilst she apostrophiz'd me in this Manner.)

Speak, added she, what Reason have you to say that I'm not a Girl of Honour?

For God's sake! Mrs. *Genevieve*, said I, give me time to consider. It's neither your being, or not being a Girl of Honour that I hesitate at, it's only your little Trunk full of Gold, and your other fine Gew-gaws, which I really believe would be as much for your Honour to be without. As your Honour was before I lik'd it well enough; but what signifies our talking at this rate? Why should you and I quarrel? Indeed you was to blame! added I with a wheedle; why could not you as well have told me the truth without disguise? There's nothing so engaging as Sincerity: and yet you are a dissembler: Had you acknowledged your little trip, why I should not have took so much Notice; because then one knows not what to trust to, and at least a Woman's oblig'd to a Man, for taking things so civilly, but to force the bit into my Mouth, and to come over me with such round-about Stories! In short it was not using me fair, you ought to have made a generous Confession. Well, *Jacob*, said she, I won't sell you a Pig in a Poke; my Master pursu'd, and I run from him; but at last

he

he threw Money, and fine Cloaths and a Houſe
ready furniſh'd at my Head ; which gave me ſuch
a dizzineſs, that I was forc'd to ſtop, and ſo I
have pick'd up the Money and the fine Cloaths
and the Houſe, will you go my halves ? You find
how I talk to you now ! Reſolve me that, and
then you ſhall hear what I have further to ſay.

Here *Genevieve*'s Tears redoubled and rain'd a
little Ocean, whilſt ſhe graſp'd both my Hands
without ſaying a Word; ſuch difficulty had poor
Truth to find an utterance !

But at laſt, as I was endeavouring to comfort
her, by preſſing her to ſpeak ; if I could but confide in thee ! cry'd ſhe, and why not ? ſaid I ;
come my ſweet Girl, have a good heart' Alas !
anſwer'd ſhe, the Love I bear you, is the occaſion of all this !

That's ſomething very ſurpriſing ! return'd I
immediately ; without that, added ſhe, I could
have deſpis'd all the Gold and all the Fortunes in
the World; but I thought to have ſecur'd thee mine
by the proviſion my Maſter promis'd to make
for us, and that thou would'ſt have been glad to
ſee me rich. But alaſs! how I'm deceiv'd !
now thou reproacheſt me with what I had never
yielded to, but thro' my over-fondneſs for thee.

Her Words were ſo many Arrows which pierc'd
my Heart. I learn'd nothing new from what
ſhe ſaid; for I could eaſily penetrate into the bottom of the Affair, without her telling me; but
for all that, when I heard it acknowledged by
her own Mouth, it appear'd like ſomething perfectly ſtrange to me, I could not help being
thunder-ſtruck as by a ſudden Surprize.

I had already vow'd that I would never concern
my-

myfelf any more about *Genevieve*, and I look'd upon it as an eftablifh'd Refolution ; but undoubtedly I had fome fparks of the old Fire ftill alive in my Heart, or I could not have been fo fhock'd as I was; but it all went out in an inftant.

However, I conceal'd what pafs'd within my Breaft from *Genevieve* : Alas ! faid I, what you tell me is a very unlucky Affair.

How ! *Jacob*, cry'd fhe, with Eyes which implor'd forgivenefs, and which inded were made to obtain it too, is not one fometimes more irreconcileable to a pretty Girl on fuch a fcore than to an ordinary one ? How ! did you only abufe me, when you made me hope that a little Sincerity would fet us right again?

No, faid I, I have fwore to fpeak loyally to you; but I'm of Opinion that my Mind is changd. And why is it chang'd ? my dear *Jacob* ! cry'd fhe ; thou'lt never find a Girl that loves thee fo well as I, and for the future thou may'ft depend upon the Prudence of my Conduct. Why, that's the misfortune, interrupted I, this prudence comes too late, it's like a Phyfician to a dead Patient.

What ! reply'd fhe, muft I lofe thee then ? As to that, faid I, I'll confider on't; but I muft have a little time to fettle with my Heart; at prefent it's upon the Chagrine, and I'm going to ufe it to bear the fatigue. Give me leave to retire, and ponder a while.

You may as well ftab me with a Dagger, faid fhe, as not take your refolution upon the Spot. It's impoffible, anfwer'd I, I can't fo fuddenly know my own Mind; have Patience, you fhall hear my Anfwer prefently, and perhaps good News with it ; yes, yes, prefently, don't be out

of

of humour: adieu, my little Heart! make yourfelf eafy, and may Heaven direct us both.

With this I left her, and fhe faw me part
with fuch a tender regret, that I was really a-
fham'd for not calming it ; but as I cared for nothing but being rid of her, I even march'd to my
Chamber, with a firm refolution to run away, if
my Miftrefs fhould fail in her promife of putting
an End to my Perfecution.

I heard the fame Day, that *Genevieve* was gone
to Bed very ill, and that fhe was feiz'd with violent Pains at her Heart, Accidents related with a
fmile, and which they run to tell me to chufe.
Six or feven of the Servants, and particularly the
waiting Maids, came to whifper it me as a Secret.

As for me, I gave them no Anfwer, I had too
much care upon my Spirits to amufe myfelf with
the chit-chat of any of them, and therefore kept
clofe to my little hole till feven a Clock at
Night.

I counted the Clock, for I lent a very watch-
ful Ear to it, becaufe I defign'd to fpeak to my
Miftrefs, whom a flight indifpofition had hinder'd from going abroad.

Accordingly I was prepraing to wait on her,
when I heard a great buftle in the Houfe; the
Servants run up and down Stairs in a great hurry ; oh my God! what a difmal Accident is this
cry'd one aloud !

This difturbance furpriz'd me, and I went
out of my Chamber to know the meaning of it.

The firft Object I encounter'd, was an old
Valet de Chambre of my Mafter's, who lifted
up his Hands to Heaven, figh'd, wept, and rav'd,
oh ! the miferable Man that I am ! oh the lofs!
oh!

oh ! the Misfortune ! What's the Matter, Mr. *Dubois*, said I ? what has happen'd ?

Alas ! my Lad, said he, my Master's dead, and I have the strongest Inclination in the World to drown my self in the River.

As he was in no danger, I would not stay to dissuade him, for there was no likelihood of his chusing the Water for his Grave, who was a sworn Foe to that Element : It could not be less than thirty Years since the old drunkard had tasted a Drop,

But upon the whole he had good Grounds for his Afliction, for he had lost a very great Benefactor ; he had been Pimp to his Master fifteen Years, and had always been lavishly paid by him, besides what he cheated him of.

Therefore I left him and his Grief together, which was half real and half maudlin (for his Skin was full of Wine when I met him) and run to enquire into the truth of what he told me.

Nothing was more certain than his Report, my Master was taken off by an Apoplectick Fit. It seiz'd him as he was alone in his Closet, so that he had no assistance ; but was found by a Servant setting dead in an Arm-chair, at his Bureau, where lay a few Lines of Gallantry, which, by what one could judge, seem'd intended for some Lady of Pleasure, for I believe there was nobody in the House but read them ; my Mistress took them up in the Closet, but drop'd them again in the Surprize which this terrible Spectacle occasion'd her.

For my part, I must frankly acknowledge, that the suddenness of his Death rather surpriz'd than afflicted me. It's likely I thought it *à propos* ;

— at

at leaſt I ſeem'd to Breath more freerly, and the Deceas'd having threaten'd me with a Jail ſerv'd as an excuſe for the hardneſs of my Heart; his Menace had alarm'd me, and his dying freed me from that uneaſineſs, and added new Motives to my reſentment againſt *Genevieve.*

Alas! poor Girl, nothing but ill luck attended her that Day. She heard the unuſual Diſturbance as well I, and call'd to a Servant as ſhe lay in Bed to enquire the Cauſe.

The fellow ſhe addreſs'd herſelf to, was one of thoſe errant Biutes, or Valets, call them which you pleaſe, who in a Family have no reſpect for anything but their Wages and their Vails, their Maſter is always a Stranger to them, and may die, rot, or flouriſh, for what they care a Farthing; whilſt they're paid they'l ſtay, and ſteal what they can.

Tho' the Deſcription I have given of him, is not very neceſſary to my Story; yet the Picture I have drawn may perhaps be of Service to my Readers, in warning them againſt entertaining any Scoundrel that reſembles him.

This then was the gloomy Animal that came at *Genevieve*'s Call; and being ask'd by her the meaning of the buſtle ſhe heard; why, cry'd he, my Maſter's dead!

The abruptneſs of this News, join'd to her former indiſpoſition, threw *Genevieve* into a Swoon.

Undoubtedly the Fellow did not amuze himſelf much in in aſſiſting her, the little Trunk of Money I have already ſpoke of, and which was ſtill ſtanding on the Table, took up all his Attention, in ſhort, from that moment both he and the

Trunk

Trunk were invifible ; they were never feen afterwards, and in all Appearance went both together.

Other Misfortunes ftill waited us ; the report
of my Mafter's Death was foon noifed abroad ;
nobody was acquainted with his Affairs ; my
Miftrefs had hitherto liv'd in an Affluence of
which fhe knew no Source ; but had enjoy'd in a
perfect Tranquillity

But fhe was cruelly undeceiv'd the next Day ;
a thoufand Creditors crouded in upon her, with
Commiffaries and the reft of their rabble. It was
a moft terrible Diforder.

The Servants grew clamorous for their Wages,
and ftole what they could in waiting till they received them.

The Memory of my Mafter was alfo ill-
treated , feveral made no fcruple to give him the
Epithet of Rafcal. Said one, he has cheated me.
Another, I trufted a great deal of Money in his
hands, what the *D--v--l's* become on't ?

At laft they infulted the Splendor of his Widow ; they preferv'd no Decency even in her
Prefence, and fhe was filent lefs thro' Patience
than Confternation.

This Lady had never known what it was to
be uneafy, and in the forrowful Experience fhe
now had of it, I verily believe, that her Aftonifhment at her Condition fav'd her half her Grief

Imagine to yourfelf a perfon fuddenly ranf-
ported into a frightful Country, of which whatever fhe had feen before, could give her no manner of Idea ; this was exactly her cafe.

As to myfelf, tho' I was neither afflicted at
the Death of her Husband, nor indeed had any
Reafon to be fo ; yet I made ample Amends for
this

this excufable Unconcern, by my Compaffion to
his Wife. I could not fee her weep, without
weeping with her, and methought if I had Mil-
lions, I could have given it her with an unuttera-
ble Sattisfaction ; for fhe was my Benefactrefs.

But of what fervice was it to her, that I was
touch'd with her Misfortunes ? it was the generous
Sympathy of her Friends that fhe ftood in need
of, and not the pity of fuch a poor wretch as
me, who could affift her in nothing.

In this World the Virtues as well as Vices are
difplac'd. Neither good nor bad Hearts are
where they fhould be   Had I been without any
Uneafinefs at my Miftrefs's Condition, fhe would
have loft nothing by it ; my Ingratitude would
only have wrong'd myfelf.   But that of the
Friends fhe had fo often entertain'd, left her
without Relief, and was a real Addition to her
Unhappinefs.

At firft fome of thefe unworthy Friends came
to vifit her ; but when they faw how her Affairs
were embroil'd, and that the Fortune of their
Friend was running to Ruin, they run too, and
without doubt advertiz'd the reft, for they ne
ver came near her

I omit the Purfuit of thefe melancholy Particulars, an account of them would be too tedious.

I ftay'd but three Days in the Houfe ; for all
the Servants were difcharg'd, except one wait
ing Woman, whom my Miftrefs perhaps had
never lov'd fo well as the others , and who
had all her wages owing her at the fame Time,
yet would never confent to leave her.

This

This waiting Woman was she with the indifferent Face that I spoke of, upon whom I endeavour'd to avoid giving my Opinion, and whose Physiognomy appear'd so little promising.

Nature often delights in this kind of Deceit, she buries I know not how many noble Souls under such sort of Faces, nobody's aware of them, and when they once find an Opportunity of shewing themselves, they look like so many Virtues rising from the dead

For my own part, penetrated, as I've told you, with all I saw, I presented myself to my Mistress, and vow'd her an everlast.ng Service, if I could be of any use to her

Alas! poor Lad, said she, the only Answer I can make thee is, that I'm sorry it's not in my power to recompence thy Affection. But thou feest to what I'm fallen, nor can I tell how much lower I have to fall, or whether I shall have any thing left or no, therefore I forbid thy Attachment to me, go and save thy self somewhere else. When I plac'd thee with my Nephew, I intended to have provided for thee; but as Affairs are, I can do nothing. Thy condition is already too trifling, thou must endeavour to mend it; don't be discourag'd; thou hast an honest Heart, which won't go without it's reward.

I persisted, but she would absolutely be obey'd; so that I was forc'd to leave her, and retir'd sheding a flood of tears.

I immediately went to my Chamber to pack up my all, and in going met with my young Master's Tutor, who was marching off with his baggage. His Scholar wept plentifully at bidding
ding

ding him Farewel ; but wept without Company.
I also took leave of the Child, who cry'd with
an Accent which pierced my Heart, what I will
every body leave me then ?

I made no return but by a Sigh, which was
the only answer I had left, and out I sally'd with
my little Booty without saying a Word to any
body. I thought at first to have bid adieu to
Genevieve ; but as I had no longer any Love for
her, but only Pity for her Misconduct, perhaps
it was more generous in the Terms we were
in, not to upbraid her with a sight of me.

My design when I went from my Mistress
was to return directly to my own Village, for I
neither knew where to go, nor what to betake
my self to.

I had no Acquaintance, nor understood any
Business, but that of a Peasant : I knew well
enough how to sow the Ground, to plough it, or
to cut a Vine, and that was all.

It is true, my stay at *Paris* had wore off a
great deal of the rustick Air I brought thither ;
I walk'd with a tolerable good Gait ; held up my
Head pretty well, and cock'd my Hat like a
Fellow that was not altogether a Fool.

In short I had learn'd a little of the Behaviour
of the World (by the World I mean those upon
my own level, who are one) these were all my
Talents, together with that promising Aspect
which Heaven had indulg'd me with, and which
play'd its part with the rest.

As I had not fix'd upon any particular Day for
my Departure from *Paris*, I went in the mean
while to lodge at one of those little Houses,
which in Contempt of their Poverty are call'd
Pack-horse Inns.   **There**

There I ftay'd two Days amongft a groupe of Carriers, who feem'd to me the greateft rufticks I had ever feen, but that was only becaufe I was not fo great a one my felf.

However they gave me a difguft againft the Country. What fignifies my returning thither, faid I to my felf fometimes ? here are numbers of People who live toppingly, and yet had nothing at firft but Providence to truft to, no more than me. Troth! I will even venture to ftay a Day or two longer, and fee what will happen. Who knows what luck I may have? My Expence can't ruin me; I can bear that this Fortnight or three Weeks longer; at the rate I live a little will go a great way. For I was naturally moderate, and was fo without Mortification. When I met with good Cheer, it was a pleafure to me, and when I met with bad, I never re-pin'd, I could conform to any thing.

And let me tell you it is of fingular Advantage for a young Fellow to feek his Fortune with this Temper, he feldom miffes of Succefs; his chance is as good as another's, and his Endeavours reward themfelves. But I have obferv'd that your gluttons fpend half their time in confidering what to eat; they have a fort of habitual Con-cern upon that account, which takes off a great part of their Attention from every thing elfe.

Thus you fee me determin'd to ftay at *Paris,* which was more than I defign'd at firft.

The next Day after my Refolution I began to put it in practice, by going to enquire after the Miftrefs I came from, but was told that fhe was retir'd into a Convent, with the generous Cham-ber-maid I mention'd; and that her Affairs had

D taken

taken fo unfortunate a turn, that fhe had hardly wherewithal to pafs her Life in Obfcurity

This News coft me ftill fome Sighs , for her Memory was very dear to me ; but there was no Remedy, and I could devife no better Courfe for my felf, than going to one Mr. *James*, who was my Countryman, and to whom my Father at my parting from him, had defir'd to be remember'd I had the Direction in my Pocket, but never thought of it till then.

He was Cook in a good Family, and you may imagine me on the March to feek him.

I pafs'd over the New-Bridge, between feven and eight in the Morning, walking very faft, becaufe it was extream cold, and having nothing but my Spark in my Head all the way.

But as I came near the *Cheval de Bronze*, I faw a Woman dreft in a plain Silk Scarf, who lean'd againft the Rails, and cry'd, oh I fhall die !

Hearing thofe Words I went up to her, to fee what Occafion fhe had of Affiftance, Are not you well, Madam ? faid I ; alas! my Lad, reply'd fhe, I can hold out no longer ; I was feiz'd juft now with a violent Dizzinefs, and was forc'd to lean here to fupport my felf.

I examin'd her whilft fhe was fpeaking, and obferv'd fhe had a round Face, which feem'd very delicately plump'd, and by what one could judge at firft fight, was no ftranger to an incarnate, when it was not clouded by any Indifpofition.

As to her Age, the roundnefs of her Face, the clearnefs of her Complexion, and the plumpnefs of her Body, made it impoffible to form any Judgment.

I

I guefs'd her in my own private Opinion, at about forty , but I was miftaken, foi fhe had already feen fifty

The Scarf untrim'd, the plain Head-drefs, the grave fuitable Habit, and the *Je ne fçai quoi*, of Devotion, which was diffus'd throughout, and fupported by the judicious placing of four or five Pins, made me immediately conclude her one of your manag'd Confciences ; for thefe fort of Women have almoft every where the fame mode of Dreffing, it's their diftinguifhing Fafhion ; tho' I muft own it's what I never lik'd.

I can't tell which the reflection properly relates to, whether the Perfons or their Dreffes, but I always think thefe Figures have fomething of a cenforious Aufterity in them, which finds Fault with all the World.

However, as this was a good agreeable Perfon, and had a round Face (which was always my Favourite,) I could not help being concern'd for her, and aiding to fuftain her, Madam, faid I, I won't leave you here ; if you think well of my Service, pleafe to accept my Arm to lead you Home; your dizzinefs may return again, and you'll have occafion for Affiftance. Pray where do you live ?

I live in the Street *de la Monnoye*, my Lad, reply'd fhe ; and I fhan't refufe your Arm, fince you offer it with fuch a good Will. You feem to be a very honeft Youth.

You're not miftaken, Madam, anfwer'd I, as we were fetting foiwards, it is but three or four Months fince I came up out of the Country, and I have not had time to fpoil and grow good for nothing yet.

It's

It's a thoufand pities you ever fhould, faid fhe, giving me at the fame time a benevolent and moft devoutly languifhing Look, you don't feem to be cut out for fuch a Misfortune.

You're in the right, Madam, reply'd I, thank God! he has given me the Grace to be downright and honeft, and to love honeft People.

One may fee it writ in your Face, faid fhe; but you are very young, how old are you? Not twenty yet, reply'd I.

It muft not be forgot, that during this Converfation, we walk'd at an aftonifhing flow Rate; and I was perfectly forc'd to lift her off the Ground, to fave her the trouble of dragging her Legs after her.

Lard! Child, how I fatigue you? faid fhe; no, Madam, anfwer'd I, pray don't let that trouble you, I take delight in paying you this little Service. I fee it, faid fhe, but prithee tell me, dear Lad! what brought thee to *Paris?* What's thy Employment?

At this Queftion it luckily enter'd my Imagination that this Adventure might poffibly turn to my Advantage; for when fhe told me it was a thoufand Pities I fhould ever be fpoil'd, her Eyes accompany'd her Compliment with fo much Bounty and fuch Sweetnefs, that I drew a good Omen from it: I could have no pofitive Affurance what confequences might attend a random Shot; but I was in Hopes of fomething, tho' I could not tell what.

In this Notion, I conceiv'd alfo, that my own Story would be a very good one to tell her, and very feafonable.

Here

Here I had refus'd to marry a handsome
young Girl, whom I really lov'd; and one who
not only lov'd me again, but offer'd to make my
Fortune, and all thro' a Pride and Difguft, which
could have affected none, but a Mind deeply
fenfible of the Impreffions of Honour and Virtue:
Wan't this giving a very advantageous Account of
myfelf? It certainly was, and I went thro' it in
the beft Manner I could, which was an artlefs
one enough, but exactly like telling the Truth.

My Defign fucceeded, for my Hiftory pleas'd
her wonderfully.

Heaven, faid fhe, will reward your upright Way
of Thinking! and you may depend upon't, my
Lad; I fee your Sentiments are conformable to
your Countenance. Oh Madam! interrupted I,
as for my Countenance, I muft be contented
with it as it is; but you fee what humour my
Heart's of.

How ingenuous is that! cry'd fhe with a Smile
full of Kindnefs. Hear me, Child, you have a great
many thanks to return to God, for having given
you fuch an upright Heart; it's a Gift more precious than all the Riches in the World, it's a
Gift for Eternity; but you muft be careful to preferve it; you are without Experience as yet, and
there are innumerable Decoys in *Paris* for fuch
Innocence as your's, and efpecially for one of your
Age. Hear me, it was certainly the Ordination
of Heav'n that I fhould meet with you. I live
with a Sifter whom I love mighty well, and fhe
loves me the fame; we live very retir'd, but thanks
to the divine Goodnefs! entirely at our Eafe, and
have an old Cook-maid, who is an honeft Girl
The Day before yefterday, we turn'd away a

Youth

Youth who difpleas'd us upon our obferving that he was irreligious, and a Libertine; and I went out this Morning, to defire a Friend of our's, a Clergyman, to fend us one he had promis'd us; but it feems, that Servant is in a Family which he won't leave, becaufe of one of his Brothers who is there with him; and now it fhall be your own Fault, if you don't fupply his Place, provided you have any body to give you a Character.

Alas! Madam, faid I, upon that footing it's impoffible for me to benefit by your good Intentions; I'm an utter Stranger here. I was only in the Family I talk'd off, where I did neither good nor harm, my Miftrefs indeed took a liking to me; but at prefent fhe has fhut herfelf up in one of the Convents, I can't tell which · that good Lady and a Cook who lives fomewhere here, and is my Countryman, but no way worthy to introduce me into your Service, are the only recommenders I have, if you pleafe to allow me Time to find out my Miftrefs, I'm fure you'll be fatisfy'd with her Report and as to Mr. *James* the Cook, he'll tell you as much again as I deferve.

I obferve, Child, faid fhe, fuch an Air of Sincerity in what you fay, that I think it ought to ferve you inftead of a Character.

She had hardly done fpeaking, when we came to her Door: Come up, come along with me, faid fhe, I'll talk to my Sifter.

I obey'd, and fhe led me into a Houfe which appear'd compleatly fitted up; the Fafhion and Order of the Furniture was exactly in the fame Tafte as the Habits of your Devotees. Neatnefs, Plainnefs and Propriety was what you faw.

Every

Every Room might be miſtaken for an Orato-
ry; and an inclination for praying naturally ſeiz'd
one at firſt Entrance Every thing was decent and handſome, and ſeem'd to invite the
Mind to the Enjoyment of a Saint-like Meditation.

We found the other Siſter in her Chamber,
reſting her two Hands upon the Arms of an Elbow-chair, where ſhe ſat to repoſe herſelf after
the Fatigue of Breakfaſt ſhe had juſt taken, waiting the benefit of a quiet Digeſtion.

The remains of this Breakfaſt were ſtanding
upon a little Table, it had been compos'd of half
a Bottle of Burgundy, two new-laid Eggs, and
a new Roll.

I fancy the detail of theſe particulars won't be
thought tedious, becauſe it enters into the Character of the Perſon I'm ſpeaking of.

Bleſs me, Siſter ! you've been an Age in returning, I began to be in Pain for you, cry'd ſhe in
the Elbow-chair, to her who was coming in.
What is this the Servant they promis'd to ſend
us ?

No, Siſter, reply'd the other; this is an honeſt young Man whom I met with on the New-
bridge; and but for him I ſhould not have been
here; for I was taken violent ill on the ſudden,
which he perceiving, offer'd me his aſſiſtance to
help me home.

Poſitively, Siſter, ſaid the other, you are continually raiſing Scruples which I can no way approve. Why would you venture to go out ſo
early, and walk ſo far, without eating ſomething?
and all foꞏſooth ! becauſe you hadn't heard Maſs :
Does God require that we ſhould make ourſelves

ſick?

fick? Can't we ferve God without killing ourfelves? Or do you think, you fhall ferve him
ever the better, by deftroying your Health
and making yourfelf incapable of going to
Church at all? Should not we preferve fome
Prudence with our Piety? And is it not our
duty to be careful of our Lives, in order to praife
that God, who is the Author of them, as long
as poffible? You're highly to blame, Sifter, and
you ought to ask Advice upon it.

Indeed, dear Sifter, reply'd the other, I'm already determin'd. I fancy'd my Srength fufficient, tho' I'd really an Inclination to eat a
Morfel before I went ; but then it was fo early
in the Morning, and befides I was timorous
of indulging myfelf too much; for where nothing is hazarded, there can be no great Merit,
but the fame will fcarce happen again, becaufe
I'm convinc'd of the Inconvenience. However,
I believe God has profper'd my little Journey,
fince it has been the Occafion of my light-
ing upon this young Man here; the other is
fix'd in his Place; it's but three Months fince
this came to *Paris*; he has told me his Story,
and I like his Morals extreamly. It's certainly
the ordination of Providence to bring him to us,
he's very fober, and will fuit our Place exactly;
what do you think of him? He has a good promifing look, reply'd the other; but we'll talk
about that, when you've eat fomething; call
Catherine, Sifter, that fhe may bring you what
you're difpos'd to have ; and do you, my Lad,
go down into the Kitchen, you fhall breakfaft
there.

At

At this order I made my Leg, and *Catherine*
being come at the Call, was charg'd with the
care of my Entertainment.

Catherine was tall, but very wan and meagre, and had a fort of crabbed Devotion in her
looks, which feem'd inclining to Choler and
Fury; but undoubtedly that proceeded from the
heat which her brain contracted, by hanging
over her Stows, and her Kitchen-fire, without
remarking, that the brain of a devotee, and efpecially that of a devotee Cook-maid, is natu-
raly dry and fiery.

I won't fay the fame by that of a real pious
Perfon, for there's a wide difference between
true Piety and what one commonly calls Devotion.

Your devotees offend the World, and your
pious People edify it, the firft are only devout
with their Lips, but the others are fo in their
Hearts ; your devotees go to Church meerly for
the fake of going, and for the pleafure of finding
themfelves there, but your pious People to pray
to God ; thefe laft are fincerely humble, whilft
your Devotees would have every one fo but themfelves. The one are the real Servants of God,
but the others are only fo thro' Affectation ; they
pray for the fake of faying, I pray , and carry
their Prayer-books to Church, to fhew how
dexterous they are at-ufing them ; then fquat
down in a Corner, to enjoy the pride of a medi-
tative pofture, where they endeavour to raife
themfelves to a pitch of divine rapture, for no
other Reafon, than to be thought Non-pareils
in Godlinefs, by thofe who happen to catch
them ; or if they feel any Tranfports, they

are

are only fuch as proceed from the vain Defire they have of exciting them, and fuch as the Devil, who never lets them want Means of delufion, takes care to furnifh them with. Then home they go, quite bloated with Self-refpect, and an infolent Compaffion for others; taking it for granted after this, that they have an undoubted Right to unbend their Devotions by a thoufand little Indulgences which ferve to fupport a pamper'd Conftitution.

Thefe are them I call Devotees ; and that none but the Devil can be a gainer by fuch Devotion I think palpable enough.

But in refpect of your truly pious People, they appear amiable even to the wicked themfelves, who can agree with them much better than they can with thofe of their own tribe ; for the greateft Enemy of a wicked Perfon, is he who refembles him moft.

What I've faid, will I hope be fufficient to exempt my Notions of Devotees from any cenfure.

But now let's return to *Catherine*, who is the Occafion of this Digreffion.

Catherine, you muft know, had a large bunch of Keys at her girdle like the Portrefs of a Convent. Bring my Sifter fome new-laid Eggs, fhe has not breakfafted as late as it is, faid Mrs. *Haberd* the Elder ; and take this young Man down into your Kitchen, and let him drink a Cup. A Cup ! reply'd *Catherine*, with a pert but good-humour'd tone, he fhall drink two becaufe of his Shape. And both of them to your Health, Mrs. *Catherine*, faid I. Good ! anfwer'd fhe, fo long as I'm well, they

can

can do me no harm, Come, let's go, you ſhall help me cook my Eggs.

No, let them alone, *Catherine*, ſaid Mrs. *Haberd* the youngeſt ; reach me the Pot of Sweet-Meats, ſome of thoſe ſhall ſuffice . but, Siſter, they don't nouriſh, ſaid the eldeſt: Eggs, ſtuff me up, ſaid the youngeſt , then Siſter this and Siſter that ; but at laſt, *Catherine* with an air which admitited no Appeal, decided in favour of the Eggs as ſhe was going out ; for a Breakfaſt, ſaid ſhe, is not a Deſert.

As for me, I follow'd her down into her Kitchen, where ſhe ſet before me the remains of a laſt Night's Regout, ſome cold fowls, a bottle of Wine almoſt untouch'd, and excellent rolls at diſcretion.

The charming Bread ! I never eat better, nor whiter, nor more ſavoury in my life ; it requires a great deal of Attention to make ſuch, and none but the Hand of a Devotee could have kneaded it ; therefore conſequently it was Mrs. *Catherine*'s.

Oh the delicious Meal that I made ! the very ſight of the Kitchen created me a Stomach, and every thing went down with an admirable Reliſh.

Pray eat, ſaid *Catherine* to me as ſhe was cooking her Eggs, it's God's Will we ſhould live. Here's wherewithall to fulfill his Pleaſure, ſaid I, and I've a ſpecial Appetite into the Bargain. So much the better, reply'd ſhe ; but tell me, are you hir'd ? Do you ſtay amongſt us ? I hope ſo, anſwer'd I, and I ſhall be very ſorry if it happens otherwiſe ; for I fancy one ſhould improve very faſt under your Direction,

Mrs.

Mrs *Catherine*, you have such a winning and such a sensible way with you. Alas reply'd she, I do the best I can, may Heav'n mend us all! every one has his Faults, and I do not pretend to be a Non-such, but the worst is, that Life soon passes, and the farther we go, the more Dust one gathers; for the Devil is always at our Elbow, we are told so by the Church; but resist and he will fly from thee. As to the rest, I shall be very glad if my Mistresses accept you; for I take you to be a very civil Person. Lack-a-day! you are as like poor *Baptist* who dy'd, as one drop of Water is like another. I thought to have marry'd him, he was just such another sweet-temper'd handsome young Man as you; but that is not what I look at, though it is very commendable. God was pleas'd to take him away from us! he's Master, none can controul him; but you are his very Picture, you talk for all the World as he talk'd. Lard! how he doated on me! I am mightily alter'd since then, and must alter for the worst still, yet my Name will always be *Catherine*, though I am not the same I was by a great deal.

Troth! said I, if Master *Baptist* was still living, he could not chuse loving you; you say I resemble him, and for my part, I have no Occasion to look twice for that Purpose. Ay, ay, said she laughing, I am a fine Object truly! pray eat young Man, pray eat, you will judge better when you have a nearer sight of me. I am good for nothing now, but to look after my Salvation, it is a very necessary Work, and what God requires at my Hands.

Saying.

Saying this she took up her Eggs, which I
offer'd to carry up Stairs for her. No, no, said
she, breakfast in quiet, that it may do you the
more good ; I will go, and hear what they say of
you above ; I conclude you are our own, and will
put in my Verdict : Our Mistresses are commonly
ten Years in knowing what they'd have, and I
am always forc'd to resolve for them at last.
Do not trouble your self about it, I will manage
that Affair. I take a pleasure in serving my
Neighbour, it is what our Lecturer recommends
to us.

I return you a thousand thanks, Mrs. *Catherine*,
said I ; but above all please to remember that I
resemble Master *Baptist* : Pray eat then, said
she, that is the only way to resemble him long
in this World , I love a Neighbour that lasts ·
And I assure you, I am very fond of lasting,
said I, at the same time drinking a bumper to her
Health.

This was the first Essay I made towards a
Commerce with Mrs. *Catherine*, from whose
Discourse I have retrench'd a little hundred *God
be thanked's* and *Lord have Mercy upon us*,
which sometimes serv'd as a Bridle, and sometimes as a Spur to her Discourse.

It is probable these compos'd a great part of
her verbal Devotion , but that was of no import
to me, I was pretty sure I had neither displeas'd
the kind Lass, nor her Mistresses, especially Mrs.
Haberd the younger, as will appear by the Sequel.

I finish'd my Breakfast in waiting what answer
Catherine would bring me, who presently came
down

down again, with a come Friend, you want nothing but your Night cap, here is a Lodging
ready for you.

The Night-cap, faid I, fhall be forth-coming,
and as for my Slippers I actually have them on. It
is mighty well, you Wag you, faid fhe, go then
and fetch your Clothes, that you may be back
again by Dinner ; whilft you breakfafted, your
Wages run on ; I concluded the Bargain. Do
they run at a round rate ? faid I ; yes, yes, I
underftand you, faid fhe laughing, they will come
in notably too. I rely fo entirely upon you, faid I,
that I won't fo much as ask the Queftion ; but
I will hold a Wager they are more than I deferve,
thanks to your good Offices !

Ah ! the merry heart, faid fhe, quite charm'd
with the Franknefs of my Compliment ; it is
Baptift himfelf come again, methinks I hear him
talk ; Stir, ftir, I have my Dinner to get ready,
do not prattle to me ; but let me mind my Bufinefs, run and fetch your Luggage ; are you return'd yet ? Prefently, faid I, as I went out, I
fhall foon difpatch ; I want no Mules to bring
my Equipage. Upon which I march'd to my
Inn.

However by the way, I made fome Reflexions
to confider whether I fhould accept the Place ;
but thought I to my felf I run no hazard, it is
only diflodging if I diflike ; at leaft the Breakfaft
I have had is a good Omen, they do not feem to
be People whofe Devotion counts every bit they
eat ; it is plain they are no bigots to Abftinence.
Befides all the Family looks pleafantly upon me,
they have no Averfion to a great Boy like me,

I

I am already in Favour with the Cook ; there is my four Meals a Day fecur'd, and my Heart tells me all will go well ; ——— Courage, my Lad !

Whilft I was reafoning in this manner, I found my felf at my Inn-Door; and as I ow'd my Hoftefs nothing but a good By-to-ye, I was not long in decamping with my Baggage.

I return'd to the Houfe, juft as they were placing themfelves at Table. Blefs my Eyes ! what a little Epicure Dinner was they diverted with ' there was a Difh of what they call Soup, without mentioning a little roaft fo delicate ' and fo perfectly well drefs'd ' ——— A Perfon muft have a Temper Proof againft Pleafure indeed, who could fit down to fuch charming Morfels, without giving into the Sin of Indulgence, when they tafted that Roaft, and then that Ragout ; for there was one fo admirably feafon'd, that I think I never met with the like —— If there was any eating in Heav'n I fhould never wifh to be better ferv'd ;——— *Mahomet* might have reckon'd this Meal amongft the Joys of his Paradife.

Our Ladies would touch no boil'd Meat, that only appear'd upon the Table, and was immediately taken off to be given to the Poor.

Catherine alfo in her turn pafs'd it by, for Charity, as fhe faid ; and for my Part, I agreed upon the Spot to be as charitable as her. Nothing is fo improving as a good Example.

I learn'd afterwards, that my Predeceffor had no fhare in Alms-Deeds as I had ; he was too much a Libertine to merit that Grace, and to be reduc'd to Roaft and Ragout.

But

But to return, I could not devife how our two Sifters manag'd in their eating ; but certainly it was Legerdemain, to eat as they did.

They never had any Appetites ; at leaft one could never fee they had any ; they perfectly juggled with their Meat; it was gone, and yet you could hardly perceive they touch'd it.

Their Forks they us'd in the moft indolent Manner in the World, it feem'd a Pain to them to open their Mouths, and they look'd with fo much indifference upon their good Cheer—I have no Stomach to Day, faid one, nor I, faid the other.——I find every thing infipid——and I too high feafon'd.

This Difcourfe of theirs drew Duft in my Eyes, in fuch a Manner, that I fancy'd I beheld the moft puny Creatures in Life, and yet the refult of all was, that the Difhes were confiderably diminifh'd when we came to remove them. For the firft two or three Days, I was at a lofs to know how to reconcile this.

But at laft I difcover'd the Cheat; for it was nothing but this Air of difguft which my Miftreffes fhew'd, that had hid from me the filent activity of their Teeth.

But what is ftill more pleafant, they really conceited themfelves to be mighty little and mighty moderate eaters ; they knew it was not decent for Devotees to gormandize, they ought to eat to live, and not to live to eat, but in fpight of this reafonable and Chriftian Maxim, their glutton Appetite would lofe nothing, and they had found out the Secret to indulge it, without being guilty of gluttony, which was no-

thing

thing, but this habit they had got of quarrelling with their Victuals, and their indolent Manner of eating it ; both which convinced them
they were moderate, and at the fame time left
them the Pleafure of being otherwife. So that
by the Delufion of this Foppery, their Devotion very innocently quitted the Field to Intem-
perance.

It muft be acknowledg'd that the Devil is
very politick , but we muft alfo own our felves
to be very filly.

The defert was agreeable to the Dinner, both
wet and dry Sweet-Meats ; and for a clofe fome
little Cordials to affift Digeftion, and rectify this
depraved Appetite.

After which, faid Mrs. *Haberd* the eldeft to
Mrs. *Haberd* the youngeft ; Come, Sifter, let us
return thanks to God! that is but juft, reply'd
the other with a Promptnefs of affent, which indeed it would have been ungrateful to have
deny'd God Almighty at that Juncture.

That is but juft, faid fhe, and immediately
the two Sifters rofe off their Seats, with a For-
mality the moft Orthodox in the World, and
which undoubtedly they thought as meritorious,
as it was lawful ; then joining their Hands fo-
lemnly together, they began an alternate Thankf-
giving, anfwering each other by Verfes, and all
in an accent, which the feeling they had of their
Well-being made extreamly pathetick.

After this the Cloth being taken away, they
funk themfelves into a Couch, whofe foftnefs and
depth of Down invited to repofe, where they
entertain'd one another, with fome reflexions
they

they had made upon one of their godly Lectures, or Morning or Evening Sermons, I cannot tell which ; but they agreed, that the Subject was very fuitable for Mr. or Mrs. fuch a one.

This Sermon could be level'd at nobody but them ; Avarice, the Love of the World, Pride, and fuch like Imperfections, were fo extreamly well inveigh'd againſt in it.

But, faid one of them, how can any Perfon attend upon hearing the Word of God and not come back with fo much as a Defign to reform ? Can you comprehend how that fhould be, Sifter ?.

Mrs. fuch a one, who came conftantly to Church during laſt Lent, I wonder what Notion fhe has of it ? I fee fhe's as much a Coquet as ever. And *à propos*, now I fpeak of Coquettery, Lard ! How I was fcandaliz'd the other Day, at the immodeſt Manner in which Mrs.----was drefs'd. How had fhe the Face to come to Church in fuch a Figure? I muſt own to you, it gave me a Diſtraction, for which I ask God forgivenefs. She diſturb'd my Prayers. Upon my Word, it was frightful !

Indeed, fo it was, Siſter, reply'd the other ; but when I fee fuch Sights, I always fix my Eyes upon the Ground ; for the Refentment I feel, won't fuffer me to look at them and I praife God for his Goodnefs, that at leaſt he has preferv'd me from thefe Sins, and intreat him with my whole Heart, to enlighten with his Grace the poor Souls who commit them.

You'll ask me perhaps, how I came to hear thefe Dialogues, where their Neighbours Faults

were

were of such Service to the Digestion of these Ladies?

Why, it was in clearing the Table, and setting Things in order in the Room where they were.

When I had taken away, Mrs. *Haberd* the Younger call'd to me, as I was going down to Dinner, and speaking very low, because of a light Slumber which began to close her Sister's Eyes, said that to me, which you shall see in the second Part of this History.

The End of the first Part.

THE

Fortunate PEASANT.

PART II.

I Acquainted you in the former Part of my
Life that Mrs. *Haberd* the younger call'd
me to her whilſt her Siſter was aſleep.

We entertain you, my Lad, ſaid ſhe; I
have prevail'd with my Siſter to conſent to it,
and have engag'd to be anſwerable for your
good Behaviour; for I'm in no fear of finding
myſelf deceiv'd either by your Looks, or your
Diſcourſe; they have given me a Friendſhip
for you, and I hope you'll take care to deſerve
it You'll be with *Catherine,* ſhe's a modeſt,
ſober Girl, and one who ſeems to like you
mighty well too; ſhe'll tell you what Wages
we have reſolv'd upon; I believe you'll have
Reaſon enough to be contented, and perhaps
in time you'll have more Reaſon to be ſo than
you

you imagine ; remember I tell it you. Go, Child, go to Dinner, always keep up to the good Opinion I have of you ; you may depend upon my Protection, and that I shall never forget how readily you assisted me this Morning in my illness.

It's peculiar to some Things, that it's impossible to describe the Spirit and Manner of them, nor is it possible for me to give a compleat Idea, either of the Meaning of Mrs. *Haberd's* discourse, or of the Air with which she accompany'd it. But this is certain, that both her Looks, her Eyes, and the tone of her Voice, spake a great deal more than her Words, or at least added to the natural Purport of them. I thought I observ'd something affectionately tender in her Expressions, and such a prepossession in my Favour, as was inconsistent with a common Esteem, which surpriz'd me, and at the same time made me curious to know what it should signify.

However, I ventur'd to shape my Thanks according to her own Pattern, and answer'd her with such a superfluity of Complaisance, as would have merited Correction had not my Observations been just ; and apparently they were, since she shew'd no sign of displeasure at my Manner of speaking to her. You'll see what Consequences attended it in the Sequel.

I was making my Bow to Mrs. *Haberd*, in order to go down into the Kitchen, when a Clergyman enter'd the Room.

This was the Director in ordinary of these Ladies ; I call him so in ordinary, because they had several other Churchmen of their acquaintance

tance who vifited them, and with whom they alfo frequently confer'd about the Affairs of their Confciences.

This therefore was their Guide in chief, and the fupreme Judge of their behaviour.

But left any one fhould be fcandaliz'd at what I fay, or induc'd to think that I ridicule without Diftinction all thofe who fubmit their Confciences to the Government of their Ghoftly Fathers, or confult them upon any Occafion; I declare once for all.

The practice is undoubtedly laudable and pious in it felf, and it's highly commendable in thofe who obferve it, if they obferve it as they ought; therefore that's not what I rally; but there are certain little Occurrences in Life, which your Directors have no Bufinefs to trouble themfelves about in the folemn Manner they do; and I only laugh at thofe who carry their Authority to fuch Extravagance.

This Director was low in Stature, but well-made as to his Shape, which inclin'd a little to the jolly; he had a frefh Colour, but a very compos'd fleek Countenance, with a brisk Eye, who's Vivacity neither fhow'd the Fool, nor the Bigot.

Have you never feen one of thofe Faces, which carry a *je ne fçai quoi*, of the conformable, indulgent, and confolative in the Air of them, and which feem to warrant the Soul within full of Mildnefs and Charity?

Exactly fuch a Face this Director had.

As for the refidue of his Picture, you may imagine to yourfelf, little fhort Hair, not one longer than another, let them fit as genteel

as may be, and play round the Cheeks in half
Curls, which to be sure proceeds from the
natural turn they have taken and not at all from
the Vanity of the Wearer, you may add a
couple of Lips pretty ruby, and a hanfome fet
of Teeth, the Handfomenefs and Whitenefs of
which, you muft alfo fuppofe entirely owing to
good Fortune, and not in the leaft to any Care
of the owner.

Such were the unaffected Attractions of our
Clergyman, who had not forgot in his drefs
neither, that Religion commands us to be very
modeft and decent in that particular, for fear of
giving Offence ; indeed he exceeded the bounds
of Decorum there a little ; but it is difficult to
know the Limits of every Punctilio, and his
Tranfgreffion in that Refpect was undoubtedly
againft his Intention.

Mrs. *Haberd* the eldeft who was nodding, rather divin'd than heard his coming in ; for he
trod very foftly in entering ; but a Devotee at
fuch a time has a remarkable quick Ear.

She wak'd in an Inftant, fmiling at the good
Fortune which had furpriz'd her napping ; I
mean altogether a fpiritual good Fortune.

As I was entirely a new Face to this Clergyman, he ey'd me very attentively.

Is this your Servant, Ladies ? faid he. Yes,
Sir, he is a Lad we hir'd to day, anfwer'd the
eldeft, and it is a Service he did my Sifter which
occafion'd it.

Upon which fhe began to relate to him what
had pafs'd between her youngeft and me : And
for my Part I thought proper to retire during the
rehearfal.

But

But when I was got about the middle of the
Stairs, reflecting upon the looks his Directorship
had given me, I was feiz'd with a violent Curiofity to hear what he'd fay · *Catherine* was
waiting for me in the Kitchen ; but no matter
for that, I went up foftly, and having before fhut
the Door after me, I laid my Ear as clofe to it
as poffible.

My Adventure with Mrs. *Haberd* the younger
was foon recounted, and every now and then I
look'd through the Key-hole, for the Director
fat in fuch a manner, that I had a full view of
his Face, as well as of the youngeft Sifter's.

I took notice whilft they were telling the Story,
that he liften'd to it with a great deal of coldnefs
and referve, look'd very thoughtful, and a little
upon the auftere.

He had no longer that mild, indulgent Countenance, which he had at firft coming in , he
offer'd indeed no Interruption , but I imagin'd he
foon would, and that my Adventure was going to
become a Cafe of Confcience.

When he had heard all, he caft down his Eyes
like a Perfon who is about to deliver fome Opinion
of Importance, and the refult of a profound
Meditation.

Then immediately · You have been very
hafty, Ladies, faid he, looking at them both in
fuch a manner as render'd the Cafe vaftly grave
and important, and almoft difpos'd my Miftreffes
to fee themfelves treated like Criminals.

I was not at all furpriz'd at this Introduction,
for I expected no better : The youngeft Sifter
colour'd, and look'd ftrangely perplex'd, but
notwithftanding I could fee fhe was not pleas'd.

E   You

You have been very hasty, repeated he a second time. Well, and what harm can there be
in that, reply'd the youngeft, with a Voice half
timorous and half revolting, if he is an honeft
Lad as we have reafon to believe he is ? Here he
wants a Place, I meet with him in the Street, he
does me a particular Service in helping me Home;
we want a Servant, and therefore we hire
him: What Offence againft God can there be in
all this ? For my Part, I thought quite the contrary, I imagin'd I was doing an Act of Charity
and Gratitude.

We know it, Sifter, reply'd the eldeft, we
know it very well, but what fignifies that ?
Since our worthy Friend here, who is more
clear-fighted than either of us, don't approve
what we have done, we ought to fubmit ; and
to tell you the Truth, when you firft fpoke to
me about keeping this young Fellow, I thought
I was of Opinion that I felt fomething of an Un-
willinefs ; I had a fort of foreboding that it
would not be according to our good Friend's
liking ; and God knows my Heart, I refer'd it
all to his Decifion.

This harangue could not perfuade the youngeft,
who return'd no anfwer to it, but by looks
which ftill perfifted, I can fee no harm in what is
done.

The Director had let the eldeft fpeak without
interruping her, and feem'd a little piqu'd at the
Obftinacy of the other.

However, affuming a ferene and benevolent
Air; my dear Lady, hear me, cry'd he to the
youngeft, you know with what a particular
Affection I have always given my Advice to——
to both of you. Thefe

Thefe laſt Words, to both of you, were divided in fuch a manner, that the youngeſt had at leaſt three Parts and a half to her ſhare, and it was only through a ſudden Recollection, that he gave any to the eldeſt; for in his firſt tranſport, the holy Man never once thought of her.

Yes truly, ſaid the eldeſt, who was aware of the unequal Dealing, and a little nettled at not being remember'd at firſt, yes, truly, Sir, we know very well that you have an equal Value for both of us; your Piety admits no Preference, neither is it juſt it ſhould.

The tone of this Speech was pretty eager, though accompany'd with a ſmile, for fear it ſhould ſeem too much like Jealoufy.

Oh! Siſter, reply'd the youngeſt briskly, I took it in no other Senſe my ſelf not I, though our worthy Friend here ſhould be more attach'd to you, than to me, I ſhould be far from finding Fault, he would only do you Juſtice; he knows the bottom of your Heart, and the Graces with which God has endow'd you, and you are undoubtedly more deſerving his Care than I am.

My dear Siſter, cry'd the Churchman, who ſaw this little Debate was occaſion'd by his Error, do not diſturb yourſelves; you are both equal to me in the ſight of God, becauſe you love God equally; and had I any Care to place more upon the one than the other, I ſhould diſpoſe of it in favour of her whom I obſerv'd the leaſt forward in the way of her Salvation; her Weakneſs would require a particular Attention, becauſe ſhe would ſtand in the moſt need of particular Aſſiſtances; but thanks to the Divine Mercy! you walk Hand in Hand the ſame Pace, neither is one behind

E 2 the

the other ; and therefore this is foreign to the
subject of our Discourse. We were talking of
the young Man you have hir'd (that Youth stuck
in his Stomach) you see no hurt in it, I am per-
suaded you do not , but pray vouchsafe to hear
me.

Here he made a little pause as if to recollect
himself.

But immediately going on ; God of his great
Goodness, added he, often permits those who are
to guide us to enjoy such lights as are refus'd to
us ourselves, which is to shew us that we ought
not to place any Confidence in our own Opinions,
and that we shall certainly go astray whenever
we neglect to hear the Voice of our Pastor.

But of what Consequence can it be you will
say, that we have hir'd a Lad apparently sober ?
Why of a very serious Consequence.

In the first Place, it is having acted against
human Prudence , for in short, you have no
knowledge of him any farther than an accidental
Meeting in the Street. You think he has an honest Countenance, and I am willing it should be
so , every body sees with their own Eyes in that
respect, though I must own mine are not altogether so favourable to him ; however I will pass
that Article ; but who would trust their Lives
and Fortunes with a Stranger upon the meer
Credit of his Countenance ? When I say Lives
and Fortunes, I do not at all exaggerate in regard
to you. Here you are only three Women in a
House , what hazard don't you run, if this
Countenance should deceive you, and if you
should have to do with an Adventurer, which is
not impossible ? Who has been answerable for his

Morals,

Morals, his Religion and his Character? May not a Rascal have the look of an honest Man? God forbid I should suspect him to be be a Rascal, Charity commands me to think to his Advantage. But Charity does not command us to be imprudent, and it is an Imprudence to trust at a venture as you do.

Ah! Sister, how sensible is what our worthy Friend advances! cry'd the eldest; really the Lad at first sight has something very promising, but notwithstanding the Gentleman is in the right, for now I think on it, he has a sort of a——I don't know what, which made me hesitate, I tell you he has.

One Word more, added the Churchman, interrupting her. You approve what I have already said; and that is nothing in Comparison of what I have to say.

This Lad is in the prime of his Youth, his looks are bold and unsettled, and you are not yet arriv'd at an Age to live free from Scandal. Have you no Apprehension what evil Thoughts may arise in the Minds of those who see him here? Don't you know how susceptible the World is of Scandal, and what a terrible Misfortune it is to occasion the least Scandal to our Neighbour? It is not I that tell you so, it is the Scripture. Besides, my dear Sisters, for it is my Duty to suppress nothing, are not we all of us full of Frailties? is not it the whole Business of our Lives to war against ourselves, to fall and to rise? I say in things of the minutest Consequence; and ought not that Consideration to make us tremble? Believe me! whilst we walk in the way of our Salvation, do not let us seek

new

new difficulties to overcome ; let us expofe ourfelves to no new Tryals of our Weaknefs. This
Lad is too young ; here you will live with him,
and you will fee him almoft every Moment , the
Root of Sin is continually in us, and I already
diftruft, (for I am obliged to difcharge my Confcience) I fay, I already diftruft the good Opinion you have of him, and this obftinate liking
which you have taken to him ; it is innocent, I
know it is, but will it always be fo ? I fay once
more, I diftruft it. I fee Mrs. *Haberd*, added
he, looking at the youngeft Sifter, is not at all
fatisfy'd with my Obfervations upon this Affair ;
but whence proceeds this Fondnefs for her own
Opinion, and this Strangenefs to mine ? I never
knew her before make a Moment's Oppofition
to any Advice, which my Confcience dictated
for the Benefit of her's. I can't approve this
Difpofition of Mind, it is fufpicious to me ; and
one may venture to fay, it is a Snare which the
wicked Spirit has fpread for her ; and therefore
in the prefent Circumftance, I am oblig'd to exhort you to part with this young Man ; for I can
have no fuch advantageous notions of his Countenance as you have. I will undertake to procure you a Servant my felf, it will be fome
trouble to me indeed ; but God infpires me for
the Work ; and in his Name, I conjure you,
that you will fuffer yourfelves to be guided. Do
you promife me you will ?

As for my part, Sir, cry'd the eldeft with an
entire Refignation to his Pleafure ; I anfwer for
my felf that you are Mafter, and you fhall fee
my Obedience; for from this very Inftant, I
proteft againft receiving any farther Service from
the

the young Man in queſtion, and I do not doubt
but my Siſter will follow my Example

Truly, reply'd the youngeſt with a Face quite
enflam'd with Anger, I do not know how I
ought to take what I hear. My Siſter's in
League againſt me already, ſhe is charm'd with
the imaginary Affront ſhe gives me; nor is this
the firſt time ſhe has behav'd thus to me, ſince I
muſt ſpeak, and ſince the manner I am ſpoke to
obliges me to it; ſhe does not doubt, ſhe ſays, but
I will conform to her Example. why! I have done
nothing but conform ſince we have liv'd together;
one muſt always conform to her Humour, or
there is no Peace. God knows, without any Reproach, I mention it, how often I have ſacrific'd
my Will to her, though at the ſame time it had
no Fault but being mine, and really, I begin to
be tir'd of a Subjection I do not owe her. Yes,
Siſter, you may make what uſe you pleaſe of what
I ſay; but you are really of an imperious Temper; and there is more occaſion for our Friend
here to alarm himſelf for you, than at what I have
done in entertaining a poor Lad to whom I am
perhaps oblig'd for my Life. I muſt turn him
away forſooth, for his Recompence, though we
have both engaged our Words to keep him. The
Gentleman objects that he has nobody to give
him a Character, but the young Man has told
me that he can produce a very creditable Perſon
for that Purpoſe, if we deſire it; therefore that
objection falls to the Ground. As to my ſelf, he
has done me ſuch a conſiderable Service, that I
cannot bid him go, indeed Siſter, I cannot do it

Well, Siſter, reply'd the Eldeſt, if that's
all, I'll undertake to diſmiſs him for you, if

you'll

you'll give me leave, and I promife to repair
my paft Imperioufnefs by an entire Condefcen-
fion to your Advice for the future, tho' you
are my Youngeft ; had you been fo charitable
as to have told me my Faults fooner, I would
have endeavour'd their Correction thro' the
Affiftance of God, and the Prayers of our good
Friend here, who notwithftanding never re-
prov'd me for that Imperioufnefs you fpeak of ;
but as you've certainly more Wit and more Pe-
netration than any body elfe, it's impoffible
you fhould be miftaken ; and I think my felf
happy that you've difcover'd thofe Foibles in
me, which have efcap'd fuch a nice Difcernment
as this Gentleman's.

I'm not come here, Madam, faid the Churchman getting up with a chagrin'd Air, to fow
Divifion between you, and fince I've been
fo fhort-fighted as to leave your Sifter's faults
unobferv'd, and fince you think I'm wrong in
my Sentiments upon your prefent Conduct ;
I conclude that I'm altogether unneceffary to
you, and that I ought to retire.

How ! Sir, you retire, cry'd the Eldeft, Oh !
Sir, my Salvation is ftill dearer to me than my
Sifter ; and I'm convinc'd it's not to be attain'd
without the Affiftance of fuch a holy Man as you
are. You retire ! my God ! No, Sir, it's my
Sifter and I that muft retire. We can live
apart one from another, fhe has nothing to do
with me, nor I with her, fhe may ftay here,
I refign her the Houfe, and will feek for another fomewhere elfe, where I hope from your
Piety, that you'll continue the fame kind Vifits with which you now oblige us. Oh good
Heaven ! where are we ?   Our

Our Churchman made no Anfwer to this devout and even tender Declaration in his Favour. To keep only the Eldeft was lofing a great deal. I thought he look'd extreamly perplex'd ; and as the Tears which the Eldeft begun to fhed, and the Clamours with which fhe fill'd the Chamber, feem'd to threaten a Storm, I quitted my Poft, and got down into the Kitchen as faft 'as I could, where *Catherine* had waited near a Quarter of an Hour for my coming to Dinner.

There's no Occafion, I imagine, to explain why the Director was fo immoveably bent upon my going, he had lectur'd them in his Sermon, that my ftaying with them was indecent, but I fancy he would have yielded up that Objection; or rather he would never have thought on't, hadn't it been for another more powerful Motive ; which was his obferving the youngeft Sifter fo obftinate for keeping me, that might fignify fhe'd a liking to me, and that liking for me might put her out of Conceit with being a Devotee, and confequently fubmiffive, and then farewel the Authority of Director: It's the delight of thofe fort of Men to domineer over others; they are charm'd at feeing them obedient and tractable, or in being their Kings, if I may fo call them, and Kings are generally the more courted, the more rigorous and inflexible they are

Befides, I was a great Lad with a good handfome Face, and perhaps he knew that Mrs. *Haberd* had no antipathy to handfome Lads ; for in fhort, a Director knows a vaft deal but to return to our Kitchen.

E 5   You

You have been a tedious long while, said *Catherine*, who was spinning and heating our Soup. What was the Matter that you talk'd so loud all of you in the Chamber? I heard somebody cry like an Eagle Hush! hark---Lord bless us! what a Hurricane is there? What have our Mistresses been quarrelling?

Troth! Mrs *Catherine*, I do'nt know, said I; but it's impossible they should quarrel,--- why that would be an offence against God --- to be sure they are not capable of such a Thing.

Ay, ay, reply'd she; they're the best Gentlewomen in the World; they live like Saints indeed; for they never fall out about any Thing but their Sanctity, there's ne'er a Day passes over their Heads but they wrangle right or wrong, and all for the Love of God, which fills them full of Scruples; sometimes I come in for a Share; but that's nothing but nuts to me; I warrant you I give them as good as they bring, then tuck up my Tail and away; God's above all still Come, come, let's eat, that's the best Business now.

What the Director had said of me, hadn't in the least spoil'd my Stomach· Happen what will, thought I to myself, I'll make sure of a good Dinner however.

Upon which I doubled my Morsels, and was just falling upon the Wing of an excellent Rabbit, when the noise above Stairs heighten'd even to the degree of a Riot.

What the Devil are they doing there? mumbled *Catherine* with her Mouth full. one would swear they were cutting one anothers Throats.

The noise continuing, I must go up, said she; I will hold a Wager now this is some Case of

Con-

Confcience, which has turn'd their Heads. How! a Cafe of Confcience? cry'd I; why have not they got a Cafuift along with them? Can't he decide the Difference? He ought to know the Bible and Teftament by heart. Yes, yes, faid fhe getting up, but neither Bible nor Teftament can anfwer the fantaftical Crotchets of fome Folks, and there's nobody has more of them than our good Miftrefles God knows. Don't ftay for me, eat on, I'll go and fee what's theMatter , and accordingly fhe went.

As for me, I obferv'd her Orders to a tittle, and continu'd my Dinner with all the Expedition imaginable; for as I told you before,I was very glad to fortify myfelf with a good Meal, in the uncertainty I was in as to the Confequence of this buftle.

In the mean time no *Catherine* return'd, and I had finifh'd my Dinner , every now and then I heard her Voice exalted above the reft; for it was very diftinguifhable by a blunt decifiveTone which fhe had ; the noife continu'd, and even encreas'd.

I ey'd my bundle which I had brought into the Houfe that Morning, and which was ftill lying in a Corner of the Kitchen : I have a great mind to carry thee back, faid I to myfelf; for I am afraid I fhall fall fhort of the fine Wages they promis'd me, and which run on whilft I breakfafted.

As I was entertaining myfelf with thefe reflections,I thought the Storm feem'd to fink into aCalm.

About a moment after, I heard the Chamberdoor open, and fomebody coming down Stairs. I plac'd myfelf in the Entrance of the Kitchen to fee who it was ; it prov'd to be our Director.

I would have fhut too the Kitchen-door to fave the trouble of pulling off my Hat, which was a

Com-

Compliment I muſt have paid him had I ſhew'd
myſelf: but I was never the better, for he open'd
it again, and came in.

My Lad, ſaid he muſtering all the Artifice together of his Vocation, I mean particularly the devout
and pathetick Tone, which is to let you know
the conſequence of the Perſon who ſpeaks to you.

My Lad, you're the occaſion of a great trouble here. Me! Sir, anſwer'd I. Why, I ſay
nothing: I have haidly ſpoke four Words ſince
I have been in the Houſe

No Matter for that, Child, reply'd he, I don't
ſay that you've actually occaſion'd this trouble, but
you're the Subject of it ; and God does not require
your being here, ſince you drive away Peace, inſtead of contributing to preſerve it.

One of theſe Ladies is very willing you ſhould
ſtay, but the other will have nothing to ſay to
you: Therefore you ſow Diviſion betwixt them ;
and theſe pious Women, who till you came,
never diſputed but with the utmoſt Mildneſs,
Complaiſance, and Humility one for another, are
now upon the point of parting upon your account ; you are a Rock of Offence to them ;
and you ought to look upon yourſelf as an In-
ſtrument of the Devil's, who makes uſe of you
to diſunite them, and to break that Band of
Peace in which they have hitherto liv'd to their
mutual Edification. As to myſelf, it touches
me to the Heart, and I declare to you on the
Part of God Almighty, that ſome ſignal Miſ-
fortune will certainly befall you, if you don't
immediately take ſome other Courſe. I am very
glad I happen'd to meet with you before I
went ; for if one may judge by your Countenance,

tenance, I believe you are a very sober Youth, and one of good Morals , and therefore you won't resist the Advice I give you for your own good, and the good of every body here.

Me, Sir, a Youth of good Morals! cry'd I, after having listen'd to him with an Air full of Indifference, and which shew'd how little I was affected with his Exhortation. You see by my Countenance, you say, that I am very sober : no, no, Sir, you are mistaken, you don't confider what you say ; for I'll maintain you see no such thing in my Countenance , on the contrary, you find that I've the Looks of a Rascal, who would not stick to plunder a House ; I'm a Person not to be trusted ; I can cut Peoples Throats, and carry away their Purses ; that's what you think of me

Pray, who tells you so, Child ? said he, and coloured. Oh, reply'd I, I'm speaking before a very discerning Gentleman, who has seen thro' me plain enough ; God inspires him that I'm good for nothing. You may put what face on't you please, but I know what you think. This same honest Gentleman has also said, that I am too young ; and that if these Ladies kept me, it might occasion ill Thoughts in their Neighbours : without reckoning that the Devil's a Sly-boots, and might make use of me as a means of Temptation to my Mistresses ; for I'm a Puppy with a handsome sort of a Face. Is it not so, Mr. Director ? I don't know what you mean, said he, and cast his Eyes upon the Ground.

Oh, as to that, answer'd I, don't you think Mrs. *Haberd* the Younger has too much Kindnefs

nefs for me on account of the fmall fervice I
did her ? perhaps there's a Sin lurking there
which may take root, do you fee : there's no occafion to be apprehenfive for the eldeft, fhe's
Obedience itfelf ; I might ftay, was there no
body but her ; fhe don't care a rufh for me nor
my Face neither ; fhe's willing enough I fhould
be kick'd out of doors : but this youngeft is
obftinate, that's a bad Sign ; fhe has too good
an Opinion of me, and fhe ought to have a
good Opinion of no body but her Director for
the Benefit of her Confcience, and the Satif-
faction of your's However, take care ; for *a
propos* now I fpeak of Confcience, had it not
been for the Charity of your's, the Peace of God
might have been here ftill , you know that as
well as I, Mr. Director.

What's your Intent in talking to me in this
manner ? faid he. Becaufe, anfwer'd I, God
does not require us to feek for mid-day at four
a-clock in the afternoon. Meditate upon that
a little , when you preach'd to thefe Ladies, I
was not far from the Pulpit. As for my part,
I've no notion of thefe Quirks of Policy , I
don't know how to get my livelihood by go-
verning a parcel of Women, I am not fo artful ; I get my bread by waiting on other folks,
whilft they eat theirs ; and let every one walk
as uprightly in their Calling as I do. Though I
fancy your's is rather a more precarious one
than mine , for I never was fo jealous of my
ftation as you are of your's, nor ever endeavour'd to give any body their difmiffion for fear
of receiving my own.

Our Gentleman made no anfwer to what I faid, but turn'd his Back and away.

There are certain little Truths againft which there's no Defence. The Confufion he was in gave him no time to adjuft a Reply ; and the fhorteft was to fave himfelf.

Mean while no *Catherine* appear'd ; and I was at leaft a quarter of an hour longer in ex-pecting her   at laft fhe came down, lifting up her Hands to Heaven, and crying, Oh, my good God ! what ftrange doings are here !

What, faid I, Mrs. *Catherine*, have they been fighting above ftairs ? is any body dead then ? Ah ! my poor Lad, faid fhe, it's our Houfe-keeping that's murder'd, it's quite knock'd on the head

How ! faid I, and pray what has murder'd it ? Well-a-day ! anfwer'd fhe, why a Scruple which has been put into their Noddles by a Ser-mon of Mr. Director's. I always faid that Man hanker'd too much after Confciences.

But once again, what's the Matter ? faid I : Why, we're all turn'd topfy turvy, anfwer'd fhe, our Ladies find they can't get to Heaven to-gether, and therefore the Conclufion of the whole is, that it's actually fo. My Youngeft Miftrefs is going to take anothei Houfe, and fhe bid me or-der you to attend here, for you muft wait upon her, and you muft both attend upon me too I think ; for this Eldeft is a very fhrew , I'm fome-times a little fretful myfelf, thefe Priefts could never cure me of that, for I was born in *Picardy*, it's the Grain of the Country ; two hot Heads will never keep a Houfe cool, mine muft ev'n bear

the

the youngeſt Company, ſhe's good-humour'd enough.

Catherine had hardly concluded her Speech, when this Youngeſt appear'd.

My Lad, ſaid ſhe, as ſhe was coming in, my Siſter won't admit of your ſtaying here any longer, but for my Part I'm reſolv'd to keep you: She and the Clergyman who parted from us juſt now, have been ſaying ſuch diſobliging Things to to me upon your Account, that I can't help reſenting them, and you ſhall reap the Advantage of the ſhocking Imprudence with which they talk'd to me. I brought you here, and beſides I'm oblig'd to you: Therefore you ſhall be with me. I'm going directly to hire other Lodgings, but you muſt aſſiſt me to walk, for I am not thoroughly recover'd yet.

When you pleaſe, Madam, ſaid I, I have no Miſtreſs here but you, and I aſſure you that I'll never give you any Occaſion to be diſſatisfy'd with my Service.

Madam, ſaid *Catherine* immediately, we won't part neither, do you underſtand me? I can toſs you up as nice Fricaſies any where elſe as I can here. Let this Eldeſt provide for herſelf, for my ſhare I begin to be tir'd, one has never done with her, ſometimes there's too much of this, and ſometimes there's too much of that. Well, well, go your Ways, hadn't it been for you, the meat might have roaſted itſelf long enough before now for *Catherine*. But you're ſo ſweet-temper'd! And then as a Chriſtian one muſt have Patience: You make one love you, whether one will or no.

I am oblig'd to you for your good Opinion of me, ſaid Mrs *Haberd*, we ſhall ſee what's to be done, when

when I've taken a Houfe. I have a great many Goods here, it will be impoffible to move them, under two or three Days, and we fhall have time enough to fettle Affairs between us . Come, *Jacob*, let's go. That's the Name I had taken, and this Lady remember'd it ftill.

Dame *Catherine* feem'd a little confus'd at her Anfwer; and as ready as fhe ufually was at a Reply, fhe could find none at that Time, but ftood fpeechlefs.

I eafily difcern'd that Mrs *Haberd* had no Intention of taking her with us; and indeed we were like to be no great Lofers; for tho' fhe babbled over as many Prayers in a Day, as would fairly have ferv'd her a Month, had fhe repeated them with the neceffary Decorum, yet her Devotion was always crabbed, and fhe was certainly as brutifh a Creature as ever lumber'd a Houfe. If fhe fpake a kind Word, it was always with the fame Tone in which other People quarrel.

But we'll leave her to digeft the Anfwer which Mrs *Haberd* gave her.

Away we went, fhe and I together; fhe took hold of my Arm, and I never in my Life affifted any body to walk with fuch a good Will. The behaviour of this generous Lady had won my Heart. There's nothing affords fo compleat a Satisfaction as the being fure of any one's Friendfhip, and of her's I was fure, abfolutely fure, tho' at the fame time, I can't defcribe in what Manner I underftood this Friendfhip, of which I was fo pofitive; it's certain I confider'd it in a very flattering Light; it touch'd me far beyond the Power of an ordinary good Will, and I found thofe Charms in it which are not in the other. Nor was I backwards in teftifying
fying

fying my Acknowledgment in as particular a Manner in my Turn; all my Actions had something caressing in them.

Whenever she turn'd a Glance towards me, I seem'd to take a Pride in myself, I adjusted my Eyes, and every look was a sort of Compliment, yet I could assign no Reason to myself for all this, what I did was the Effect of meer Instinct, and Instinct explains nothing.

We were already got about fifty Paces from the House, and had neither of us spoke a Word; but the walk seem'd very agreeable to both. I held her with Joy, and she receiv'd my Service with Pleasure: At least I imagin'd so, nor was I mistaken.

Whilst we went forwards in this mute Manner, which proceeded, I believe, from our not knowing how to begin the Conversation, I perceiv'd a Bill which seem'd, to promise very commodious Lodgings for Mrs *Haberd*; and immediately seiz'd the opportunity to break a Silence, which appear'd only troublesome to both of us.

Madam, said I, will you please to see what Apartments they have in this House? No, no, Child, answer'd she, I should be too near my Sister; lets go farther on, we'll look in another Quarter.

Lord! Madam, reply'd I, how is it possible this Sister of your's could differ with you? You are of such a winning Temper, was one a *Turk* one could not help loving you. For example, I who never saw you till to day, was never so light-hearted in my Life.

Indeed! *Jacob*, said she. Oh! Madam, said I, you may soon know the Truth of that, it's only

looking

looking in my Face for't. So much the better, said she, it is then as it should be ; for you are more oblig'd to me than you're aware of.

So much the better again, said I, for there's nothing gives one so much Pleasure, as the being oblig'd to those who have won our very Souls.

Why, *Jacob*, said she, you are to understand, that my parting from my Sister is entirely upon your Account. Once more I tell you so, but you assisted me this Morning with so much Concern, that I was really sensibly affected with it.

What Happiness is mine ! cry'd I, with a Transport which made me hug the Arm I held a little. God be prais'd for having directed my Way over the new Bridge ! But as to the Assistance I gave you, Madam, that's no such extra-ordinary Matter: Who could see such a Lady as you taken ill, without being in Pain for her? For my Part, I was in a perfect fright. Pray, Madam, excuse my Expressions; but there are some People whose Faces make every body their Friend who sees them ; and one of those Faces, your Mother in her Bounty has bestow'd upon you.

Thou expresseft thyself pleasantly, said she; but so artlesly that I can't help being diverted : Tell me, *Jacob*, what are thy Parents in the Country? Alas! Madam, said I, they're not Rich, but for Gentility, they're the Cream of our Parish; nobody can deny that. As to Profession, my Father is Vine-Dresser and Farmer to our Lord of the Mannor. But I'm out there, I don't know what he is, he has neither Vineyard nor Farm now ; for our Master's dead, and it was his House in *Paris* that I came from. For my other
Rela-

Relations, they're none of your small Fry neither, they call them *Mr.* and *Mrs.* except an Aunt I have who's always call'd Madam, because of her having been marry'd to a Surgeon of our Country, who dy'd on the Wedding Day; and for grief of his Death, this Aunt of mine has betaken herself to teach School in our Village; they generally pull of their hats to her when they see her. Besides this, I've two Uncles, one of them's a Vicar, and has always a good Stock of Wine by him, and the other was in Hopes of being so two or three Times; but he still follows the Trade of Curate till he can get something better. The Attorney of our Town is also our Cousin, at least; and there's a Talk in the Country, that our Grandmother was a Gentleman's Daughter: It's true indeed, not to lie for the Matter, that's the Left-Side; but for the Right-Side is not far from it; we come into the World which Way we can, and it's always on the Left-Hand of Gentility. As to the rest of them, they're all fine Folks; and this is all the Account I can give you of my Relations, only I forgot a little Poppet of a Cousin, who is not out of his swaddling Cloaths yet.

Why, answer'd Mrs. *Haberd*, one may call this a good Country Family, and there are a great many a People who make a Figure in the World, and yet can't boast such an honest Descent. We, for Example, are deriv'd from such a one ourselves, yet I think it no Disgrace to me. Our Father was a wealthy Farmer's Son, who left him wherewithall to carry on a considerable Trade, and my Sister and I have very easy Fortunes.

That's

That's apparent, faid I, from your good House-Keeping, Madam; and I'm overjoy'd at it for your fake who deferve all the farms belonging to the City and Suburbs of *Paris*; but this makes me think what a Pity it is that you won't leave fome of your Breed behind you; there's fo much bad Grain in the World, that it's a S n not to beat good when we can, one would make amends for the other, and you could no more want Suiters than the Rivers want drops of Water.

Perhaps it might have been fo, reply'd fhe laughing; but not at this time of Day; I'm without them at prefent, *Jacob.* —

You without them, cry'd I! No, no, Madam, that can never be; you muft hide you Face in a Mask then! So long as they fee the Honey, the Flies will be buzzing. Odds my Life! who would not marry his Face to your's, tho' even no Parfon was to be at the Wedding? Had my Father been the Son of a wealthy Farmer, and capable of driving a great Trade; troth! we'd foon fee, whether this Face of your's fhould pafs by the Shop without having Bufinefs with me.

Mrs. *Haberd* made no other Anfwer, than by laughing outright, but it was a Laugh which proceeded lefs from the Pleafantries I fpake, than the Compliments couch'd under them. I could fee her Heart was not at all chagrin'd at the Humour mine was in.

The more fhe laugh'd, the fafter I talk'd. By degrees, I grew bolder in my Expreffions, from complaifant, they were already become flattering; and prefently they were fomething more lively; and immediatly they begun to foften into tendernefs. and then troth it was downright Love, the

bare

bare Word excepted, which I durft not venture upon, as thinking it rather too grofs, but I gave her the full Value of it without bating her a Doit.

She feem'd not to underftand what I faid, but let it all pafs under Pretence of the innocent Pleafure fhe took in hearing my comical Prate.

I made my Advantage of her hypocritical Way of liftening to me. I then begun to open my Eyes upon my good Fortune, and concluded upon the Spot, that fhe muft certainly have an Inclination for me, fince fhe never once offer'd to filence fuch an amorous Difcourfe as mine.

Nothing makes one fo amiable as the thoughts of being belov'd; and as I was naturally lively. befides as that Vivacity fpur'd me on, and as I was ignorant in the Arts of Difguife; in fhort, as I had no other reftraint upon my Tongue, than a little awkard timoroufnefs, which was diminifh'd ev'ry Moment by the Impunity it met with, I let fall moft aftonifhing Careffes, and all with a Courage and Ardour which at leaft perfuaded her that what I faid was fincere, and this Sincerity is always fure to pleafe, tho' it even comes from thofe we've no Value for.

We were fo entirely wrap'd up in this Converfation, that we had forgot the Houfe we were to hire.

But at laft a ftop which we met with in one of the Streets, oblig'd us to break it off; and I took notice that Mrs. *Haberd*'s Eyes were more gay than ufual.

During this Interruption, fhe faw a Bill in her Turn. I like this Quarter very well, faid fhe (it was towards Saint *Gervais*) here are Lodgings to be let, we'll fee what they are.

Accordingly

Accordingly we went in, and ask'd to fee the Apartment to be let.

The Perfon who own'd the Houfe dwelt in a Part of it herfelf, fhe came to us.

She was an Attorney's Widow, who had lef ther a very handfome Maintenance, and fhe liv'd according to it. As to the reft, the Woman was a likely Woman enough, much about Mrs. *Haberd*'s Age, had the fame frefh Colour, but was fomething fatter; fhe was a little upon the goffip with her Tongue, but then fhe was an exceeding good-natur'd one; fhe took a Friendfhip to you at firft fight, open'd all her Heart to you, told you her Affairs, ask'd after your's, then return'd to her own, and immediately to you again: talk'd to you about her Daughter, for fhe had only one; inform'd you that fhe was eighteen Years of Age, run over the Actions of her infancy, what Sickneffes fhe had: Then fell upon the Subject of her deceas'd Husband, begun the Hiftoryof his Childhood, proceeded to their Court-fhip, told you how long it lafted; pafs'd from that to their Marriage, gave you an Account of the Life they led together; he was one of the beft Men in the World! Mightily addicted to his Study; therefore he got a great deal by his Know-ledge and good Management · He was naturally a little jealous, occafion'd too by the extraordina-ry Love he bore her; very fubject to the Gravel; God knows what he fuffer'd! The Care fhe took of him In fhort, he dy'd in a very Chriftian Manner. Speaking this fhe wip'd her Eyes, for fhe really fhed Tears; which was becaufe this melancholy Part of the ftory requir'd it, not be-caufe of the Lofs itfelf; for directly, fhe want to fomething elfe, which made it as neceffary to laugh, and accordingly fhe laugh'd.

It coft me no other Trouble in drawing this Picture than only to recollect all the Difcourfe with which this good Widow entertain'd us. For as foon as we had feen the Apartment in queftion, fhe took us into the Room where her Daughter was, till we fhould fettle a little Scruple about the Price; very cordially made us fit down, plac'd herfelf by us, and there o'erwhelm'd us, if I may ufe the Expreffion, with that Deluge of Confidence and to-no-purpofe Stories which I juft now repeated.

For my part, I was exceffively tir'd with her prate, tho' at the fame time I could not help being delighted with her Character; becaufe I was fenfible fhe only talk'd, for the pleafure of hearing herfelf talk: it was purely the fuperfluous bounty of a tittle tattle Heart.

She offer'd us a Collation, order'd it to be brought in, tho' we refus'd it; made us eat, tho' we had no inclination; and affur'd us that we fhould not leave her before we were agreed. I fay we; for it muft be remember'd that I was drefs'd in an uniform Suit without Livery; the fame which my former-Miftrefs had given me; and in this habit, which was agreeable enough to my looks, I might very well be taken either for fome young Tradefman, or a relation of Mrs. *Haberd*'s The plain, tho' genteel manner in which fhe herfelf was drefs'd, allow'd their doing me that honour. Befides, during the converfation, that Lady would often turn towards me, with a familiar friendly Air, and as for me, I behav'd hav'd as conformably as if fhe had given me the word.

She had her reafons for acting thus, which I could not then dive into ; but without troubling my head about them, I took the hint, and was charm'd at her proceeding.

We fat there two tedious long Hours at leaft, which was partly Mrs. *Haberd*'s fault, who was no enemy to your prolix Narrations, but threw away her time with as much good will as any Body. Tho' allowances muft be made; for every Woman's a goffip, or takes a pleafure in hearing thofe who are ; the love of prattle is a tribute which fhe pays to her Sex. There are a few filent Women indeed, but I can't believe them to be natuaral Characters; it's either Experience or Education which has taught them to be fo.

At length, Mrs. *Haberd* bethought her felf that we had a confiderable way to walk before we reach'd home; fhe got up.

When we were upon our legs the Converfation renew'd again for fome time ; at laft we got to the door, where me made another ftand, which finally terminated the debate ; for Mrs. *Haberd* having been fufficiently carefs'd and flatter'd upon the fweetnefs and modefty of her air ; the high opinion which the other had of her good Qualities, Chriftian Morals, and amiable Character, ftruck up the bargain for the Apartment.

It was agreed that fhe fhould come to lodge there within three days, they neither ask'd her with who, nor how many perfons fhe was to bring with her; that queſtion was forgot amongſt the croud of other things which they talk'd of. It was lucky enough, for we ſhall ſee that Mrs. *Haberd* would have been per-plex'd had ſhe been oblig'd to have made an immediate anſwer to it

We were now in our return home, I paſs by an infinite number of things which Mrs *Haberd* and I diſcours'd of. Among the reſt, we talk'd of our Landlady with whom we were to lodge

I like that Woman, ſaid ſhe, I fancy we ſhall agree very well together, and I almoſt long till I am there: We have nothing to do now but to provide ouiſelves with a Cook, for I own to you, *Jacob*, I will have no *Catherine*; ſhe is of a rude, untractable Temper, and beſides ſhe'd be continually intriguing with my Siſter, who is naturally very inquiſitive, without reckoning that all our Devotees are ſo; they make themſelves amends for the Sins they do not commit, by the Pleaſure they take in diſcovering the Sins of other People; they account it ſo much Gain to them, but it is I who make this remark, it is not Mrs. *Haberd*, who continuing to ſpeak to me about her Siſter, ſince we muſt part, ſaid ſhe, it ſhall be once for all, that I am reſolv'd on; but thou haſt no notion of Cookery, and even if thou had'ſt, it is not my Intention to employ thee in it.

You ſhall employ me in what you pleaſe, ſaid I; but now we are got upon this Subject, is it becauſe you think of ſome other Buſineſs for me?

This

This is not a proper place to tell you my thoughts in, reply'd she; however, you muſt have obſerv'd that I mention'd nothing before our Landlady, that could give her any Item of your being a Servant; neither is it poſſible ſhe could divine it from your Dreſs; therefore I charge you when we go there, to regulate your Behaviour by mine. Ask me no more now, this is all the Satisfaction I can afford you at preſent.

May Heaven reward your good Intentions! anſwer'd I, quite charm'd with this little Diſcourſe, which ſeem'd a lucky Omen to me: But harkee, Madam, there is another Affair to be adjuſted ſtill; perhaps I may be ask'd a few Queſtions concerning my ſelf; they may ſay, Who are you? or, Who are you not? Now, who would you pleaſe to have me be? Here you have made me a Mr., but this Mr. who is he? Mr Jacob? Will that ſound well? Jacob's my Chriſtian Name, and a very good Name it is, we may even leave that as we find it, for it is not worth while to change and get nothing; therefore I will keep it; but I want another; my Father is call'd Goodman la Vallée, and if you think proper, I'll be Mr. de la Vallée's Son

Thou art in the right, ſaid ſhe laughing, thou art in the right, Mr. de la Vallée, call thy ſelf ſo: But this is not all, reply'd I; ſuppoſe they ſhould ſay, Mr. de la Vallée, what Buſineſs have you with Mrs. Haberd? what anſwer muſt I make them?

Oh! ſaid ſhe, that difficulty is not great; I ſhan't leave Matters long undecided; in the Apartment I have taken, there is a Room very

diſtant

diſtant from that which I deſign for my ſelf, you ſhall be there, under the decent pretence of being a Kinſman of mine who lives with me and manages my Affairs; beſides, as I have already told you, we will ſoon make our ſelves eaſy upon that Article; a few Days will ſuffice to determine my Thoughts, and indeed I muſt be ſudden; for Circumſtances won't admit a Delay. Be ſure ſpeak nothing of all this at my Siſter's, but behave as uſual during the little time we have to be there; you muſt return to morrow Morning to our Landlady's, ſhe ſeems to be a very obliging Woman; you ſhall deſire her to get us a Cook Maid; and if ſhe asks you any Queſtions in regard to yourſelf; why, anſwer her agreeable to what we have been talking of; call thy ſelf *de la Vallée*, and my Kinſman; you make a good Figure enough for that.

Oh! cry'd I, how the Plot tickles me! what Joy gallops through my Heart for I do not know why! I muſt be your Coſin then, muſt I? But yet, my fair Coſin, was I to chuſe my own Quality, it ſhould not be that of your Kinſman; no, no, I have a better taſte than that comes to, the Relationſhip does me a great deal of Honour, but ſometimes Honour and Happineſs go together, is not it ſo?

We were drawing very near Home when I ſpoke this; but I perceiv'd that ſhe immediately ſlacken'd her pace to gain time to anſwer me, and to make me explain my ſelf.

I do not rightly underſtand you, Mr. *de la Vallée,* ſaid ſhe, with an accent full of

good

good Humour, I cannot apprehend what this Quality is which you would chufe.

Oh! Cofin, faid I, I muft beg your Pardon for that; I dare not advance a Step farther; I am not of a Humour to forget the Refpect I owe you, though you are my Relation, but if by Chance, one time or other you fhould have a fancy to take a Partner in Houfekeeping; I mean one of thofe whom they do not fend into Chambers apart, and who are bold enough to fleep upon the fame Pillow; what do they call the Profeffion of thofe fort of People? They ftile them Husbands with us: have they the fame Names here? For Example now, would this Partner of your's, when you took him, change his Qual ty of Cofin with which you have honour'd me? Anfwer in Confcience. You have my Riddle, can you guefs it now?

I will tell you that fome other time, faid fhe, turning towards me with an indulgent look; but thy Riddle is a very diverting one. Yes, troth! faid I, and a great many pretty things might be made of it, if we would but take it in it's right Meaning.

Hufh! cry'd fhe immediately, this is no time to talk of fuch Waggeries; and the Moment fhe ftopp'd me, we found our felves at her Door, where we got about the Dusk of the Evening.

Catherine let us in, big with Curiofity to know Mrs. *Haberd*'s Intentions concerning her.

I fhall fay nothing of the extraordinary fufs which fhe made with us, nor of the diflike

which

which she exprefs'd for the eldeft Sifter's fervice; and this diflike was certainly fincere, becaufe the removal of the youngeft Sifter would leave her alone with the other · But for all that, whilft they were together, Dame *Catherine* only made her Court to the eldeft, whofe haughty and imperious temper requir'd fuch Subjection, and who befides had always the Government of the Houfe.

But the Union of the two Sifters being diffolv'd, alter'd the Cafe, and it was much the moft engaging to ferve the youngeft whom fhe might govern.

Catherine inform'd us that the eldeft was gone out, and that fhe defign'd to lie at a Devotee's of her Acquaintance, for fear God fhould be angry if the two Sifters fhould fee one another again in the prefent Circumftance : I am glad fhe is gone, faid *Catherine*, we fhall fup with the better Stomach, fhan't we Madam ? Affuredly, my Sifter has done very prudently, reply'd Mrs. *Haberd*, fhe is as much Miftrefs of her Actions as I am of mine.

To this fucceeded a hundred little Queftions from the complaifant Cook You were out along while, have you taken a Houfe ? Does it ftand pleafant ? Is it far from hence ? Shall we be near the Markets ? is the Kitchen convenient ? Is there a Chamber for me ?

She extorted a few anfwers in the laconic ftile ; I had alfo my fhare in her cajoleries ; to which I reply'd with my ufual gaiety, without telling her a Syllable more than Mrs. *Haberd* told her, by whom I regulated my conduct.

We'll

We'll talk of thofe things another time, *Catherine*, faid fhe, in fhort, I'm too much fatigu'd at prefent, let me have Suppei as foon as you can, that I may go to bed.

Upon which fhe went up into her Chamber, and I to lay the cloth, as alfo to efcape the importunate interrogatories of *Catherine*, from whom I expected a perfecution as foon as we fhould be together.

I was a long while in my office ; for Mrs. *Habei d* being come into the Room where I was laying the Cloth, I jefted with her about *Catherine*'s uneafinefs ; if we fhould take her along with us, faid I, adieu Relationfhip ' there could be no Mr. *de la Vallée.*

I amus'd her with fuch fort of difcourfe, whilft fhe drew up a little Memorandum of the Goods which belong'd to her, and which fhe intended to remove from her Sifter's ; for upon the Strangenefs which the other fhew'd in abfenting herfelf from the houfe, fhe defign'd, if poffible, to lodge in her new Apartment the next Night.

Mr. *de la Vallée*, faid fhe, laughing, go to morrow Morning as early as you can, and get me an Upholfterer to unfurnifh my Chamber, and my Clofet ; tell him to bring carriages with him, and every thing neceffary to remove my goods ; they may carry them all in a day, if they make any ufe of their time.

I wifh they were already carry'd, faid I, fo impatient I am till we drink together ; for yonder, my plate muft be plac'd oppofite

to

to your's, the Kinfman muft eat with his Kinfwoman; therefore depend upon't, ev'ry thing fhall be ready for the march by feven a clock in the Morning.

What was concluded, was executed. Mrs. *Haberd* fupp'd; and being grown hardy with her, I invited her to drink the laft Glafs, which I fill'd her to her Cofin's Health; whilft *Catherine*, who every now and then came up for fomething or other, was gone down into the Kitchen.

The Cofin's Health was drank, and I did her Juftice upon the Spot; for as foon as fhe had taken off her Brimmer, (and it was one) I pour'd out another of all Wine; and then, to your Health, Cofin, after which I went down to fup in my turn.

I eat a great deal, but chew'd little, fuch a hurry I was in to have done; for I rather chofe to run the hazard of an Indigeftion than to ftay long with *Catherine*, whofe impertinent Curiofity plagu'd me to death. Therefore under pretence of being obliged to rife early in the Morning, I retir'd, leaving her moft forrow-fully amaz'd at all fhe faw, as well as at my precipitate hafte in cramming down my Victuals, without anfwering her any other ways than by Monofyllables.

But, *Jacob*, tell me this; tell me that. Troth, Madam *Catherine*, faid I, Mrs. *Haberd* has taken a Houfe, fhe hung upon my Arm, we went, and now we are come back again; that's all I know; good night. Oh, how fhe long'd to rail at me! But fhe was in hopes
ftill,

ftill, and the Brute durft not make a noife.

It's time I proceed to events of more moment ; therefore let us make hafte to our new Houfe.

The next Morning the Upholfterer came, and mov'd our Goods off the Ground, we made a running dinner, deferring a more regular Meal till we could fup at our new Lodgings. At laft *Catherine* being convinced that fhe was not to go with us, treated us agreeable to the Indifference we fhow'd her, and as our Defertion of her deferv'd, fhe difputed the Propriety of I don't know how much Linen with Mrs. *Haberd*, affirming it belong'd to her eldeft Sifter, and would have beat me ; me ! who was fo like the deceas'd *Baptif*, whom fhe told me fhe lov'd fo dearly. Mrs *Haberd* wrote a Note, and left it upon the Table for her Sifter, in which fhe acquainted her that fhe would come in feven or eight Days, to fettle with her, and to difcufs fome little accounts which they had together. A Hackney-Coach came to take us, in we went without Ceremony, I and my Cofin ; and then, Drive away Coachman.

We are now at our new Houfe ; and henceforwards you may expect to find my Adventures more grand and important. Mr *Jacob*, your humble Servant, we have no Bufinefs now but with Mr *de la Vallée* ; a Name which I bore for fome time, and which was really my Father's, though ufually join'd with another to diftinguifh him from one of his Brother's ; and it's this other Name that I am

E 5   known.

known to the World by, which I think proper to conceal, and which I did not aſſume till after Mrs. *Haberd's* Death; nor then, becauſe I was diſſatisfy'd with my former, but becauſe my Countrymen obſtinately perſiſted in calling me by no other. Let us paſs to the new Houſe.

Our Landlady receiv'd us as if we had been her moſt intimate Friends. Mrs. *Haberd* found her Chamber in nice Order; and I had a little Campaign Bed ready prepar'd for me, in the ſeparate Apartment I ſpoke of.

The Affair was now, what we ſhould have for Supper; there was a Cook liv'd at the next door, who could have furniſh'd us with any thing; but our obliging Landlady, whom I had inform'd in the morning of our being to come that evening, had provided for us, and abſolutely inſiſted upon our ſupping with her.

Mrs. *Haberd* began immediately to eſtabliſh my Quality of Coſin; to which I anſwer'd directly, by calling Coſin again: and as I had ſtill a Spice of the Village in my Accent and Expreſſions, we remedy'd that by ſaying I was juſt come out of the Country, and that I had not been above two or three Months at *Paris*.

But tho' I had hitherto a few clowneries in my diſcourſe; yet I had learn'd to correct that fault above a Month before whenever I had a mind, and I only preſerv'd that rural turn with Mrs. *Haberd*, becauſe I perceiv'd it was of ſervice to me, and that I could ſay what I would to her under colour of that

ruſtick

rūſtick Dialect, but it's certain I could ſpeak better *French* when I pleaſed. I had already acquir'd a tolerable Phraſe, and thought my ſelf oblig'd to endeavour at as polite a one as poſſible

Our repaſt was one of the gayeſt in the world, and I was more gay than any body.

I thought myſelf in a flattering Situation; there were great likelihoods of Mrs *Haberd*'s being in love with me, ſhe was very amiable as yet, ſhe was an extraordinary Match for me; ſhe enjoy'd an yearly income of four thouſand Livres and upwards, and the proſpect before me was a very ſmiling one; it was enough to rejoice the heart of a young Peaſant like me, at almoſt the firſt jump from the Plough tail, to be capable of throwing myſelf into the honourable rank of a good Burgeſs of *Paris*, in ſhort I was upon the very criſis of being a Gentleman, upon having my rents to live on, with the careſſes of a Wife whom I was far from hating, and for whom I at leaſt felt a Gratitude ſo extreamly like Love, that I never troubled myſelf to examine the difference.

I was naturally of a ſprightly temper, you may perceive it by the account which I've given of my Life, and when this natural Sprightlineſs is join'd by new Motives of Vivacity, God knows how it tranſports one! it's certain I was in tip-top Spirits; to which you may add a little Wit, an ingredient I never wanted; heighten the whole with an agreeable Countenance, and then tell me, whether

ther I was not qualify'd for a pleafant table Companion ? Don't you think I became my place ?

Undoubtedly I appear'd to be fomebody; for our Landlady was a great friend to Mirth, indeed more capable of enjoying, than furnifhing it ; for her converfation was too rambling to be poignant ; and at table we fhould have Words, not tedious Stories.

Our Landlady therefore could not tell what compliment to make me worthy, fhe faid, of the pleafure fhe receiv'd from my Company; fhe melted into open tendernefs when fhe look'd at me, I had won her Heart, and fhe frankly own'd it, fhe conceal'd no-thing.

Her Daughter who as I've told you, was feventeen or eighteen years of age, I forget which, and who was more referv'd and cunning than her Mother, alfo gave me a great many Leers ; fhe affected rather an hypocritical than a modeft Carriage, and would not fhow above half the liking fhe had for my difcourfe.

Mrs. *Haberd*, on the other fide, feem'd perfectly aftonifhed at the Vivacity I difcover'd ; I could fee by her looks, that fhe had believ'd me to have a pretty deal of wit, but never fo much as I had.

I took notice at the fame time that it encreas'd her efteem and inclination for me ; tho' this augmentation of her good Opinion was not without it's uneafinefs neither.

The

The encomiums of my frank Landlady diſturb'd her, nor were the ſly artful Glances of the young Girl unobferv'd by her. Perſons who' love, have their eyes every where, and her heart was divided between the Anxiety of feeing me ſo lov'd, and the fatisfaction of feeing me ſo amiable.

I perceiv'd it at once, for this talent of looking into Peoples minds, and reading their fecret thoughts, is a gift which I always poſſeſs'd, and which has fometimes done me admirable fervice.

I was immediately charm'd to find Mrs. *Haberd* in ſuch a diſpoſition; it was a good' fign for my hopes, it confirm'd me that ſhe'd an inclination for me, and might probably haften her deſigns in my favour, eſpecially fince the leers of the daughter and the amorous compliments of the Mother, feem'd to put me up, at, Who bids moſt?

Therefore I redoubled my agreements as faſt as poſſible to continue Mrs. *Haberd* in the alarms ſhe had taken; but as it was neceſſary ſhe ſhould be afraid of their liking me, and not of my liking them, I manag'd the matter in ſuch a manner, as not to appear blameable in any reſpect, and fo as ſhe ſhould conclude that my intention was barely to divert myſelf, not to pleaſe, or that if I took any pains to be agreeable, it was only to make my advantage in her heart, not in that of either of the others

For a proof of this, I took care to look at her very often, as if to demand her approbation

probation of what I faid; fo that I had the addrefs to make her contented with me, to leave her in thofe uneafineffes which might be ufeful to me, and to continue my civilities to the Widow and her Daughter, to whom I alfo found the fecret of infinuating that I thought them agreeable, which was to excite them to pleafe me in their turns, and to preferve them in thofe inclinations which they difcover'd for me, and which I ftood in need of to prefs Mrs. *Haberd* to explain herfelf, and if I muft tell all, perhaps I had a mind alfo to fee how the adventure would turn out, and to make the beft of every thing; one's very glad, as the faying is, to have more than one ftring to one's bow.

But I forgot one thing, and that's the young Girl's picture, which it's very neceffary I fhould give you.

I have already told her age. *Agatha*, for that was her name, according to her Cit Education, had abundance more wit than her Mother, whofe opennefs of heart and tittle tattle humour feem'd ridiculous to her; which I perceiv'd by certain little malignant fmiles which every now and then peep'd out, and whofe meaning efcap'd the artlefs Mother, fhe was too good-natur'd and too frank to be fo intelligent.

Agatha was not handfome, but fhe had a good deal of delicacy in her features, with Eyes very fparkling and full of Fire; but then it was a fire which the little Soul fupprefs'd prefs'd, and never let appear but by halves, which altogether gave her a very poignant, but a very fly look, and fuch a one as a Perfon would miftruft at firft fight, becaufe of a *je ne fçai quoy* of craftinefs which was diffus'd thro' the whole, and which made it not much to be depended upon.

Agatha was inclin'd to love at the firft view, fhe was rather difpos'd to be amorous than tender, had more Hypocrify than Morals, and more regard for what was faid of her, than for what fhe really was : She was the moft intrepid lyar I ever met with ; I never knew her at a lofs for expedients ; you would have imagin'd her timorous, but there never was a more daring, refolute Spirit, nor a more unfhaken countenance in the World ; there was nobody troubled themfelves lefs for being guilty of a Fault; and nobody took more pains to conceal, or excufe it , nobody was lefs fearful of reproach when fhe could not avoid it , and then you talk'd to fo calm a delinquent, that her fault no longer appear'd any thing.

It was not upon the Spot that I unravel'd this myfterious Character, I only knew *Agatha* by feeing her often.

It's certain fhe found me to her liking, as well as her Mother,who was wonderfully taken with me, and was one of thofe good natur'd Women whom you may lead by the Heart any where , thus on both fides, I faw a fine Field open for my Gallantries, had I been difpos'd to have attempted the Succefs of them.

But

But Mrs. *Haberd* was more fure than all this; fhe was refponfible for her Actions to no one, and her Intentions, if they were favourable to me, were fubject to no Contradiction. Befides, I ow'd her my Gratitude, and that's a Debt which I've always very faithfully difcharged to v ery Body.

Therefore, in fpight of the Favour I had acquir'd in the Family, and the Appearances there were of my being able to make myfelf valu'd, I refolv'd to keep my Heart at home, and to preferve an entire freedom in my Determinations.

It was Midnight when we rofe from Table; they waited upon Mrs. *Haberd* to her Chamber, and in the little Space we had to walk for that purpofe, *Agatha* found at leaft a dozen opportunities to ogle me in her flattering, referv'd Way, which I could not help anfwering in my Turn, and all fo rapidly one to the other, that they were imperceptible to any Body but ourfelves.

For my Part I only anfwer'd *Agatha*, becaufe I had no mind to mortify her Vanity; it's barbarous to play the cruel with a handfome Girl who courts you.

The Mother had hold of my Arm, and never ceas'd crying, go, you're a pleafant Wag, one fhould never be tir'd of you.

I never faw him in fuch a merry Humour, reply'd the Cofin, in a Tone which faid you've too much on't.

Troth, Ladies, I am always of a merry Humour, anfwer'd I, but good Wine, good Cheer, and good Company, are enough to make

a Man gayer than ordinary; are not they, Cofin?
added I, giving a little hug to her Arm which
I held.

With this fort of Difcourfe we got to Mrs
Haberd's Apartment.

I believe I fhall fleep found, faid fhe, as
foon as we came there, affecting to be more
weary than fhe really was, on purpofe, to engage our Landlady to take her leave.

But this Landlady of our's was not fo expe-
ditious with her Good-Breeding; and thro'
the Abundance of her Friendfhip for us, there
was not a fingle Convenience in the whole
Apartment, which fhe mifs'd pointing out to
us.

She afterwards propos'd feeing me to my
Chamber; but as I read in my Cofin's
Looks, that this excefs of Civility was not very
agreeable to her, I refus'd it in as handfome a
Manner as I could.

At length our Ladies went out, perfectly
drove away by the hints which Mrs. *Haberd*
gave them, and which at laft were fo broad
that they could not avoid taking Notice of
them.

As for me I retir'd at the fame time to go
decently to my own Room, when my Cofin
call'd after me.

Mr. *de la Vallée*, cry'd fhe, ftay a Moment;
I've fome Affairs to charge you with for to
morrow Morning; upon which I went back,
having wifh'd the Mother and Daughter a good
Night, who both of them drop'd me very low
Courtefies, and particularly *Agatha*, who wouldn't
confound

confound her's with her Mother's; but made it apart, that I might the better diftinguifh it, and obferve all the expreffive, obliging Things which fhe put in it.

When I was return'd to Mrs. *Haberd*, and we were alone, I imagin'd the Bufinefs would be fome chagrin Reflections or other upon our Table Adventures, and the Advantages I had made by appearing fo diverting.

However, I was miftaken; tho' not as to her Intentions; for what fhe faid to me plainly fhew'd, that fhe only kept that Part of the ftory in referve.

My merry Cofin, faid fhe, I want to dif-courfe you a little; but it's late now and the Hour indecent, therefore, we'll defer it till to Morrow; I fhall rife earlier in the Morning than ufual to put fome Linen in order which is in thefe bundles, and will expect you here between eight and nine, that we may confult what Meafures to take about a thoufand Things which I'm thinking of: Do ye hear me? Don't fail; for this Landlady of ours has all the Air of threatning a Vifit in the Morning to enquire after my Health, and perhaps after your's; we can have no time for talking, un-lefs we're beforehand with the fury of her Compliments.

This little Difcourfe, as you may perceive, was a fort of Prelude to a jealous, or at leaft an uneafy fit; therefore I never doubted a Mo-ment what was to be the Subject of our next Day's Parley.

I

I was punctual to my Appointment; I went even before the time, to witnefs an Impatience which could not chufe but be agreeable to her; and I had the Satisfaction of feeing that she took it as I intended.

Oh! it's mighty well, faid fhe, as foon as fhe faw me coming; you are very exact, Mr. *de la Vallée*, have you feen our Land-ladies fince you have been up?

How! cry'd I, it never enter'd my Head whether there were any fuch People in the World: What Bufinefs have I with them? Troth! I had fomething elfe to think of.

What then is this fomething which you have been thinking of? reply'd fhe. Why our Appointment, faid I, I have dream'd of nothing elfe all Night.

I have alfo been very thoughtful myfelf, faid fhe; for what I'm going to fay to you, *la Vallée*, is of great Confequence to me. Then for God's Sake! my dear Cofin, reply'd I, fpeak quickly, you make me fick with Im-patience. Since the Subject regards yourfelf, I cannot live without knowing it; Does any Thing afflict you? Is there any Remedy? Is there none? I fhall run diftracted unlefs you tell me immediately.

Do not difturb thy felf, faid fhe, it is nothing which ought to make you uneafy. Madam, anfwer'd I, my Heart is no more capable of hearing Reafon than a new born Babe's, to-wards you, and it is none of my fault. Why have you been fo good too me? I could not keep it within bounds.

But

But Child, faid fhe, looking earneftly at me, as if to conjure me to be fincere; do not you exaggerate your Attachment for me? Do you fpeak as you really think? May I believe you?

How! cry'd I, ftepping back with Surprize; do you doubt me, Madam, when I'd ftake down my Life, and a hundred Lives to it, if I had fo many, to procure the Health and Continuance of your's; do you doubt me? Farewell Comfort! I had nothing valuable but my poor Heart; and fince you queftion that, it is the fame as if I had nothing at all. Is this the cafe, after all the Favours which you heap'd upon me, after the Relationfhip you gave me for nothing? Had you faid, Do you love me, Cofin? why I fhould have immediately anfwer'd, yes, Cofin, I do; and had you reply'd, perhaps no, Cofin: Why then your Cofin is worfe than a Bear; there's not a Beaft in the Foreft, fo favage and unnatural as him. What a fine Kinfman have you introduc'd into your Family? Go, Madam, may God forgive you! I wifh I had never feen you. Would to Heaven I had never fet fight on you! Rather than to hear my felf accus'd in this manner by a Perfon who was the firft Object of my Affection, except Father and Mother, whom I reckon as nobody, becaufe one's of their Blood, and becaufe the Affection one has for them does not interfere with that which we conceive for others: It was all the Confolation I had to think you knew the bottom of my Heart; pray God help me, and you too! As merry as I was, you fee me melancholy enough now.

I

I perfectly well remember that whilſt I talk'd thus to her, I felt nothing within my ſelf that could give the lie to what I ſaid. I acknowledge at the ſame time that I affected as moving an Air and Accent as poſſible; I aſſum'd the Tone of a Man who cries, and endeavour'd to adorn the Truth a little; but what is very ſingular, my Invention prevail'd upon me firſt. I acted my Part ſo well, that I deceived my ſelf, and had nothing to do but to go on without adding any Thing to my real Conceptions; it was the Sentiment which ſtruck me, and that's more powerful than all the Art in the World.

Nor was I miſtaken in my Aim; I ſo thoroughly convinced and perſuaded Mrs. *Haberd*, that ſhe cry'd thro' meer Tenderneſs, comforted me for the Affliction I ſhew'd, and even aſk'd my Pardon for having queſtion'd my Sincerity.

But I was not to be pacify'd at once; I had my Heart full a conſiderable Time, it was what the Sentiment led me to, and it led me right; for when we're upon the ſubject of Complaints, and eſpecially tender ones, they are not eaſily to be appeaſed; we continue to complain even after we have pardoned; it is like the firſt Mvement which you give to any Thing, it does not end preſently, it diminiſhes by degrees, and then ceaſes

But at laſt my tender reproaches being vented, I yielded to the many obliging Things which ſhe ſaid to pacify me.

Nothing

Nothing is fo affecting either on one Part or the other as fuch fcenes as thefe, and efpecially in the beginning of an Amour . It occafions Love to make an infinite Progrefs, it ungari- fons the Heart of all it is refervednefs, and makes it fay more in a quarter of an Hour, than according to the rules of Decorum, it would dare to fay in a Month, and that without feeming to fpeak any Thing too foon, tho' it fpeaks every Thing.

At leaft this was my Cafe with Mrs *Haberd*, I am perfuaded fhe had no defign of making the Advances fhe did, and that fhe would not have told me my good Fortune under feveral Confe- rences ; but fhe was no longer her own Miftrefs to obferve that Oeconomy : her Heart flew open, and I drew from it her moft fecret In- tentions concerning me ; and perhaps fhe alfo in her Turn, drew more Tendernefs from me than I really had for her ; I was aftonifh'd my felf at the excefs of my Paffion, tho' I loft no thing by it, as you'll find by the fequel of our Converfation, which it is neceffary I fhould ac quaint you with, becaufe it is that in which Mrs. *Haberd* declar'd her felf.

Child, faid fhe, after having repeated the Word twenty times over ; I believe Thee, in- deed I believe Thee ; Child, faid fhe again, I fancy you can guefs now upon what our Bu- finefs turns , Alas ! my gracious Cofin, faid I, methinks I fee fomething ; but the fear of amu- fing my felf perplexes my Sight, and what I fee confounds me becaufe of my little Merit: Is it poffible, God forgive me, that my Perfon is not

not difpleafing to your's ' Can fuch a Happinefs be the Portion of a poor Country Lad ? This is what it feems to me, and if I was certain of it, why I fhould die for Joy

Yes, *Jacob*, anfwer'd fhe directly, fince you underftand me, and fince it affords thee fo much Satisfaction, enjoy it in full Security.

Softly then, faid I ; I fhall fwoon away with pleafure elfe ' There's only one Confideration which checks me How ' What is that ? faid fhe, why, anfwer'd I, you might fay, thou haft nothing, neither eftate, nor money, nothing to let, every thing to buy, and nothing to fell, no lodging but thy Neighbour's Houfe, or the Street, nor even fo much as a Month's Bread beforehand : After which, my pretty Sir, is not it extream kind in you to be fo overjoy'd at my loving you ? And do not you think I ought to thank you for the Fatigue of your Raptures ? This, my precious Kinfwoman, is what you may reply to the exceffive Joy with which I receive your Affection. But God's my Witnefs, Cofin, it is not the Love of thefe Provifions which tranfports me thus.

I believe it, faid fhe, thou wouldft never think of telling me fo, if it was not true, my dear Child.

Hear me, Cofin, added I, I no more think of the Bread, the Wine, and the Lodging, than if there was neither Corn, Vines, nor Houfes if the World ; I fhall take them to be fure when they offer themfelves ; but then it will be only becaufe I find them in my Way. As for money, I concern my felf about it juft as much as

I

I concern my felf about the Mogul; my Heart
is no Merchandife, nor would I fell it tho' any
one would bid me a thoufand Crowns more for
it than it is worth; but it fhall go *gratis*, where
it likes, as it has done to you without demanding any Thing in Return. Be you angry or
pleafed with this Heart, it is all one, it has
fix'd its Choice, and will abfolutely be your's.
I confefs indeed that it is in your Power to
be of infinite Service to me, becaufe you have
wherewithall: But I had no fuch Arithmetick
in my Head when I furrender'd my felf to your
Merit, lovely Afpect, and Sweetnefs of Behaviour;
and as to your Affection, I look'd for that, as
I look for Saturday's being Sunday. Mine is
an Affair which begun upon the *New Bridge*;
from thence to your Houfe, it gather'd new
Strength and Vigour; when we came there it
was at the Height, and two Hours after, was
incapable of any Addition, this is the plain
Truth of the Story.

How! reply'd fhe, had you been rich and
in a Condition to have told me, I love you,
Madam, would you have told me fo, *Jacob*?

Who! me? cry'd I; mercy on my Life!
I would have told you fo before I fpoke to you,
as indeed I've already done, begging your Pardon; for had I been worthy of your Attention, you might eafily have read in my Eyes
what my Tongue was afraid to utter, they
never yet look'd upon your's but they talked
to you as I talk to you now: I was always
in love, I adore you; words which are wrote
in every Feature of my Face. Well, Child,

anfwer'd

anfwer'd fhe, fetching a deep Sigh which parted from the Abundance of her Tendernefs; you have open'd your Heart to me, I muft now open mine to you.

When you met with me, I had been a long Time weary of living with my Sifter upon Account of her unfociable Temper , but I neither knew which way to take, when I fhould part from her, nor what kind of Life to addict my felf to , I had fometimes an Inclination to go to boarding , but that is attended with its inconveniences, for there one's generally oblig'd to facrifice one's Humour to the Humours of other People, which I could not away with. Sometimes again I thought of marrying ; I am not yet of an Age to renounce that State, faid I to my felf ; I can bring a handfome Fortune to whoever lights upon me ; and if I could meet with an honeft Man of a good Temper and good Character, I fhould be happy for the reft of my Days. But this honeft Man, where muft we find him ? I faw feveral Gallants follicitous for an Opportunity to flatter me, and fome very rich, but none of them were to my tafte; one was of a Bufinefs I did not like, another I was inform'd was extravagant; this lov'd Wine, that Gaming, and a third loofe Women : fo few there are in the World who live in the fear of God, and who marry with a Defign to difcharge the duties of their Station ! Amongft thofe who were free from thefe Vices, one was a Coxcomb, another was fullen and melancholy, and what I fought for was a Man of an open, gay Temper, one of a grateful,

G   fincere

fincere Heart, and one who would anfwer the Affection I fhould have for him with mutual Tendernefs. I valued not whether he was rich or poor, whether he was of Diftinction, or no Diftinction. Nor was I more curious concerning his Family, provided it was a creditable one; that is, provided it was only obfcure, not vile and defpicable; and I had Reafon to think modeftly in that particular, for my own Parents were only fubftantial People, they made no Figure. Therefore I waited till Providence, to which I entirely referred my felf, fhould guide me to the Man I fought for; and it was then I found him, when I met you upon the *New Bridge.*

In this Part of her Difcourfe I interrupted her.

I'm refolved, faid I, I'll buy a Pocket Book, and write down the Year, the Day, the Hour, and the Moment, with the Month, the Week, and the Time which compofed the Day of that happy meeting.

The Pocket Book is already bought, Child, faid fhe, and I'll give it Thee; let me go on.

I was exceeding weak when you met me, and it muft be acknowledged that you affifted me with a hearty good will.

When by your care I was a little recovered, I confidered you very attentively, and your Countenance feem'd altogether promifing.

Thank God! who has bleft me with fuch a one, cry'd I. Yes, faid fhe, it ftruck me at once; and the Inclination I felt for thee was fo fudden, and fo natural, that I could not help reflecting upon it. What can be the meaning

ning of this? thought I; I find my self perfectly compelled to love this young Man!
Upon which I recommended myself to God
who is the Difpofer of all things, and entreated
him, that he would manifeft his holy Will
to me in an Adventure which appeared fo extraordinary.

How! Cofin, cry'd I immediately, why
our Prayers took wing together then that Day;
for whilft you was faying your's, I alfo put up
my little private Ejaculation. My God! faid
I, who haft brought *Jacob* upon this *New
Bridge*; my God! faid I, who art ever mer-
ciful towards me, how happy fhould I be, if
thou wouldft infpire this good Lady with the
Refolution of keeping me all her Life, or at
leaft all mine, in her amiable Service!

Is it poffible, cry'd Mrs. *Haberd*, that fuch
a Thought fhould come into thy Mind, my
dear Child?

Yes, troth, faid I,; I did not perceive it
come into my Mind; I found it already
there

How remarkable is that! reply'd fhe. However, you help d me to walk home; and as
we went, the difcourfe fell upon your Station
of Life. I afk'd you feveral Queftions, and
it's impoffible to exprefs how fatisfy'd I was
with your Anfwers, and the Sentiments you
difcover'd. I perceiv'd a Sincerity and Candour in you which charm'd me; and I continually return'd to the fame Inclination,
which I could not avoid having for you; begging God to enlighten me, and to manifeft

his

his Pleasure to me. If it is his Will that I should marry this Youth, thought I, something or other will happen to prove it to me during his stay with us.

And I reason'd very justly God did not leave me long in Uncertainty. The same Day that Clergyman of our Acquaintance came to see us, and I've already told you our Quarrel together.

Ah! my dear Cosin, the precious Quarrel, cry'd I; how vastly I am obliged to the good Director for being so fantastical! how strangely it all hangs in a string! Here's a Street where we meet, a Prayer on one side, and an Ejaculation on the other, a Priest who comes to see you, and who reprimands you: your Sister, who would drive me out; you, who bid me stay: then a Separation between two Ladies for a Lad sent by God. how wonderful it is! and yet you ask me whether I love you! Why how is it possible I can do otherwise? Don't you clearly perceive that my Affection for you is of divine Ordination, and that it was determin'd before we saw one another? nothing is so glaring.

Truly, reply'd she, thou speak'st like an Oracle; and it seems as if God had furnish'd thee with these Arguments to compleat my Conviction. Go, Child, I am no longer in doubt; you are he for whom God has reserv'd me, you are the Man I sought, with whom I ought to live, and to whom I give myself.

And

And I humble myfelf, faid I, before this invaluable Gift, this bleffed Marriage, which I no way deferve; only as it is ordain'd you by God, and you are too good a Chriftian to refift his Pleafure. All the Advantage is mine, and all the Charity your's.

I was upon my Knees whilft I fpoke this, and printed a thoufand Kiffes on her Hand, which fhe devoutly thought it was her Duty to abandon to the Tranfports of my Gratitude.

Rife, *la Vallée*, yes, added fhe, I will marry thee. and as we can't put ourfelves too foon into that State to which God calls us, and as our living together may be liable to Cenfure, notwithftanding our Relationfhip, we muft haften our Marriage.

It is but morning yet, reply'd I; is it not poffible, if we make good ufe of the Day, to difpatch with the Notary, and get the Parfon to blefs us before Midnight? I don't underftand how thefe Affairs muft be managed.

No, Child, faid fhe, Things cannot be done at once; it is neceffary that you firft write to your Father for him to fend you his Confent.

Why! reply'd I, my Father is not againft it; he would give his Confent, though he was in his Grave, fo glad he would be at my good Fortune.

I do not doubt it, faid fhe; but begin by writing your Letter this morning. We fhall want Witneffes too, and I would have them

difcreet;

difcreet; for I defign to conccal our Marriage for a little while becaufe of my Sifter, and I do not know who to get

Let us take our Landlady, faid I, and one of her Friends; fhe's an obliging Sort of a Woman, and will keep your Counfel.

I agree to it, faid fhe, and the rather becaufe it will put an end to thofe impertinent Advances which fhe made you yefterday, and which perhaps fhe might otherwife continue, as well as her Daughter, who is a young ill-bred huffey in my Opinion, and to whom I defire you'll behave very cold.

Juft then, we were interrupted by a noife, it was our Landlady, attended by her Cook, who was bringing us Coffee.

Are you up? Neighbour, cry'd fhe. Yes long fince, faid Mrs. *Haberd* opening the Door for her, come in, Madam. Oh! good Morrow to you, faid the other. How do you do? Have you refted well? Mr. *de la Vallée*, I'm your humble Servant. I pafs by the reft of our Compliments, as well as the Converfation over our Coffee.

When the Cook had carry'd back her Equipage: Madam, faid Mrs. *Haberd*; you feem one of the beft Women in the World, and I have a fecret to difclofe to you, concerning an Affair in which you may be of fervice to me.

Oh! my God, my dear Lady, what fervice can I do you? reply'd our Landlady with a profufion of Zeal and good Nature which were very fincere. Pray fpeak. But not yet, added fhe she directly, stay till I've shut the Doors, since it's a secret, nobody ought to over-hear us

She got up as she spoke this, went out, and immediately from the Top of the Stair case, call'd to her Cook; *Javote!* said she, if any body comes to enquire for me, tell them I'm gone out; let nobody come up into the Gentle-woman's Room neither And be sure keep my Daughter away, for we've a secret to talk of together, do you hear? And after having taken these discreet Measures against Intruders, back she came to us, fastening all the Doors and Bolts in her way, so that out of meer Respect to the Secret to be confided in her, she acquainted all her Family that she was going to be trusted with one; her Zeal and good Meaning knew no better, and it's very much the Character of the best sort of People in the World. Your excessive good Tempers are voluntarily imprudent thro' the Excess of their good Nature, and on the other Hand, your prudent Tempers have rarely any good Nature at all.

Oh! Madam, said Mrs. *Haberd*, you should not have told your Cook that we had a Secret to talk of; there was no Occasion to inform her that I had any thing in particular to tell you.

Oh! no Matter, said she, do not let that trouble you. If I had not given her this Charge they would have interrupted us; and besides, had it been only upon my Daughter's Account the Precaution was necessary. Come,

G 4   Madam,

Madam, what is this Affair? I defy you to produce any body who wishes you better, without reckoning that I am the Confidant of all my Acquaintance, when they have once told me a Secret, why mum for that! I have my Mouth sow'd up; I am speechless. Yesterday Mrs. such a one, who has a Husband that devours all before him, brought me a thousand Livres to keep for her; he'd devour them too if he knew were to find them; but I will warrant him from that! they are safe enough! ay, ay, pray speak.

All these proofs of our good Landlady's Discretion were no great encouragements to Mrs. *Haberd:* But after having promis'd her a Secret; it was perhaps worse to refuse it her than to tell it; therefore she lay under a Necessity of speaking.

I shall have done in two Words, said Mrs. *Haberd*; we are going to be marry'd, Mr. *de la Vallée* that you see here, and I.

Together! cry'd our Landlady with an Air of Surprize; yes, answer'd Mrs *Haberd*, I have consented to take him for a Husband.

Ay, ay, said she; why, it is mighty well! he is young, he will last a long time. I wish I could meet with such another, I'd do the same my self. Have you been long Sweet-Hearts! No, reply'd Mrs. *Haberd* blushing. Oh! continu'd she, it is so much the better in making Love, there is nothing like being Man and Wife But have you got your Dispensation? You are Cosins.

No,

No, we have no need of one, anſwer'd I ⸳
We were only Relations through decency, and
to hinder the reflections of the World.

Ha! ha! that is pleaſant enough, ſaid ſhe.
Why, you tell me things which I ſhould never
have dream'd of. It is your Wedding then
which you would conſult me about?

That is not all, ſaid Mrs. *Haberd,* we
would keep our Marriage private, becauſe of
my Siſter, who perhaps might make a Diſturbance elſe.

A Diſturbance! for what? Becauſe of your
Age? reply'd our Landlady. Truly, that
would be pretty indeed! was not it laſt Week
pray, that a Woman of threeſcore and ten and
upwards, was marry'd in our Pariſh Church to
a young Cadet of twenty? Age is for the old,
what Buſineſs have other People to trouble their
Heads about it?

I am not ſo old neither, ſaid Mrs *Haberd,* in
a little Confuſion which had not left her all the
time. No, no, God forbid! reply'd our Landlady; you are of an Age to marry, if you ever do.
After all, one loves what one loves, they may
think you have a young Husband. But what of
all that? you meet with him young If he is but
twenty, that is no more your Fault, than his.
Let me tell you, Neighbour, the younger the
better, he will have youth enough for you both.
Ten Years more, ten Years leſs, tho' it was
twenty, tho' it was thirty, he will have forty good
ſtill; and the one is no more offence to God than
the other. Why what can they ſay? That you
are old enough to be his Mother? Well, and

                                                    the

the worft of that is, that he is young enough
to be your Son. If you had one, perhaps, he
might not prove fuch a handfome Spark, and
would have Coft you dearer into the Bargain .
Ay, ay, laugh at People's idle prate, and tell
me what farther.

You would keep your Marriage private, is
not it fo ? Why, that will be very eafy ; you
have no blab to fear, I have taken care of
that, nothing can betray you . But go on.

If you make fuch long Comments upon
every Article, cry'd Mrs. *Haberd*, a little
nettled at her Difcourfe, I fhall have no time to
tell you. But in regard to my Age, I am very
glad to acquaint you, Madam, that I have no
occafion to be afraid of People's idle prate ;
for at five and forty, which I am----

Five and forty ! cry'd the other, interrupting her Why, that is nothing It is but five
and twenty more than he is ; truly, I took you
to be fifty at leaft ; but it was his looks which
deceiv'd me in Comparifon of your's : Five and
forty is nothing, Neighbour ! oh ! your Son may
very well make you a Mother yet. Juft over-
againft us, lives a Lady who lay in laft Month
at four and forty, and I warrant fhe won't ftick
out at five and forty, though between you and
I, her Husband is threefcore and twelve. Oh !
it is mighty well, you are comely, and he is
young, I will engage you will have Children.
But tell me, would you have me help you to a
Notary to draw the Contract ! I will wait on
you to mine by and by, or fhall I bid *Javote*
go and defire him to ftep here ?

Why,

Why, no! Madam, faid Mrs. *Haberd*, don't you remember I would have my Marriage kept a Secret? Oh! yes, I had forgot, faid fhe; we will go to him in private then. Are there any Banns publifh'd this Morning?

That is the very Affair, faid I, in which Mrs. *Haberd* begs your Affiftance, as alfo to procure us fome Witneffes, and to fpeak to the Parfon of the Parifh.

Leave all that to me, faid fhe, after to Morrow comes *Sunday*, the Banns muft be publifh'd; I will go prefently and take Order about it. I know a Clergyman who will fuit you exactly; do not be uneafy, I will fpeak to him this Morning. I will go and drefs me this Inftant, without taking leave, Neighbour. Five and forty, and afraid of People's prate about your marrying! No, no, Neighbour, never let that difturb you. Adieu, adieu, my good Friend; your Servant, Mr. *de la Vallée*. But now I think on it, you fpoke to me yefterday concerning a Cook, you fhall have one immediately; *Favote* told me, that fhe went to engage one this Morning; fhe is an Acquaintance of her's, they are Countrywomen. They come both from *Champagne* as well as my felf; we are three of us now, and you will make the fourth. For I think you are of *Champagne*, are not you? added fhe laughing. No, it is me, faid I; you are miftaken, Madam. Oh! very well, faid fhe, is it fo? I knew it was one of you; no matter which. Good-Morrow, till I fee you again.

As

As foon as fhe was gone, What a ridiculous Woman this is, faid Mrs. *Haberd* with her Age, and her Mother, and her Son! I am forry I difcover'd our Affair to her, *Jacob*, if I am as old in thy Eyes as I appear to be in her's, I would not advife thee to marry me.

Oh! faid I, do not you perceive a little rancour at the bottom of all that? Harkee, Cofin, between you and I, if you was to drop me, I believe fhe would gladly pick me up, in cafe I was willing, which I never fhould be; for after you, all the Women in the World would be as nothing to me. But ftay, I am going to fhew you your Age. Upon which, I run to fnatch down a little Glafs which hung againft the Tapiftry Here, faid I, look at your five and forty, and fee if it does not refemble thirty; I will venture a Wager you are nearer thirty than you fay.

No, my dear Child, replyd fhe, I am really of the Age I mention'd; though few People indeed take me to be fo much. I do not fpeak it becaufe I pride my felf in a frefh Colour, or a good Mein; I might have heard a great many flatteries upon that Subject, if I would have liften d to them: but I would neverthrow away my Attention upon fuch Cajoleries.

We had no time for any farther Converfation, being interrupted by *Agatha*.

So! Madam, cry'd fhe as fhe came in to Mrs. *Haberd*; do you take me for a blab then? fince you durft not truft me with what you told my Mother? She fays fhe is going to the

Notary's

Notary's for you, and afterwards to the
fon's.   What, is it for a Wedding ?

At the Word Wedding, Mis. *Hab*
blufh'd, without knowing what to reply.
is for a Contract, faid I, taking the anfv
upon my felf, and to haften it, I muft write a
Letter this Inftant to be fent away directly :
Which I faid on purpofe, that the little huffey
might leave us in Quiet ; for I faw her Company was difagreeable to Mrs. *Haberd*, who
could not recover her felf out of the furprize
into which the aftonifhing Imprudence of the
Mother had thrown her.

Accordingly I look'd for Paper, and fet
my felf down in earneft to write to my
Father Mrs *Haberd* feigning to whifper to
me what I fhould write, fo that *Agatha* was
forc'd to retire.

As indifcreet as the Mother was, fhe ferved us to a Miracle. In fhort, all the neceffary Meafures were taken, the Banns were
publifh'd the next Day, and that very Afternoon we went to the Notary's, where the
Contract was drawn up, by which Mrs. *Haberd* fettled all fhe had upon me during my
Life. My Father's confent arriv'd four Days
after, and we were now come to the Eve
of our private Wedding, when for fomething, I forget what, we were oblig'd to
go to fpeak to this Clergyman of our Landlady's acquaintance. It was he who was to
marry us the next Morning, I mean, after
Midnight; and he had charg'd himfelf with
feveral little Matters, out of refpect to our
Landlady,

Landlady, to whom he had some Obligation.

Mrs. *Haberd* was to give a Supper that
Night, to her, and her Daughter, and four
Witnesses. It was agreed that we should rise
from table at eleven a Clock, and that the
Mother and Daughter should retire to their
Apartment, where *Agatha* should be left a-
sleep, and that two hours after Midnight, we
should set out, our Landlady, the four Witnesses her Friends, Mrs. *Haberd* and I, to go
to Church.

Accordingly we went about six in the Evening, to wait upon this Clergyman we were
to speak to ; he had been appriz'd of our
coming, but could not possibly stay for us, and
had left word with one of his Fraternity,
to tell us, that he would be at our Lodging in
an hour or two.

We returned, and were just sitting down
to table, when we were told that the Clergyman in question was coming up. We had
neither heard his Name, nor he ours.

He came in. Imagine to yourself our
Astonishment[1] when instead of a Person whom
we thought we should know nothing of, we
saw the Director, who at Mrs *Haberd*'s had
declar'd for my being turn'd out.

My Intended gave a sudden Scream, as
soon as she saw him, which was imprudent
enough, but is one of those Emotions which
are quicker than Reflection. For my part,
I was in the Middle of a Bow which I left
unfinished : He had his Mouth open to speak,
but

but ftood fpeechlefs. Our Landlady was
going to meet him, but ftopp'd fhort with
her Eyes fix'd to fee us fo immovable ; and
one of our Witneffes, a friend of our Landlady's, who was advanc'd towards the Clergyman to embrace him, remain'd with his
Arms ftretch'd out. So that altogether, we
compos'd one of the moft fingular Scenes in
the world. We were fo many Statues.

Our filence lafted for at leaft two Minutes.
At laft the Director broke it, and addreffing
himfelf to our Landlady · What' Madam,
faid he, are not the parties in queftion here
then ? (for he never imagin'd that we were
the Subjects of his Miffion, I mean, the Perfons he was to marry, five or fix Hours after.) Yes, truly, reply'd fhe, here they are
both, Mrs. *Haberd* and Mr. *de la Vallée*

He could hardly believe what he heard ·
And really it was odd enough, that it fhould
happen to be us. 'Twas of that fort of News
which a Perfon may enquire after, and yet
not doubt of at the fame time.

What ' cry'd he, after having look'd upon us, for a Moment or two, with Aftonifhment, do you call that young Man Mr.
de la Vallée, and is it he who is this Night
to marry Mrs. *Haberd* ?

The very fame, reply'd our Landlady, I
know of no other, and to be fure the Gentlewoman won't marry two.

Neither my Intended nor I anfwer'd a
Syllable, I held my Hat in my Hand with
as carelefs an Air as poffible, and alfo look'd

with

with a fmile at the Director whilst he in-
terrogated our Landlady · But it was only
a fmile of Affectation, it was not genuine;
and I'm perfuaded, that for all my carelefs
Air I made but a filly Figure. One muft
have a furious Stock of Affurance, to hold
out againft fome things, and I was naturally
no more than bold, I was not brazen.

As for my Intended, fhe had her Eyes rivetted to the Ground, with a Countenance
which one can't eafily defcribe. It was a
Mixture of Chagrin, Confufion, and Timi-
dity, which proceeded from the remains of
a devout Refpect for the Director; and yet
over all, was diffus'd the penfive Air of a Perfon, who has a mind to fay, I don't value
it of a rufh; but is too much fhock'd, to be
fo refolute.

This Prieft, therefore, having gaz'd at us
with all the Eyes he had. Madam, faid he,
addreffing himfelf to our Landlady, this affair
deferves a little Confideration: Pray let me
fpeak a word or two in particular to you.
If you pleafe, we'll juft ftep into the next
Room, I fhall not detain you a Moment

Oh dear! Yes, Sir, reply'd fhe, quite charm'd
to find herfelf every way a Perfon of fuch importance in the adventure Don't be impatient,
Madam, cry'd fhe to Mrs. *Haberd* as fhe
was going out, the Gentleman fays we
fhall not be long.

Upon which fhe fnatch'd up a light, and
went out with the Prieft, leaving my Intended,

tended, our Witnesses, who witness'd nothing, *Agatha*, from whom she had conceal'd every thing, and my self in the Chamber.

Mr *de la Vallée*, cry'd one of our Witnesses immediately, what's the Meaning of this? Does Mr. *Doucin*, speaking of the Priest, know you then? Yes, said I, we have seen one another at Mrs. *Haberd*'s.

Ha, ha! Shall you be marry'd then? said *Agatha* in her turn. Yes, answer'd I, but not yet, as you will see presently.

Till then not a Word came from Mrs. *Haberd*: But during her Silence, her Confusion wore off, and Love reassuming its Place, calm'd all those Emotions which had alarm'd her at first: It shall neither be better, nor worse, cry'd she, plucking up her Spirit courageously.

Do you know, said one of our Witnesses, a Friend of our Landlady's, what Mr. *Doucin* is gone to say to Mrs *d'Alain*? (that was our Landlady's name.) Yes, Sir, reply'd she, I believe I can guess, but I don't care a straw.

He's a very good Man, a saint-like Man, this Mr. *Doucin*, said the malicious *Agatha*; he's my Aunt's Confessor. Well! Madam, I know him better than you, cry'd my Intended, but we were not talking of his Sanctity, they'll canonize him if he is such a Saint. What's that to the Purpose?

Oh dear! reply'd the little Hussey, what I said was only to shew you the esteem we have for him, I spoke of nothing else:

It's

It's none of my Bufinefs. I'm forry you
don't like his Behaviour : But undoubtedly,
one ought to believe, it's for your Good , he's
fo prudent ——

Juſt then, her Mother return'd You come
without Mr. *Doucin*, faid our Witneſs , I
thought he would have fupp'd with us.

Sup with us ! reply'd Mrs. *d'Alain*, truly,
that's a likely Story ! Come, come, there wiſl
be no Wedding to night ; and if it nevei
is, why fo much the better . Let's fup, fince
it's before us. It's an upright S ul this Mr.
Doucin, and you are very much oblig'd to
him, Madam, faid fhe to my Intended ;
you can't think how he loves you, both
you and your Siſter · Poor Man ! He fhed
Tears when he went away ; I could not
help crying my felf ; I have done nothing
but wipe my Eyes What News for this
Siſter ! oh good God ! what will become of
us ?

What do you mean, Madam, with your
Exclamations ? faid Mrs. *Haberd.* Oh ! nothing at all, reply'd fhe ; but I am aftonifh'd !
no matter for your feparation, one is not
oblig'd to live always together. You may be as
well here as there . But to marry in private ,
and then this *New Bridge* where the firſt meeting was ; a Husband upon the *New Bridge* !
you who are fo pious, fo reafonable, of a
Family, and fo rich ! oh, oh, do not trouble
your felf ! I fhall fay no more ; for I was
defir'd to talk to you in fecret ; this is an
Affair which fhould not be known to every
body.

body. And yet you tell it to every body, cry'd Mrs *Haberd*, with a tone of refentment

No, no, reply'd the difcreet Mrs. *d'Alain*, I fpeak of nothing but the meeting upon the *New Bridge*, and there is nobody knows what that means; ask my Daughter, ask this Gentleman, added fhe, pointing to our Witnefs, if they apprehend a Syllable? Nobody but you, and the young Man with you, underftand what I fay.

Oh! as for me, I underftand nothing faid *Agatha*, only it was upon the *New Bridge* where Mr. *de la Vallée* and you came firft acquainted, that is all.

Befides it is but fix Days ago, reply'd the Mother, and that is what I fhan't fay a Word about. Six Days! cry'd our Witnefs. Yes, fix Days, Neighbour: But fpeak no more on it, for you fhall know nothing from me; it is in vain to ask me any Queftions; it is fufficient for us to talk, Mrs. *Haberd* and I; come, let's fit down to Table, and let Mr. *de la Vallée* fit down too, fince it is Mr. *de la Vallée*. Not that I defpife any body; he is a good young Man, and a well behav'd young Man, and there is no profperity which I do not wifh him. If he is not a Mr. yet, perhaps he may be; a Servant to Day, and a Mafter to morrow; there is a great many befides him who have receiv'd Wages, and have afterwards come to pay Wages.

Mr. *de la Vallée* receive Wages! cry'd *Agatha*. Hold your Tongue, you little Huffey, faid the Mother? what muft you be meddling

for?   Did

Theme of class Rangerout (handwritten)

Did he receive Wages of the Gentlewoman who is prefent? cry'd our Witnefs directly. Oh! no matter, no more of that, Neighbour; mum· It is to Day, Mr. *de la Vallée*, you have him for fuch, take him for fuch, and let's to Supper.

As foon as you pleafe, reply'd he Only one loves to fit down with People of one's own Rank. However, Neighbour, I will do as you do; one cannot be wrong in following your Example.

This little Dialogue was handed to and fro, fo fwift, that Mrs. *Haberd* and I had had no leifure to recollect ourfelves; every word was a new Shock to us; and upon fuch an occafion the time can be only fpent in blufhing Imagine to yourfelf the Confufion we were in, to hear our Story repeated Article after Article, by this Woman, who was to fpeak of it to no body but Mrs. *Haberd*, who kill'd herfelf with faying, I won't mention a Syllable; and who told every thing, in protefting fhe would tell nothing.

Melodrame (handwritten)

For my part I was aftonifhed, I was ftruck dumb, I was ftupify'd; and all my intended Wife could do, was to throw herfelf back into her Arm-Chair, and to vent her Affliction in Tears.

However, I immediately recover'd myfelf at our Witnefs's Expreffion, that he lov'd to fit down with People of his own Rank.

Snobbery (handwritten)

This honeft Gueft of ours had no very impofing Mien, notwithftanding a new Cloth Suit which he had on, with a long white Neckcloth,

Neckloth, which was as ftarch'd and ftiff a himfelf. He was alfo equip'd in a new Pe ruque, which his Head bore with Refpeé and which rather feem'd to perplex than cov it; to be fure it was becaufe they were not familiar as yet; in all likelihood, they had not been acquainted above a Sunday or two at moft.

The good Man (a Grocer who liv'd at the Corner of the Street, as I found afterwards) had put himfelf in this Garb on purpofe to honour our Wedding, and his own defign'd Function of Witnefs; I fhall take no notice of his Cuffs, which had alfo their peculiar Gravity, I never faw their Fellows.

Well, but you, Sir, who talk to People of your own Rank, faid I, of what Rank are you pray? for my Heart tells me that I'm as good as you, for all I wear my own Hair, and you other Peoples. Yes, yes, faid he, we are both very good in our Places, one to ask to drink, and the other to bring the Cup: but you need not ftir now, I am not dry. Good night to you, Mrs *d'Alain*, I wifh you a good night, Madam: and away went our Witnefs.

Pride (sins of those who look down on couple, though hypocrits. Lucifer.)

The End of the fecond Part.

THE

Fortunate PEASANT.

PART III.

OUR other Witneſſes had remained ſilent
till now, and, I believe, would have
ſtay'd with all their hearts, had it been
only for the ſake of the good Cheer , for an
Entertainment is not a matter of indifference
to ſome People a good Supper is of Conſequence to them.

But this Witneſs, who had juſt left us, was
their Friend and Companion ; and ſince he
had refuſed to ſit down with me, they thought
themſelves obliged to follow his Example, and
to ſhew themſelves as ſcrupulous in this Affair
as him.

Since Mr ſuch a one . . . . (ſpeaking of
the other) is gone, ſaid one of the three, who
was

was a thick fhort Man, to Mrs. *Haberd*, we can be of no farther Service to you, Madam, and therefore I believe it will be proper we fhould take leave of the Company.

The Air with which he deliver'd this, was almoft as forrowful as grave, it feem'd to fay, we go with regret, but we don't know how to act otherways.

And what render'd their Retreat ftill more perplexing, whilft their Orator was fpeaking, our firft Service was brought up, which they lik'd extremely, as I could fee by their manner of eying it

Gentlemen, anfwer'd Mrs. *Haberd* coldly, I fhould be forry to incommode you, you are your own Mafters.

What fhould you go for, cry'd Mrs. d'*Alain*, who delighted in numerous Companies, and faw herfelf on the point of being depriv'd the Pleafure of goffiping a whole evening at difcretion · marry! fince Supper's here, we have nothing to do but to fit down to Table.

We are very forry, but it cannot be, reply'd the thick fhort Witnefs, it cannot be, Neighbour.

His Brethren, who had rang'd themfelves on each fide him, faid nothing, but hung down their Heads; and fuffered themfelves to be guided, without being able to pronounce a Syllable. This good Cheer had ftruck them fpeechlefs. He made his Bow, they made theirs; he went out firft, and they follow'd him.

We

We were now left with only Mrs. *d'Alain* and her Daughter.

See what it is! cry'd the Mother looking grumly at me, see what it is to answer People with ill Manners! had you so said nothing, they would have been here still, and would not have went away so discontented.

Why did their Companions speak with ill Manners to me then? reply'd I; what did he mean by his People of his own Rank? must he despise me, and I say nothing?

But between you and I, Mr. *de la Vallée*, answer'd she, how was he so much in the wrong on it? Lookee, he is a great Shopkeeper, a Burgess of *Paris*, and a Man of good Business, truly how are you his equal? Why, he is Churchwarden of the Parish!

What do you call him, Madam, said I, Churchwarden of the Parish? Do you think my Father has not been Churchwarden of his? Or do you think I should have miss'd being one my self, had I stay'd at our Village, instead of coming hither?

Well, well, said she, but this is a Parish, a great Parish, Mr. *de la Vallée*. Troth! said I, I fancy our Saints are as good as your's, Mrs. *d'Alain*; St. *James* is as good as St. *Gervase*.

However they are gone, reply'd she in a milder tone, for she was not pertinacious, it signifies nothing you and me disputing, that won't fetch them back again, as for my part I have no pride in me, I do not refuse sitting down to Supper. Your Wedding must be when God pleases, I only spoke my Opinion

H   through

through Friendſhip, I had no deſign of affront-
ing any body.

Yet you have affronted me in the higheſt degree, cry'd Mrs. *Haberd* ſobbing, and if it was
not for fear of offending God, I ſhould never
pardon your Behaviour ; to tell all my Aſſairs
to People whom I never ſaw before, to inſult
a young Man whom you knew I valu'd, to
ſpeak of him as if he had been the meereſt
wretch upon the Face of the Earth, and to
treat him like a Footman, though he never
was one only for a minute or two by Accident,
and becauſe he was not rich, and then to quote
the *New Bridge*, to make me paſs for a Fool,
for a Woman without Senſe, or Conduct, and to
repeat all the tittle tattle of a Prieſt who has
not acted according to God. Upon this Occaſion, for what Reaſon has he told you all
theſe idle Stories pray ? Let him ſpeak in his
own Conſcience, is it for Religion ? Is it for
any Concern he has for me or my Actions ?
If he has ſuch a Friendſhip for me, if he in-
tereſts himſelf ſo chriſtianly in what relates to
me, why did he always ſuffer my Siſter to uſe
me ill whilſt we liv'd together ? Was it poſſible
to ſtay with her ? Was there any ſuch thing
as bearing with her Humours ? He knows the
contrary, had not I reſolv'd to marry one Day,
I muſt another, and perhaps I ſhould not have
met with ſuch an honeſt Man Mr. *de la
Vallée* has ſav'd my Life, I ſhould have dy'd
perhaps had not it been for him, he is of as
good a Family as I am ; what would they have ?
What does Mr. *Doucin* mean ? Intereſt is a

fine

fine thing truly; becaufe I leave him, and becaufe he can have no more of thofe Prefents which I us'd to make him every Day, he muft perfecute me forfooth! under pretence of his extraordinary care for me, and here a Perfon under whofe roof I lodge, and in whom I plac'd all my Confidence, muft expofe me to one of the moft cruel infults in the World! for can any thing be more mortifying than what has juft now happen'd?

Here Tears, Sobbs, and Sighs, and all the Accents of a moft violent Affliction ftopp'd Mrs *Haberd*'s Voice, and prevented her going on.

I alfo wept my felf, inftead of comforting her, I paid her tear for tear, upon which fhe redoubled her's to recompence me for thofe I fhed; and as Mrs. *d'Alain* was fuch a good natur'd Woman, that every one who wept was in the right with her, we gain'd her over upon the Spot, and nobody was to blame now but the Prieft.

Oh my good God! my dear Friend! cry'd fhe to Mrs *Haberd*, going to her! oh my good God, how fretted I am, that I was not acquainted fooner with all this which you tell me! Come, Mr *de la Vallée*, courage Man! come and help me to comfort this dear Lady, who torments herfelf for a Word or two which I let fall unawares; but what would you have of me? I cannot conjure; here a Prieft draws one afide, and fays it is pity it fhould be a Match, truly I believe him, I had no notion of his little Reafons for being fcandaliz'd at it

H 2   But

But as for his being a dear lover of Prefents, oh I do not doubt it ' it is the Coffee, the Tea, and the Sugar. Ay, ay, I have a Friend who is a great Devotee, and fhe fends him all thefe things ; your mentioning of it makes me recollect her , you us'd to prefent him too, that is infallibly the cafe , you fhould do as I do, I talk of God as much as they will, but then I give nothing ; there is three or four of them frequent here, I receive them civilly : Good morrow to you, Sir ; Good morrow to you, Madam , fometimes they drink Tea, fometimes they take a Dinner, then a Game at Quadrille, a Word or two of Edification by the by, and after that your humble Servant, I may marry twenty times inftead of once, and they never trouble their Heads about me ; but come, my dear Friend, be comforted, what you are no minor ! you are in the right to marry Mr. *de la Vallée* , and if it is not to Night, it fhall be the next, and that is only one Night loft. I warrant you, let me alone , how, you fhould have dy'd had it not been for him ' oh it is no more than Confcience ' he muft be your Husband , I fhould be the firft to blame you, if he was not.

Juft then, we heard Mrs. *Haberd*'s Cook coming up, for Mrs. *d'Alain* had procur'd her one, which I forgot to tell you

Come, my dear, added fhe, careffing Mrs *Haberd*, let's fit down to Table, wipe your Eyes and fhed no more Tears , place her Armchair nearer Mr *de la Vallée*, and be merry , fit you there, Huffey

She fpoke that to *Agatha*, who had not open'd her Mouth fince her Mother's return.

Agatha was not in the leaft touch'd at our Situation, for to pity her Neighbour was not her Weaknefs, fhe had only kept filence to obferve us more at her leifure, and to amufe herfelf with the Figures we made in weeping. I faw by her Looks that the little Diforder we were in diverted her, and that fhe took a Pleafure in our Pain, notwithftanding the forrowful Air which fhe affected.

There are a great many People in the World of this Character, who love their Friends better in Affliction than in Profperity; when they congratulate you it is out of Compliment, but when they condole with you they are happy.

However, at laft as fhe was fiting down to Table, *Agatha* drop'd a little Exclamation in our favour, and it was an Exclamation worthy the hypocritical part which fhe took in our uneafinefs, one fhews one's felf in every thing, and the little Soul inftead of faying this is nothing, cry'd, oh how vexatious this is! Your malignant Tempers always take this turn; it is their Style.

The Cook enter'd, Mrs *Haberd* dry'd up her Tears, and carv'd for us, Mrs. *d'Alain*, her Daughter and me, and we all fell on with a pretty good Appetite, mine indeed was an extraordinary one, but I fupprefs'd part of it for fear of fcandalizing my Intended, who fupp'd very foberly, and might have accus'd me perhaps with being but little affected, had I fed too

H 3 heartily.

heartily One ought not to be hungry when one's afflicted.

Therefore I laid a restraint upon my self through decency, or at least I had the address to make them often cry, Pray eat! Mrs *Haberd* herself press'd me, and from entreaty to entreaty, I had the Complaisance to make a very hand'ome Meal, without any body's being able to find Fault with it.

Our Conversation during Supper had nothing particular in it, Mrs *d'Alain* as usual launch'd out into a great many unnecessary repetitions, talk'd over our Story in a very plain, though as she thought a very enigmatical manner, took notice that our Cook listen'd to her Discourse, and told her that Servants ought not to overhear what their Masters say.

In short Mrs *d'Alain* acted in every thing with her accustom'd Discretion, supper ended, she embrac'd Mrs. *Haberd*, promis'd her her Friendship, her Succour, and almost her Protection, leaving us if not comforted, at least more easy than we should have been without these assurances of her Service. To morrow, said she, in default of Mr. *Doucin*, we will get some other Parson to marry you. We thank'd her for her zeal, and she retir'd with *Agatha*, who put nothing extraordinary in the Curtley she made me that Night.

Whilst *Cathos* was taking away (that was the Name of our Cook) Mr. *de la Vallée*, said Mrs *Haberd*, softly to me, you must retire, it is not proper that this Girl should leave us together. But do you know any body who

can

can protect you here? For I am afraid my
Sister will occasion us some trouble; I will
engage Mr *Doucin* has carry'd her the News
already, and I know her Temper so well, that
I do not expect being left at quiet.

Troth! Cosin, answer'd I, provided you
protect me, what harm can she do me? If I
have your Heart, what occasion have I for
any thing else? I have wrong'd nobody, my
Parents are honest People, my Father has
consented, you have consented, and I have
consented, sure I think we are the Principals.

But above all, said she, do not suffer thy
self to be intimidated, whatever happens, I
charge thee, for my Sister has a great many
Friends, and perhaps they may threaten you.
you are unexperienc'd, Fear will seize upon
you, and then you will desert me for want of
Resolution.

Desert you! cry'd I, yes when I am dead,
but I shall hardly leave you till then, for whilst
my Soul and Body are together, go where you
will they will follow you, do you understand
me, Colin? It is not my nature to be timorous;
wrong nobody and fear nobody; let them come,
I love you, you are amiable, who can say to
the contrary? Love is common to all the
World, you are in Love, I am in Love, who
is there exempt from it? And when one loves,
why one marries, honest People do so, and we
do so, that is all!

Thou art in the right, reply'd she, and thy
Intrepidity gives me new Life, it is God who
inspires thee with it, and I plainly see his Hand

is in this Affair ; I should be guilty of an un-
pardonable scruple to doubt it , go, Child, let us
place our whole Confidence in him, and let us
thank him for the visible care which he takes of
us , bless, oh my God! a Union which is thy
Work. Adieu, *la Vallée*, the more Obstacles
we meet with, the dearer thou art to me.

Adieu, Cosin, the more they cross us, the
more I love you, answer'd I in my turn ; oh!
that this Instant was to morrow ! that I might
be able to call this dear Hand which I hold my
own , I was in hopes by and by to have been
in Possession of that and the whole Body belonging to it , what a cruel trick this Priest has
play'd me ! added I squeezing the Hand, whilst
she look'd at me with Eyes which seem'd to
repeat, what a cruel trick he has play'd us '
but then they repeated it in the most Christian
manner possible, considering the Love of which
they were full, and the difficulty there was in
adjusting all that Love with Modesty.

Go, said she, still speaking softly, and ac-
companying her Words with a Sigh, go, this
is not a proper time for us to melt into such
Tenderness ; it is true we ought to have been
marry'd to Night, but we are not, *la Vallée*,
nor can we till to morrow, therefore go.

Just then *Cathos* had her back towards us,
and I seiz'd the Opportunity to kiss her Hand,
a Gallantry which I had often seen practis'd,
and which one easily learns ; mine cost her
another Sigh, after which I got up and wish'd
her a good Night.

She

She had charg'd me to say my Prayers, nor was I in the least forgetful of that Duty; I even pray'd with more than ordinary Fervour, for one never loves God so heartily as when one has occasion for him.

I went to Bed extreamly satisfy'd with my Devotion, and with a firm persuasion that it was very meritorious; nor wak'd again till eight a Clock the next Morning.

It was near nine when I enter'd Mrs. *Haberd's* Chamber, who was also up later than usual; and I had scarcely wish'd her a good Morning, when *Cathos* came to tell me that somebody wanted to speak with me.

I was surpriz'd, for I had no Business with any body. Is it one of the Family? cry'd Mrs *Haberd*, who was more inquisitive than I.

No, Madam, reply'd *Cathos*, it is a stranger just this minute come in. I was going to see who it was, stay, said Mrs. *Haberd*, you shall not stir, let him come here to speak to you, bring him up.

Accordingly *Cathos* brought him up; he was a well made Man, a sort of a Valet de Chambre, with a Sword by his side.

Do not you call yourself Mr *de la Vallée?* said he to me. Yes, Sir, answer'd I, pray what service can I do you?

I come from Mr. President----(that is one of the chief Magistrates at *Paris*) who desires to speak with you, said he.

With me! cry'd I, you mistake sure, it must be with some other Mr. *de la Vallée*, for I neither know Mr. President, nor ever saw him in my Life.   H 5   No,

No, no, reply'd he, it is you he wants, it is the Person who courts a Gentlewoman call'd Mrs. *Haberd*, I have a Hackney Coach waiting below for us, and you cannot difpenfe with going, for they will oblige you to it. Therefore it fignifies nothing to refufe, befides there is no harm meant you, he only defires to fpeak with you

I have the Honour to know a Lady who is related to the Prefident, and lives in the fame Houfe with him, faid Mrs. *Haberd*; and as I imagine this Affair concerns me too, I will follow, you Gentlemen Do not difturb yourfelf, Mr *de la Vallée*, we will go together, this is all owing to my eldeft Sifter, fhe would fain crofs us I am certain we fhall find her at the Prefident's, and perhaps Mr. *Doucin* with her. Come, let's fee what the matter is. You fhall not wait long, Sir, I will only juft flip on another Gown.

No, Madam, faid the Valet de Chambre, (for he was one) I am precifely order'd to bring nobody but Mr. *de la Vallée*; I fuppofe they forefaw that you would be for coming with him, fince they gave me that pofitive Order, therefore you muft not go, I beg Pardon for the refufal, but I muft obey.

Ha! what precautions are here! what ftrange meafures are thefe! faid fhe. Well, Mr. *de la Vallée*, you fhall go firft then, and go boldly, I fhall be there almoft as foon as you, I will fend for a Chair this Minute.

I would not advife you to it, Madam, reply'd the Valet, for I am alfo commiffion'd to tell you, that in that Cafe you will fpeak to nobody

To nobody ' cry'd fhe, how ' what is the meaning of that ? The Prefident has the Reputation of being a very worthy Gentleman, every body fpeaks well of him ; how can he act fo contrary to his Character ' Where is his Religion then ? Does his being a Prefident empower him to fend for a Man he has no Bufinefs with, and that as peremptorily as if he fent to apprehend a Criminal ? Truly, I do not know what to think on it ; God can never approve fuch Actions, and it is my Advice he fhould not go I intereft my felf in what Concerns Mr. *de la Vallée,* I own it , and though he has neither Poft nor Employ, yet he is the King's Subject as well as another, and we are not permitted, to ufe the King's Subjects ill, nor to force them to come where we pleafe, under pretence that one is a Prefident, and they nothing ; it is my Opinion he fhould ftay.

By no means, Madam interrupted I, I am afraid of nothing (which was true enough) no matter whether it is right or wrong, his fending for me in this manner ; what have I to take State upon ? ought not every one to confider what he is . . . . . when I am a Burgefs of *Paris,* it will be another Cafe , but at prefent as I am a little Fellow, I muft vail my Bonnet, and take all in good part · To your little Fellows, they fay , the Prefident commands you to come, why let it be fo ; the Prefident fhall fee me, his Prefidentfhip fhall tell me is Reafons, and I will tell him mine; what ' we are in a Chriftian Country,

Country, I carry a good Confcience with me, and God's above all ftill · Come, Sir, let us march, I am ready.

Well, I confent, cry'd Mrs. *Haberd*; for indeed, what can he fay to you? But before you go, let me fpeak a Word or two with you in my Clofet, Mr. *de la Vallée*.

I follow'd her, and as foon as we came there, fhe open'd a Cabinet, and putting her Hand into a Bag drew out a quantity of Gold, which fhe bid me take. I fufpect, added fhe, that thou haft not much Money, Child, at all adventures put this in thy Pocket Go, Mr. *de la Vallée*, may God conduct you there, and fafe back again, be fure do not ftay, but return as foon as poffible, remember I fhall expect you with Impatience

Yes Cofin, yes Miftrefs, yes my charming Intended, and all that is dear to me in the World, yes, I will return immediately; I fhall be undone till I come back; I cannot live till I fee you again, cry'd I, feizing the generous Hand which fhe had juft empty'd into my Hat; had one a Heart of Flint, you would foon mollify it into Flefh, you and your endearing ways! What Bounty! oh my God! the charming Woman! how I fhall love her when I am her Husband! I die with Pleafure at the very Thoughts on it; come all the Prefidents in the World, I'd fay the fame. Adieu, Queen of my Soul, Idol of my Thoughts; I have fo much Love that I cannot utter it till we are marry'd, my Heart will be overcharg'd till then.

The

The only anfwer fhe could make me, was to throw her felf weeping into her Arm-Chair: and away I march'd with the Valet who waited for me, and who feem'd to be a courteous fort of a Man.

Do not alarm your felf, faid he to me as we went, it is no crime to be a Lady's Favourite, it is only out of Complaifance that the Prefident fends for you, he was defir'd to do it in hopes of frightning you; but he's a very equitable Magiftrate, and will hear Reafon; therefore do not be uneafy, but make a handfome Defence, and ftand your Ground boldly

Dear Sir, faid I, it is my Refolution; I thank you for your Advice, and hope fome time or other it will be in my power to fhew my Acknowledgement, but I affure you that I am as merry as if I was going to my wedding.

Talking in this manner we arriv'd at his Mafter's. Undoubtely my ftory had made a noife in the Houfe, for I found all the Servants got together in a croud upon the Stair Cafe to receive me.

I was not in the leaft bafh'd; every one fpoke his Opinion of me; and as it luckily happen'd amongft all their fpeeches, I heard nothing that could fhock me, I had even fome very obliging ones from the Females. He has not the Air of a Fool, faid one, truly the Devotee has made a good Choice, he is a handfome Youth, cry'd another.

To the right, it was, I am glad at his good Fortune; to the left, I like his looks, I fhould not fall out with fuch a one my felf; I am of

your

your mind, cry'd a third, you have no ill tafte, faid a fourth.

In fhort, I may fairly affirm that my way was pav'd with Compliments, and tho' it was like running the Gantlope, yet it was the moft agreeable Difcipline in the World, and I had no Reafon to be diffatisfy'd, except with an old fpoil-all of a Governante, whom I met at the Top of the Stairs, and who undoubtedly was piqu'd at feeing me fo young, whilft fhe her felf was fo old, and fo far remov'd from Mrs. *Haberd*'s good Fortune.

Her lafh was by no means a favourable one, for cafting a haggard look at me, and lifting up her Hands, hum! cry'd fhe, the doating old Fool! that it fhould ever enter her Head to marry fuch a Butterfly as this! fure fhe has loft her Senfes!

Softly, Mother, you'd be glad to lofe them too upon the fame Condition, reply'd I, encourag'd by the Flatteries of the others.

My Anfwer fucceeded, nothing was heard but a general laugh, from the top of the Stairs to the bottom, and we enter'd the Apartment, the Valet and I, leaving an eftablifh'd Quarrel between the Governante and the reft of the Family, who hifs'd her in my Favour.

I do not know how the old Woman rid her felf of it: but as you fee, my Repartee was not an unpleafant one.

The Company was affembled in in Mrs. Prefident's Chamber, where they expected my coming, and thither it was my Guide brought me.

Modefly

Modefty and Courage were the Equipage with-
which I enter'd. The Perfons I found there,
were Mrs. *Haberd* the Eldeft, whom I name
firft, becaufe it was fhe I was to plead againft.

The Prefident, who was a middle-aged Man.

Mrs. Prefident, whofe fingle Countenance
was fufficient to have reaffur'd me, had I been
afraid ; there needs only one fuch as her in a
Company to make one love all the reft,
not that fhe was handfome, fhe was not ; neither can I fay fhe was ugly ; I dare not offer
it, for if Franknefs, good Nature, and all the
valuable Qualities which compofe an amiable
Spirit were to chufe an ordinary Face, they
would chufe no other than Mrs. Prefident's.

Methought I heard her whifper to the Prefident ; Lord ! Sir, this poor young Man trembles ; fpeak to him mildly, I beg of you ; and
immediately fhe turn'd towards me with an
Air which feem'd to fay, do not be frighten'd.

Thefe are things of fuch a fenfible Nature
that one cannot mifapprehend them.

But the Obfervation has made me wander from
my Subject. I was reckoning up the Affiftants;
I have already nam'd three, we now come to
the others.

The next was an Abbot of a very courtly
mein, and dreft with all the galantry his Habit
would admit of, decent, yet graceful ; in fhort,
he was a polite little Clergyman, but I fhall
fay no more of him, becaufe I never faw him
afterwards.

Befides thefe, there was a Relation of the
Prefident's, the fame Lady whom Mrs. *Haberd*
faid

said she was acquainted with, and who liv'd in part of the House; she was a Widow of about fifty Years of Age, a tall Woman and extreamly well made. I'll give you her Picture presently. These were all.

But it's proper to advertise you that this Lady whose Picture I promise you was also a Devotee, how many Devotees are here ! may any one cry, but I cannot help it, it was by this means that Mrs. *Haberd* the Eldest came to know her, and to interest her in the Affair in Question; they both went to the same Confeffional.

And *à-propos* of your Devotees; it was on this Occasion that I may safely affirm (such rancour enters their devout Souls !) I never saw such an enrag'd Countenance of that of Mrs. *Haberd* present; it was chang'd to that Degree that I hardly knew it again.

The truth is, your violent Emotions are peculiar to these sort of People, and to be in a Paffion belongs solely to them, perhaps they believe themselves the Favourites of God; and that therefore they have a Licence to indulge in such transports; or perhaps they imagine that what is Sin in us profane Wretches, changes its Nature, and purifies itself in its Paffage thro' their Souls. In short I do no know what they think, but this I'm sure, the Wrath of your Devotees is very formidable.

In all likelihood their holy Exercise breeds a great deal of Choler; I only speak of your Devotees, I always except the Pious; for they have no Choler at all, their Piety entirely cleanses them from it.   I

I was not in the least disturb'd at the furious looks which Mrs *Haberd* gave me, I cast my Eyes as indifferently upon her as upon the rest of the Company, and advanc'd bowing to the President

What! said he, is it thee then, that this Lady's Sister is about to marry?

Yes, Sir, at least I've her Word for't, and to be sure I shan't be against any thing which is so much for my Honour and Happiness, answer'd I with a modest, but resolute and composed Air, I took a little Notice of the Language, but that *en passant*.

Marry thee! reply'd the President, thee! art thou qualify'd so be her Husband? Dost forget that thou art only her Servant?

I should not find any difficulty in forgetting it, said I, for I was only so for a Moment by accident.

See the Brazen-Face! how he answers you, Mr. President, interrupted Mrs. *Haberd*.

Oh, not at all, Madam, you are in a Passion, cry'd Mrs. President immediately with a Tone exactly conformable to the Countenance I spoke of, Mr. President questions him, he must have leave to answer, there's no harm in that, let us hear what he says.

The Abbot could not help smiling at this Dialogue in a sprightly manner; and the President cast down his Eyes with the Air of a Person who would fain be grave, but can hardly forbear laughing.

The other Lady, the Relation, was knotting, I believe, but every now and then she lifted

up

up her Head and gazed ftedfaftly at me ; I obferved that fhe meafured me from Head to
Foot.

How! reply'd the Prefident, why doft tell
me that thou wa'ft only her Servant for a
Moment, fince thou art actually in her Service?

Yes, Sir, at her fervice, as I am at your's, I
am very much her Servant, her Friend, and
her Suitor, that is all.

Why, you little, forry Rafcal, cry'd my
Sifter-in-law that was to be, not fatisfy'd
with the Prefident's way of talking to me,
can you lie then fo impudently at your Age?
Come, lay your Hand upon your Heart, and
remember that you are in the Prefence of God
who hears us both. Did not my Fool of a
Sifter meet withyou in the Street? Wasnot you a
Vagabond without knowing where to go when
fhe picked you up? What would have become
of you but for her? Muft not you have been
forc'd to have begg'd your Bread, had not fhe
took you out of Charity? Poor Woman! it
would have been happy for her to have had no
Pity on you, it's plain her Charity wasn't pleafing to God, fince it is follow'd by fo great a
Misfortune to her felf: what a Wandering,
Mr. Prefident, how terrible are the Judgments
of God! here fhe paffes over the *New Bridge*
one Morning, meets with this little Libertine,
brings him home; for my Part I did not like
him, but keep him fhe would in fpight of my
Advice, and the Infpiration of a holy Man who
endeavour'd to diffuade her, fhe quarrels with
him,

him, feparates from me, takes a Houfe in another Place, there goes to lodge with this
Scoundrel (God forgive me for calling him fo)
doats on him, and muft be his Wife forfooth!
the Wife of a Footman at fifty Years of
Age !

Oh ! Age is nothing in that refpect, faid the
Devotee Lady, who was not at all pleafed with
the Article fifty, for fhe was in her fiftieth
Year her felf, and was afraid the Difcourfe
fhould make them think of her. And befides,
continued fhe, is your Sifter fo old, Madam?
You are in a Pet. I think I heard her fay fhe
was about my Age, and if fo, fhe muft be at
leaft five Years younger.

I faw the Prefident fmile at this Calculation;
undoubtedly it appear'd none of the exacteft to
him

Oh ! Madam, reply'd Mrs. *Haberd* the eldeft, a little piqu'd, I know my Sifter's Age
very well, I am her elder, and I'm almoft two
Years older than fhe ; yes, Madam, fhe's fifty
wanting two Months, and I think at that Age
one may pafs for an old Woman; for my
Part I own I look upon my felf as fuch ; it is
not every one that bears their Age like you,
Madam.

Another folly which efcap'd her, either thro'
fpleen, or for want of Attention.

Like me ! Mrs. *Haberd*, reply'd the Lady
reddening ; why where are you rambling ? Am I
call'd in Queftion pray ? I bear my Age, fay you !
I believe I bear it as well as another. God
knows I do not trouble my Head about it , but
there's

there's no great Miracle in a Perfon's bearing their Age well at my Years.

Indeed, cry'd the Prefident drolling, Mrs. *Haberd* makes the *bel âge* very fhort, wrinkles don't come fo foon as that neither, but let's difmifs the Difcuffion of Ages

Yes, Sir, reply'd our eldeft, it is not her Years that I regard in this Affair, it is the Condition of the Husband fhe's about to take, it is the Bafenefs of her Choice ; confider what a Scandal it will bring upon the Family. I know very well that we are all equal in the fight of God, but amongft Men it's a different Cafe, and God requires us to conform to the Cuftoms eftablifh'd amongft us. We are forbid to difhonour our felves, and People will fay that my Sifter has marry'd a Beggar, that's what they'll call this young Fellow here, and I intreat that you'll kinder a poor run-away from loading us with fo much Difgrace, it will be a Labour for her good, and we ought to have Compaffion on her; I have already recommended her to the Prayers of a holy Community; Mr. *Doucin* has promifed me his, this Lady alfo, added fhe, looking at the Devotee, who appear'd not to relifh her Apoftrophe much ; and Mrs. Prefident and Mr Abbot, whom I have not the Honour of knowing, won't refufe me theirs , (the Prayers of the Abbot feem'd fomething ungrantable upon this Occafion ; he was ready to burft into a laugh, and therefore thank'd her for the Invitation, with an Air which put that Value upon them they were worth;) and you will have your Part in this good Work, continu'd
fhe

she to the President, if you'll be so kind as to assist us with your Authority.

Do not disturb your self, Madam, said the President, he shan't marry your Sister; he dares not carry things to that Extremity; and if he has a Mind to run that length, we shall find a way to hinder him, but he won't give us the trouble; and to make him amends for what we deprive him of, I'll take care of him my self.

I had held my peace hitherto, because I would give my answer all at once, but I lost no time during that Silence, I often cast my Eyes upon the Devotee Lady, who not only took notice of it, but return'd my stolen Glances, and why did I think of looking at her? Why, because I saw that she frequently gaz'd at me, and that made me reflect that I was a handsome Lad; one was the natural Effect of the other; one acts thousands of things in Consequence of such confused Ideas which come into the mind I do not know how, but lead you insensibly, and which we have no notion of restraining

Nor did I forget to look at Mrs. President, but that was in an humble suppliant manner; my Eyes said to one We take a Pleasure in seeing you, and she believ'd it, to the other, protect us, and she promis'd her Protection; at least I think they both understood me, and answer'd what I tell you

The Abbot had also his share in my Attention, some very modest looks had disposed him too in my Favour, so that I had already two thirds of my Judges for me when I began to speak

Im-

Immediately I demanded Silence, for the Gesture I employ'd for that Purpose was as much as to say, Hear me.

Mr. President, said I, I have let Mrs. *Haberd* speak without Interruption, and have patiently heard all the injurious things she has been pleased to say of me; if she was to talk an Hour longer, she could say no more than she has, therefore at present it's me to speak, every one in their Turn, which is but reasonable.

You say, Mr President, that if I resolve to marry Mrs. *Haberd* the younger, you'll hinder me, to which I answer, that if I'm hinder'd, I must desist of Necessity, there's no encountering with Impossibilities, but if I'm not hinder'd I will marry her, that's certain, and any one would do the same in my Place.

We now come to the Aspersions which have been cast upon me, I do not know how far they are consistent with Devotion, for that I shall leave entirely to her Conscience who spoke them; she says that God hears us, and so much the worse for her, I'm sure the Expressions she us'd were not very decent to be heard by him In short according to her, I'm a Scoundrel, a Beggar; her Sister a Fool, a poor old Run-a-way, none of which can belong to any but the meer Offscowrings of the Earth. therefore, to speak of my self. For Example, Mr. President, you see Mrs *Haberd* here, suppose you was to talk to her in the same Stile as you talk to me, thee this, thee that, who art thou, who art thou not, she'd think it very strange, she'd say, you treat me with ill manners, Sir,

and

and you yourſelf would acknowledge her in the Right, Madam is the proper Word· you uſe it, Madam this, Madam that, always complaiſantly Madam, and to me always thee, and thou. Not that I complain of this, Mr. Preſident, I have nothing to ſay againſt it, it's the Cuſtom of you great ones, thee is my Portion and that of the poor World; that's the Caſe but why is it the poor World? I know it's not your fault, and what I've ſaid is only by way of Compariſon. Becauſe Madam here, to whom it would be rude to ſay thee, is hardly any more a Madam, than I am a Sir, indeed it's the ſame thing.

How, Mr. Impudence, the ſame thing cry'd ſhe.

'Troth, yes, anſwer'd I, but that's not all, permit me to go on.

Was Mr. *Haberd* your Father? God's Peace be with his Soul' a Beggar then, Madam? No, he was the ſon of a good Farmer of *Beauce,* and I am the Son of a good Farmer of *Champagne ;* there's Farm for Farm; you ſee your Father and I as much Beggars one as another; he was a Tradeſman, was not he? perhaps I may be one; and then there will be Shop for Shop. As it is, you Ladies his Daughters, are but a Shop better than me; but if I take this Shop, my Son will be able to ſay, my Father kept one, and then my Son will be upon a Level with you. You are ſtepping from the Shop to the Farm, and I am ſtepping from the Farm to the Shop; the odds is'nt much, you are only a

degree

degree above me; and am I a Scoundrel for being only one degree beneath you? Do such People as you then who serve God, and profess Humility, stand upon degrees? and especially when there is but one to object against.

As to what relates to the Street where your Sister met me; why, why it's a Street which all the World passes thro'; I pass'd thro' it, she pass'd thro' it, and it's as well meeting there as any where, when one's to meet at all. You say I must have begg'd but for her; oh! not the same Day by a great many, nor so soon as that neither? had not I went with her indeed, I must have return'd to the Farm, I frankly own it, for I do not understand your Evasions, it's a fine thing to be rich, but none but Fools are vain upon that Account; and after all, is my Adventure such a mighty Wonder? here a Person is young, and has a Father and Mother, whom he leaves to seek his Fortune, what riches can you expect him to have? He has little enough to be sure, but he goes in quest of more; and I was in quest of more, when your Sister comes, and asks me, who I am? I tell her, will you live with us? cries she; we are two Sisters fearing God. With all my Heart, replies I, and till I should mend my self follows her. We chat by the Way, I acquaint her with my Name, my Sirname, my Station in Life, and give her a detail of my Family; our's says she, is made of the same Stuff, I rejoice, she is pleas'd, I answer her, she answers me, I praise her, she returns it; you seem to be a sober young Man, and you, Madam,

dam, the moft deferving Woman in *Paris*; after which we come to you, and you quarrel with her upon my Account; you tell her you'll part from her, fhe parts from you firft; fhe takes me with her, and as foon as fhe's by her felf grows tir'd ; the thoughts of Matrimony feize her, we mufe a little, I find my felf entirely that way inclin'd, fhe efteems me, and I revere her, I am a Farmer's Son, fhe's a Farmer's Grandaughter, fhe ne'er cavils for a degree more, or a degree lefs, a Shop here, or a Shop there; fhe has means enough for us both, and I have gratitude enough for a dozen; the Notary is called; I write into the Country, am wrote to again, every thing's ready, and now I ask Mr. Prefident, who knows Juftice by Heart, Mrs. Prefident who hears us, that Lady who is fo difcerning, and the Abbot who has fo good a Confcience, where is this great Injury I do you ?

A profound Silence enfu'd, nobody anfwer'd a Word. Our Eldeft, who waited for the Prefident's fpeaking, look'd with aftonifhment at him to find he faid nothing; what! Sir, will you abandon me then ? cry'd fhe.

I fhould be very proud to ferve you Madam, faid he, but what would you have me do in this Cafe ? I underftood the Affair quite different, and if what he fays is true, it is neither juft nor poffible to oppofe a Marriage againft which there's no Objection but its being liable to ridicule on Account of the Difproportion of Ages.

I   Without

Without reckoning, cry'd the Relation, that one fees more difproportion'd Matches every Day, and this won't be vifible but by a few Years, for your Siftei is very comely ftill.

And befides, faid Mrs Prefident, with a conciliating Air, the Gentlewoman's her own Miftrefs, and this young Man has nothing againft him but his youth in reality.

And there's no ciime in having a young Hufband, faid the Abbot in a bantering Tone.

But is not this a notorious Folly, which fhe's going to commit? cry'd Mrs *Haberd*; (whofe Head was a little difoider'd at the Genealogies I had run over) and is not it a Charity to prevent her? You, Madam, who promifed me fo cordially to engage Mr. Prefident to interpofe his Authority, added fhe fpeaking to the Devotee Lady, won't you prefs him to act for us? I depended fo much upon you!

But, good Mrs. *Haberd*, reply'd the Lady, one muft hear Reafon. You reprefented this young Man as a meer Vagabond, who belong'd to nobody, and I took Fire at that, but it is far from it, it is quite another thing; he is the Son of honeft Parents of a good Family in *Champagne*, and befides he's a fenfible Youth, and I own to you I fhould fcruple to hurt his little Fortune.

Immediately the fenfible Youth made his bow to the fcrupulous Lady, my Reverence parted off the Spot.

My God! what's the World come to? cry'd my Sifter in law that was to be, for only telling

lling

ling this Lady that she bore her Age well at my Sister's Years, see! I've lost her good Graces already! who could ever divine that one was still a Nymph at fifty? Adieu, Madam; Mr. President, I am your Servant.

Upon which, she courtes'd to the rest of the Company, whilst the Devotee Lady look'd at her with a scornful Air, and without vouchsafing her an Answer.

Go, Child, said she, as soon as the other had left the Room, get marry'd, there's nobody has a word to say against you.

I would also advise him to make haste, said Mrs. President, for this Sister has very ill Intentions. Let her take what Method she will, her ill Intentions will signify nothing, said the President coldly, I can't see what she can do.

Just then Notice was given of some body's arrival. Come, said the Nymph of fifty, rising from her Chair, you must carry a Letter for me to Mrs. *Haberd*, she's a very good Woman, I always lov'd her better than the other, and shall be glad to inform her how Things have pass'd here. Mr. President, pray give me leave to step into your Closet for a Moment to write, and immediately she went, and I follow'd her not a little pleas'd at my Embassy.

When we were in the Closet, indeed Child, said she, taking a Sheet of Paper, and trying some Pens, I was against you at first; this enrag'd Creature that's just gone had spoke so much to your Disadvantage, that

I 2   your

your Marriage appear'd the moſt aſtoniſhing
Thing in the World ; but I was of another
Mind as ſoon as I ſaw you, your Countenance deſtroy'd all the ill ſhe ſaid of you ;
and really you have a handſome one, a very
happy one; Mrs. *Haberd* the youngeſt is in
the Right.

I am very much oblig'd to you, Madam,
for your good Opinion of me, anſwer'd I,
and will endeavour to deſerve it.

Yes, ſaid ſhe, I think mighty well of you,
extreamly well! I am charm'd at your
Adventure ; and if this croſs Siſter ſhould
play you any new Tricks, you may depend upon it I'll ſerve you againſt her.

She was trying the Pens all the while during this Diſcourſe, but could find none to
pleaſe her.

What wretched Pens are here ! cry'd ſhe,
trying to make, or rather to mend one ; how
old are you? Almoſt twenty, Madam, ſaid
I ; That's the right Age to make your fortune,
reply'd ſhe; you only want Friends to puſh
you, and I'll recommend you to ſome ; for
I love your Mrs *Haberd,* and I like her
the better for her Choice of you ; ſhe has
a good Diſcernment. But is it true, that
you have been no longer than four or five
Months at *Paris ?* one would not believe
it to look at you, you are not in the leaſt
tann'd, you have nothing of the Air of the
Country, you have the fineſt Complexion in
the World.

At

At this compliment the Rofes of the fine Complexion bloom'd afrefh; I blufh'd a little thro' Modefty, but much more out of a certain Sentiment of Pleafure which I could not help being affected with at hearing myfelf prais'd by a Woman of her Condition.

We are never happier, nor more contented with ourfelves than when we pleafe by our Perfons, for that's a Merit which cofts us no trouble to preferve and continue; this Perfon is ftill the fame, your Attractions are durable; and when it's only that you are valu'd for, you are in no fear of People's being deceiv'd in you, which gives you a becoming Affurance.

I fancy fhe's taken with my Perfon, thought I to my felf, and immediately I felt all the fweets and convenience of this way of pleafing; it gave me an eafy and more liberal Air.

Mean time the Pens ftill prov'd bad; and finding her endeavours to mend them unfuccefsful, fhe threw them up in a pet, and continu'd the Converfation.

I can't tell how to write with this, faid fhe, can't you make me one?

Yes, Madam, faid I, I'll try; and accordingly I took a Quill, and began to fhape it.

Shall you Marry to Night? rep'y'd fhe, whilft I was making the Pen. I believe I fhall, Madam.

I 3

But

But tell me, added she smiling, Mrs. *Haberd* has a great love for you, Child, I don't question, nor am I at all surpriz'd at it; but between you and I, do you love her a little again? have you any Love for her? what one properly calls Love? I do not mean Gratitude, for of that she deserves a great deal at your Hands, and you are under no Obligation as to the other; but has she any Charms in your Eyes, quite old as she is?

These last words were pronounc'd with a tone which dictated my Answer, and seem'd to excite me to say no, and to be merry upon those Charms. I saw it would please her not to discover any Impatience to possess them; and troth! I had not the power to refuse her what she desired.

Tho' one's never so strictly engag'd in an affair of Love, yet the vanity of pleasing elsewhere will give the Mind this turn to Infidelity, and make one guilty of this false Complaisance.

For my part I had the weakness to be wanting both in Honour and Sincerity upon this Occasion; for really lov'd Mrs. *Haberd*, at least I believ'd so, and that struck upon me at the same time as a Punishment for my Hypocrisy; and tho' I had not lov'd her, yet the Circumstances we were in together, the Obligations I had; and was going to have to her, were not they Motives sufficient to make me say without hesitating, yes, I love her, and with all my heart?

However,

However I did not, for this Lady would not have me love her, and her Uuwilling-ness flatter'd me.

But as I was not of a brazen Difpofition, nor capable of a downright Falfity in a cafe of this Nature, I took what I imagin'd a Medium, which was to fmile without faying any thing, and to anfwer with a Look inftead of a Word.

Yes, yes, I underftand you, cry'd the Lady, you have more Gratitude than Love, I don't doubt it ; but the Woman has not been difagreeable formerly.

Whilft fhe was fpeaking I try'd the Pen which I had made; it was not to my lik-ing, and therefore I retouch'd it to prolong a Converfation which amus'd me, and of which I had a mind to fee the end.

Yes, fhe's very paffable, and I think fhe has been comely, continu'd the Lady, and as her Sifter fays, fhe is fifty; it was no fault of mine that fhe was not a great deal Younger, for I reprefented her of my Age to make her the more excufable. Had I fided with the eldeft Sifter, I fhould have hurt you with the Prefident, which was not my In-tention.

I very well obferv'd, Madam, faid I, the Protection you honour'd me with ; true, re-ply'd fhe, I declar'd myfelf openly enough ; this poor youngeft Sifter, I put myfelf in her place, it would have been too much Af-fliction for her at her Age to have loft you ; and befides I wifh you well.

Oh!

Oh! Madam, reply'd I with a frank Air, I could fay as much to you if it was worth the trouble of hearing · And why not? anſwer'd ſhe, I negleſt the Friendſhip of nobody, my dear Child, and eſpecially of thoſe who are ſo well to be lik'd as you are; you really pleaſe me, you have prejudiced me in your favour; I don't regard the conditions of People, not I; I don't regulate my Taſte upon that footing.

Tho' ſhe ſpoke theſe words in the manner of a Perſon who takes the firſt which come without being curious what ſhe ſays; yet the force of the diſcourſe oblig'd her to caſt down her Eyes, for one can't trifle with one's Conſcience

Mean while I was at a loſs how to behave about this Pen; it was high time to have made it good, or to let it alone.

I ſhall think myſelf happy, Madam, ſaid I; if you will always pleaſe to preſerve the ſame favourable Sentiments for me; good fortune will never be ſo welcome to me from any where, as from you.

Speaking this I gave her the Pen, which ſhe took and try'd; it fits mighty well, ſaid ſhe, to be ſure you write a very legible Hand. A tolerable one, ſaid I; that's enough, reply'd ſhe, and I've a great mind to give you ſome things to copy which I want to be fair wrote out. Whenever you pleaſe, Madam, ſaid I.

Upon which ſhe begun her Letter to Mrs. *Haberd*, and every now and then took her Eyes off to look at me. Your

Your Father, is he a handſome Man ? is it him you reſemble, or your Mother ? ſaid ſhe, after two or three Lines writing. My Mother, Madam, ſaid I.

Two lines after ; your adventure with this old Maid whom you are going to marry is very ſingular, added ſhe, as thro' reflection, and with a ſmile, ſhe muſt have good Eyes, as retir'd as ſhe has liv'd, and I'm glad on't , pray behave well to her, I exhort you, Child, and afterwards diſpoſe of your Heart as you will, for at your Age it's ſeldom kept.

Alas ! Madam, ſaid I, what would it avail me to diſpoſe of it ? who would have any thing to ſay to a Peaſant like me ?

Oh ! reply'd ſhe, nodding her Head, that's not the difficulty. Pardon me, Madam, ſaid I, but it is, becauſe it would not be my Equal I ſhould love, I ſhould never look there, it muſt be my Superior ; nothing elſe could engage me.

Mighty well ! cry'd ſhe, why you think tranſportingly ! and I eſteem you the better for it ; that Sentiment becomes you, never part from it, it's an honour to you, and will turn to account, I foretell you it will ; what ! I know the World, and you ought to believe me ; have a good Courage ! and that ſhe accompany'd with a very perſuaſive look. But à propos of Hearts, added ſhe, are you naturally a little tender ? it's the ſign of a good temper.

Troth!

Troth! then I am of the beſt temper in the World, rep'y'd I, ay, ſaid ſhe, ha, ha, ha, ---- the great Boy! with what a pleaſant Vivacity he anſwers me? but tell me ingenuouſly, have you any one in view at preſent? do you actually love any body?

Yes, ſaid I, I love every one that I've Obligations to, as I have to you, Madam, whom I love more than any other.

Take care, ſaid ſhe, I am talking of Love, and you have none of that for them any more than for me, if you love us it's out of Gratitude, and not becauſe we are amiable.

Where Perſons are like you, Madam, it's becauſe of both, rep'y'd I; but it is not for me to ſay ſo, Oh! ſpeak, Child, ſpeak; ſaid ſhe, I'm neither vain nor a Fool; and provided you are ſincere, I'll forgive you.

Troth! then, anſwer'd I, if I did not, I ſhould think myſelf very difficult. Softly however, ſaid ſhe, clapping her Finger to her Lips, tell nobody ſo but me; for they'd laugh at us, Child, and beſides, you'd put Mrs. *Haberd* out of Humour with me, if ſhe knew it.

I ſhould hardly ſpeak it, if ſhe was within hearing, reply'd I. Indeed theſe old Women are very jealous; and the World is very cenſorious, added ſhe, concluding her Letter, and we muſt always keep a Guard upon our Tongues.

Juſt then we heard a noiſe in the next Room.

Is not there some Servant who over-hears us ? said she, folding up her Letter ; I should be fretted at that ; let's go out, give this Billet to Mrs *Haberd*, and assure her of my Friendship, do you hear ? and as soon as you are marry'd come and acquaint me with it here, where I live ; my Name's at the bottom of the Letter which I've wrote ; but don't come till the Evening, I'll give you some Papers to copy out, and we'll consult some way or other to serve you. Go, my dear Child, be discreet, I have good Intentions for you, added she with a soft low Voice, and at the same time giving me the Letter with an Air which seem'd to say, I give you my Hand too, at least I understood it so, and in taking the letter, kiss'd the Hand which seem'd to present itself, and which was not at all cruel ; notwithstanding the lively and affectionate Gratitude with which I kiss'd it, it was a very handsome Hand.

Whilst I held it, see, here's something else which you must not talk of neither ! said she leaving me Oh ! Madam, I'm a very honest Fellow, answer'd I confidently, I'm a downright Peasant at boxing, can behave well when I'm us'd well, but can't live so modest as the Ladies.

The Expression was brutish, she blush'd slightly, for I was not worthy she should blush much ; I was insensible of the Indecency I was guilty of, therefore she soon recover'd herself, and all Reflexion past, I

saw.

faw fhe was not difpleas'd at the Clownery
which had efcap'd me, for it fhew'd I underftood her Meaning, and that was faving
her the Trouble which fhe muft have been
at fome other time in explaining herfelf.

We feparated; fhe went in to Mrs. Prefident's Apartment, and I retir'd full of agreeable Tranfports.

Was that becaufe you defign'd to love
her? you may ask me. Why, really I
had no determinate Defign at all; I was
only charm'd at finding myfelf lik'd by a
great Lady, I fparkled by Anticipation, without knowing what it would come to, or fo
much as once thinking how I fhould behave in the affair.

I can't tell you that this Lady was indifferent to me; neither can I tell you I lov'd
her, for I believe I did not. What I felt
for her can hardly be call'd Love; for I
fhould never have taken notice of her, had
not fhe taken notice of me firft, nor even
then fhould I have regarded her attention,
had not fhe been a Perfon of Diftinction.

Therefore it was not her, it was her
Rank I lov'd, which was very great in Comparifon of me.

I faw a Woman of fafhion of a certain
Air, which fpoke an Equipage and Attendants
belonging to it; who permitted me to kifs
her Hand, and would have nobody know
it; a Woman in fhort who rais'd both me
and my Vanity from their original Nothing;
for

for till then had I look'd upon myfelf as any thing? had I ever felt the fweets of felf-love?

It is true I was going to marry Mrs *Haberd*; but fhe was a little Cit, who had fpoil'd all at firft dafh by telling me, I was as good as her felf; fhe had given me no time to grow proud of my Conqueft. and except her Fortune, I almoft confider'd her as my equal.

Had not I already been her Cofin? The means after that to fee any vifible Diftance between us!

But here the Diftance was immenfe, it was beyond my power to judge of; and I was loft in the bare thought; that a Woman fo much my Superior fhould ftoop to me, or that I fhould find my felf in a Moment advanc'd to her; was not it enough to turn my Head? and to give me Senfations very like thofe of Love!

I lov'd her then thro' Refpect and thro' Amazement at my Adventure, thro' the Drunkennefs of Vanity, thro' excefs of Pleafure, and thro' the infinite Value I fet upon her Charms; for I imagin'd that I had never before feen any thing fo beautiful. Notwithftanding fhe was really fifty; and I had fix'd her at that Age in Mrs. Prefident's Chamber: but that was forgot an in inftant; I could fee nothing amifs in her, and had fhe been twenty Years younger, it was impoffible I could have thought her more amiable; fhe was a Goddefs, and your Goddeffes are never old.

Thus I return'd penetrated with joy, puffed up with vain Glory, and full of my ridiculous Exaggerations upon the Merit of this Lady.

It

It never once enter'd my mind, that thefe Sentiments were injurious to thofe I ow'd Mrs. *Haberd*, for my Heart had fuffer'd no Change in Refpect to her, and I went to fee her again with as much Tendernefs as ever ; I was charmed at the thoughts of marrying the one, and pleafing the other , and one may feel two pleafures at once very well.

But before I had put my felf in the road to return to my Intended, I fhould have given you the Picture of this Goddefs from whom I juft parted ; if you pleafe we'll place it here, it won't be a long one.

Her Age you know already, I have alfo told you that fhe was well-made, but that was faying too little ; for I have feen few Women of fuch a noble Prefence, or fo grand an Air.

Her Drefs was modeft, but adjufted in fuch a manner as not to rob her of any of thofe natural Attractions which fhe had left.

A Woman may drefs her felf in this Mode to pleafe, without being accufed with a defign of pleafing ; I mean a Woman who is inwardly a Coquette, for that fhe muft neceffarily be to reap any Advantage from this way of dreffing ; there are a great many little fecret Arts to make it engaging as well as decent, and perhaps more alluring than the moft glaring Attire.

She had handfome Hands, and handfome Arms without ruffles ; which made them more obvious, and more affecting.

Her Face was a little ancient but ftill very comely, it would have look'd old in a coftly Head-drefs, but in a plain one it was altogether

amiable

amiable. Will any one fay it was neglecting it too much to adorn it fo little?

She had a lovely Bofom (for we muft not forget that Article which is almoft as confiderable in a Woman as her Face) a lovely white Bofom, clofe cover'd, but of which the covering took an opportunity to difclofe it felf every time fhe turn'd her Head to difplay the Lillies; and the little one faw of it gave one the moft tranfporting Idea in the World.

Her Eyes were large and black, which fhe conrain'd to be grave and prudent, in fpight of them felves; for naturally they were lively, tender and amorous.

I fhan't define them entirely; there's too much to be faid of thofe Eyes, there was fo much Nature, and fo much Art in them, that I fhould never leave off if I was to pretend to tell all, and perhaps even then I fhould be ne'er the better, for is it poffible to fpeak all one feels? Thofe who imagine fo, feel next to nothing, and apparently fee but half what they might fee.

Let's now come to the Countenance which refulted from the whole.

At firft Sight you would fay of the Perfon whofe it was, this is a very fober difcreet Woman.

At the fecond Glance, this Woman has acquir'd this Air of Prudence and Gravity, it is not genuine. Is fhe virtuous? her Countenance fays yes, but it cofts her deal; fhe behaves her felf better than fhe is often tempted to do; fhe refufes pleafure, but fhe loves it, ten to one

one she's not impregnable! so much for her Morals.

As to her Wit, one would suspect her to have a great deal, and the Suspicion would be just, but my Acquaintance with her was too short to say any more upon that Head.

In regard to her Character, that would also be very difficult for me to define; but the following little Sketch will give you a general, as well as a very singular Idea.

She really lov'd nobody, but wish'd more harm to her Neighbours, than she directly did them.

The Honour of being esteem'd a good Woman, would not permit her to shew her self a bad one; but then she had the Address to excite Malignity in others, and that serv'd her instead of exercising her own.

Wherever she went, the Conversation turn'd upon nothing but Scandal, and it was always she who put her Company into that Humour, either by crying up, or defending somebody or other *mal-à-propos* · In short by a thousand Innuendoes, which still seem'd in Favour of those she would have pull'd to pieces, and then whilst they were pulling to pieces, it was nothing but charitable Exclamations, tho' at the same time encouraging ones, but you do not tell me so? Are not you mistaken? is it possible! so that she always return'd innocent of the Crimes she made others commit, (I call all Satyr so) and was always the Protectress of those whose Reputations she murder'd with other Peoples Tongues.

But

But what is moſt pleaſant, this Woman, ſuch
as I've deſcrib'd her, was a perfect Stranger to
the badneſs of her own Diſpoſition, the bot
tom of her Heart had eſcap'd her, and her
Addreſs had deceiv'd even herſelf; becauſe
ſhe affected to be thought good, ſhe believed ſhe
was really ſo in earneſt.

Such then was the Lady I parted from; I've
drawn her from what I afterwards heard of her,
from the little Commerce we had together, and
from the Reflection I have ſince made.

She had been a Widow eight or ten Years;
her Husband is reported not to have dy'd
very well ſatisfy'd with her; he accus'd her
with ſome Irregularities in her Conduct. and
to prove that he injur'd her, immediately
upon her Widowhood ſhe abſconded from
the World, and enter'd into a ſtate of Devotion, which ſhe ſtill continued as much
thro' Pride as Habit, and becauſe of the In-
dency of appearing again upon the Stage of
the Publick with Charms which would no
longer be acknowledg'd as ſuch, which time
had a little impair'd, and which even Retirement itſelf had tarniſh'd; for it has always that Effect upon thoſe who leave it.
Retirement, and eſpecially a Chriſtian one,
fits well upon none but thoſe who perſevere
in it; a Perſon's Face is never in the Fa-
ſhion afterwards, it always becomes either ridiculous or ſcandalous.

I return'd then to Mrs. *Haberd* my Intended,
and joyfully doubled my Steps to get the
ſooner to her, when I was ſtop'd by a great
Croud

Croud of Coaches and Chairs at the entrance
into a Street, I would not engage myfelf
amongſt them for fear of being wounded;
and in waiting till the hurry ſhould be over,
went into an Alley, where to paſs away the
Time, I ſet myſelf to read the Letter which
Mrs. *Ferval* (for ſo I ſhall call the Lady I
have been ſpeaking of) had given me for Mrs.
Haberd, and which was not ſeal'd.

I had ſcarce begun to read the firſt Line,
when a Man came down a Stair-caſe which
was at the bottom of the Alley, fled thro'
it with full ſpeed, ruſh'd againſt me in paſ-
ſing, drop'd a naked Sword which he held
at my Feet, and ſav'd himſelf by ſhutting
the Street-door upon me.

I was now ſhut in this Alley, not without
ſome Apprehenſions at what I had ſeen.

My firſt Care was to run to open the Door;
but I try'd in vain, I could not effect it.

On the other ſide, I heard a Noiſe above
Stairs. The Alley was alſo very dark, which
increaſ'd my Uneaſineſs.

And as in a Caſe of this Nature, all our
Actions mechanically tend to our Preſervation,
and as I had neither Cane nor Stick, I ſnatch'd
up the Sword, without well knowing what
I did.

The Noiſe above Stairs redoubled; it
ſeem'd to me that the Cries came from a
Window in the Houſe upon the Street, nor
was I miſtaken I could hear them cry,
Stop, Stop; and at all Adventures I ſtill
kept the naked Sword in one Hand, whilſt
with

with the other I continu'd endeavouring to open this miserable Door which at last I got open, without once thinking to drop the Sword.

But I was never the better, for a whole Croud of People were assembled together about it, who seeing my frighted Air, and the naked Sword which I held, made no Question but I was either an Assassin, or a Robber.

I would have escap'd, but it was impossible, and my Endeavours for that Purpose, only serv'd to render their Suspicions the more violent against me.

At the same time some Archers or Sergeants run from the next Station, pierc'd thro' the Croud, snatch'd the Sword out of my Hand, and seiz'd me.

I would have spoke, and told my Reasons; but the Noise and Tumult were so great that I could not be heard; and in spight of my Resistance, which was not very prudent, they dragg'd me into the House, forc'd me up Stairs, and I enter'd with the Archers who led me, and some of the Neighbours who follow'd us into a little Apartment, where we found a young Lady lying upon the Floor, in a Swoon, extreamly wounded, and an old Woman who was endeavouring to raise her up against an Arm-chair.

Over against her lay a young well-shap'd Man, wounded also, and fallen cross a Sofa, who as his Blood flow'd from him, still cry'd out for help for the young Lady, whilst

the

the old Woman and a fort of Servant fill'd the Room with Shrieks.

Oh! quick, Sirs, quick, a Surgeon, cry'd the young Man to thofe who held me; make hafte, and help her, fhe's dying, perhaps you may fave her (he fpoke of the young Lady.)

The Surgeon was not far off; there liv'd one juft oppofite to the Houfe, whom they call'd out at Window, and he came in an inftant with a Commiffary with him.

But as I talk'd very faft, and protefted that I had no part in this Adventure, and that it was unjuft to detain me, they dragg'd me into a little contiguous Clofet, where I waited till the Lady's Wounds and thofe of the young Man were drefs'd.

The Lady was recover'd out of her Swoon, and when they had taken all the neceffary Care they could, I was brought back again out of the Clofet into the Chamber.

Do you know this young Man? faid one of my Archers to them; obferve him well. we found him in the Alley, the Door of which was fhut upon him, and he open'd it holding this Sword in his Hand which you fee. It's ftill bloody, cry'd another immediately, who examin'd it, and undoubtedly this is one of thofe who wounded you.

No, Gentlemen, reply'd the young Man with a very feeble Voice; we don't know this Man, it's not he who has reduc'd us to the deplorable Condition we are in, but we know our Affaffin; it's one Mr.----- (he mention'd a Name a Name which I've forgot) but fince this Perfon was in the Houfe, and fince you feiz'd him with that Sword ftill reeking with our Blood, perhaps our Affaffin might bring him to fupport him in cafe of Need, and therefore by all Means keep him in hold.

Miferable Wretch! cry'd the young Lady in her turn, without giving me time to anfwer, what's become of him whofe Accomplice to be fure thou art? Alas! Gentlemen, he has efcap'd you; ---- fhe had no Power to go on, fhe was wounded to Death, and could be brought to herfelf no more.

I imagin'd then I might have Liberty to vindicate myfelf; but had hardly begun to open my Lips, when the Archer who firft fpoke interrupted me

It is not here thou moft juftify thy felf, faid he; March, and directly they haul'd me below where I ftay'd till the coming of a Hackney Coach which they were gone to call, and in which they hurry'd me to Prifon.

The Place where I was confin'd was not altogether a Dungeon, tho' it wanted little of it.

As it luckily happen'd the Man who lock'd me in, as much a Jailor as he was, yet had no inexorable Look, he did not fright me; and at fuch a Time one's glad to catch at ev'ry Thing, and a Face a little lefs Morofe than another, feems a good-natur'd one; therefore addreffing myfelf to this Jailor, Sir, faid I, putting into his Hand, to engage him to hear me, fome of thofe Pieces of Gold

Gold which Mrs. *Haberd* had given me, and which I had preserv'd, though every thing else was taken from me, for the bottom of my Pocket had a Hole in it, and in plain Terms they had slipt down lower ; nothing besides was left me except my Letter which I had clap'd into my Bosom, after having held it a long time rumpled up in my Hand.

Sir, said I, you are at your Liberty to go and come where you please; do me a Favour : I am guilty of nothing, you will find I an't, this is only a Misfortune which has befallen me. I just came from Mr. President's---and a Lady his Relation gave me a Letter for one Mrs. *Haberd* who lives in such a Street, in such a part, and as I cannot deliver it my self, I give it into your Hands ; be so good as either to carry or send it to the Lady, and at the same time let her know where I am ; hold, added I, pulling out some more pieces, here is wherewithal to pay the Messenger, if there is occasion, and this is a trifle, you shall be much better re-compenced when they fetch me from hence.

Stay, said he, drawing out a little Pencil, Mrs. *Haberd* you say, in such a Street Yes, Sir, answer'd I ; put down too at Mrs. *d'Alain*'s a Widow's.

Well, reply'd he, make your self easy, I shall go out presently, and in an Hour at far-thest your Business shall be done.

Upon which he bluntly left me, and I re-main'd weeping between my four Walls, rather out of Consternation than Fear ; or if I had any Fear, it was entirely owing to the violent

Shock

Shock which this Accident had given me, for I had no notion of being apprehensive for my Life.

Upon such occasions we are immediately seiz'd with those emotions which we deserve to feel, our Consciences, if I may use the Expression, do themselves Justice. An innocent Persons sighs, and a Criminal trembles , the one is afflicted, and the other tormented.

Therefore I was only afflicted, I deserv'd to be no more ; what a Disaster, cry'd I to my self? oh the cursed Street with its Throng of Coaches and Chairs ! what Business had I in that miserable Alley ? It was certainly by the Impulse of the Devil that I enter'd it.

And instantly the Tears trickled down . Oh my God! where am I ? O my God ! deliver me from hence, cry'd I. The Wretches' this Mrs. *Haberd* the eldest, and Mr. *Doucin* ; what plague have they given me with their President? Why I must needs go forsooth ' and then I sobb'd and wept afresh , but after a short silence, my poor Father, added I, he little thinks I am in Prison on my Wedding Day ' and dear Mrs. *Haberd* who expects me, are not we in a fine way to meet again ?

I was lost in Grief at these Considerations; but at last, some other Reflections coming to my aid; I ought not to despair, said I, God will not leave me here. If this Jailor gives Mrs. *Haberd* my Letter, and informs her of my Misfortune, she will spare no pains for my Deliverance.

And

And I had Reaſon to encourage my ſelf as
you will ſee. The Jailor was punctual to his
Word, and Mrs. *Ferval*'s Letter was carry'd to
my Intended an Hour or two after, he was the
Meſſenger himſelf, and told her where I was ;
as ſoon as he return'd he came to acquaint me
with it, bringing me at the ſame time ſome
Food, which was not at all tempting.

Have a good Heart ! ſaid he, I have given
the Lady your Letter ; I told her you was in
Priſon, and when ſhe heard it ſhe ſwooned away
directly, farewel This was exact a Jailor's
Style, as you may perceive.

But hold a Moment, cry'd I ſtopping him,
was there any body with her to aſſiſt her
then ?

Oh ! yes, ſaid he, that need not concern
you ; there were two Women in the Room
with her. What and did ſhe ſay nothing to
you ? reply'd I. Why no, anſwer'd he, how
could ſhe when ſhe was ſpeechleſs ? Eat, and
hope the beſt.

I have no Stomach, ſaid I, but I am exceſ-
ſive thirſty, I wiſh I had a little Wine, is there
no ſuch thing as getting any ? yes, reply'd he,
lug out, I will ſend you ſome preſently.

After all the Money which I had given him,
in any other place than that where I was, the
Word lug out would have ſounded ungrateful
and raſcally , but in a Jail, it was I who was
to blame, and who did not know how to
live.

Alas, ſaid I, pardon me, I had forgot the
Money, pulling out another *Louis d'Or* ; for I
had no other Coin. Would

Would you have me, faid he, as he was going out, inftead of returning your change,
fupply you with Wine whilft this lafts ? You
will have leifure enough to drink it.

Juft as you pleafe, reply'd I fubmiffively,
and pierc'd to the Heart to find my felf in
Commerce with thefe new fort of Gentry,
whom you muft thank for the very Kindnefs
you do them.

The Wine came very *à propos*, for I was
juft ready to faint away when they brought it
me, but by the help of that I recover'd, and
the only uneafinefs I now felt was an extream
impatience to fee what would be the event of
this News which I had fent the charitable Mrs.
Haberd.

Sometimes her fwooning difturb'd me, for I
was afraid it fhould put her out of a Capacity
of acting herfelf, and I depended more upon her
than all the Friends fhe could employ for me.

But on the other hand this fwooning was an
argument of her Affection, and of the fpeed
fhe would make to my affiftance.

Three Hours were already paft fince their
bringing me the Wine, when I was inform'd
that two Perfons below wanted to fpeak with
me, that they would not come up, but that I
muft go down to them.

My Heart beat the March of Joy, and I
follow'd the Jailor, who led me into the Chamber, at the entrance of which I was receiv'd by
Mrs. *Haberd* who embrac'd me, burfting into
Tears.

Clofe by her ftood a Man dreft in black,
who was a ftranger to me.

Ah ! Mr. *de la Vallée*, my dear Child, by
what accident are you here? cry'd fhe, do not
be furpriz'd, Sir, at my embracing him ; we
were to have been marry'd as to Day, added fhe
to the Gentleman who accompany'd her , and
immediately returning to me, what has befallen
you ? what is the matter ?

I could not anfwer immediately ; Mrs.
Haberd's reception of me had melted me into
Tendernefs, and it was fome time before my
Tears would give me leave to fpeak.

Alas ! faid I at length, it is a furious Story
this of mine ; would you imagine that it is nothing but an Alley which is the occafion of my
being here ? Whilft I was in it the Door was
fhut upon me, and two Murders were committed above Stairs . I was fufpected to be con-
cerned in them, and fo they hurry'd me hither.

How ! concern'd in two Murders for only be
ing in an Alley, anfwer'd fhe, what doft mean
by that, Child? Explain thy felf ; who is this
Murderer? I do not know, reply'd I, I faw
nothing but the Sword which I inadvertently
took up in the Alley.

This carries a very grave Face with it, interrupted the Gentleman in black ; but we can
learn nothing from what you tell us ; pray fit
down, and relate the whole Affair to us dif-
tinctly as it happen'd ; what of all this Alley ?
What are we to underftand by it ?

Look

Look ye, faid I, the cafe was this, and immediately I begun my Narrative with my leaving the Prefident's, fiom whence I proceeded to my ftoppage in the Street, the Alley I fpoke of, the unknown Perfon who efcap'd thio' it and fhut me in, the Sword which he drop'd and which I took up, and in fhort to all the reft of my Adventure.

I neither know, faid I, the Killer nor the kill'd, they were not dead when I was brought before them, and they own'd that they knew nothing of me; this is all the Account I can give you why I am imprifon'd.

My Flefh perfectly trembles, faid Mrs. *Haberd*; what then would not they hear Reafon when the wounded parties acknowledg'd they did not know you? What could they fay to you? That perhaps I was an accomplice of their Murderer, tho' I never faw any thing of him but his back, anfwer'd I.

The bloody Sword with which they feiz'd you, faid the Gentleman in black, is an ugly Article, it is a perplexing one; but your Story has occafion'd me a thought.

We heard them talk below that a Prifoner was brought in here about three or four Hours ago, for the Murder of two Perfons in the fame Street you fpeak of; and very likely this may be the Man who rufh'd by you in the Alley. Stay here both of you, I'll go and endeavour to inform my felf more particularly, perhaps I may learn fomething.

Upon which he left us. Poor Child! faid Mrs. *Haberd* as foon as he was gone, in what a Situation do I find thee? the news of it affected me in fuch a manner that I thought I fhould have dy'd; I never expected to fee another Day. But, dear Child, when you faw this Step, why would not you take fome other Street?

Oh! my dear Cofin, faid I, I was willing to keep in the direct Road that I might get the fooner to you. Who would imagine any Street could be fo fatal? When one goes to fee a Perfon one loves, it is natural for one to be impatient, and to take the fhorteft way one can.

Saying this I bath'd her Hands in tears, and fhe alfo rain'd as faft as fhe could.

Who is this Gentleman you have brought with you, faid I, and where have you been, Cofin? Alas! reply'd fhe, I have done nothing but run up and down fince I receiv'd the Letter you fent me, Mrs. *Ferval* exprefs'd her felf fo obligingly in it, and offer'd me fo many fervices, that I immediately refolv'd to addrefs my felf to her, and to intreat her Affiftance. She's an exceeding good Lady, fhe could not have acted with more Vigour had it been for her own Son; poor Woman! fhe was almoft as much afflicted as I was· Do not trouble your felf, faid fhe, this is a thing of nothing, we have Friends enough, and I warrant we'll get him out; ftay here, I'll go and fpeak to Mr. Prefident

Away fhe went without lofing time, and in a Moment after return'd with a Letter from the Prefident to Mr-- (he was one of the Principal Magiftrates for fuch Affairs as mine) I took tne Letter and directly carry'd it to that Magiftrate,

giftrate, who as foon as he had read it, call'd
for one of his Secretaries, fpoke fomething to
him apart, and afterwards bid him wait on me
to the Prifon to procure me the Liberty of feeing
you, and here we are come both together to
know what has befallen you. Mrs. *Ferval* alfo
promifed to join with me, and to accompany
me wherever there fhould be Occafion

The Secretary who had left us, return'd juft
as Mrs *Haberd* had finifh'd her Detail of thefe
particulars.

I was right in my Notion, faid he, the Man
who was brought hither this Morning, is certainly the Affaffin of the Parties in Queftion;
I have been talking to one of the Archers who
ftop'd him as he fled without either Hat or Sword,
and purfu'd by a croud of People who had feen
him rufh in a diftracted manner out of a Houfe
in the fame Street where you met with your
Obftruction; it was a confiderable while before
they could take him, becaufe he had the heels
of them, but at laft they feiz'd him, and carry'd him back to the Houfe he came out of,
and whence they fay another Man had been
juft before fent to Jail on Sufpicion of being his
Accomplice. Now agreeab'e to what you have
told us, this other Man believ'd to be his Accomplice is in all Appearance your felf.

Yes, it's me, anfwer'd I, I am the Man of
the Alley; that's the very Reafon of my being
here, nobody knew it was in going home that
I had the Misfortune to be cram'd up there.

This Prifoner will be foon examin'd, faid
the Secretary, and if he knows nothing of you,

and

and anfwers conformably to what you tell us, as I do not doubt but he will, you'll foon be at liberty, and we'll haften your releafe. Return, Madam, and make your felf eafy; let's go. As for you, added he fpeaking to me, ftay in this Chamber, you'll be better here than where you was, and I'll go and order them to bring you fome Dinner.

Alas! faid I, they have already brought me a forry Pittance in my hole above there, but its mouldy, and I can have no Appetite to it.

They left me with Exhortations to eat, and we embrac'd one another, Mrs. *Haberd* and I, fhedding a new Flood of Tears. Let him want for nothing, cry'd the good Woman to him who lock'd me in; and they had been gone two or three Minutes, before I could get the Noife of the turning the Keys out of my Ears. There's nothing fo harfh as the lockings in thefe Places, and I believe they are much more difpleafing to the innocent than the guilty; the laft have fomething elfe to do than to attend to fuch things.

A few Moments after, my Dinner came up; and upon comparing it with that which had been brought me before I found my felf comforted; it was a Charge of a good Omen, one defires to live, it's a natural inftinct, and therefore after a few carelefs Glances at a pullet of a pretty good Mein, I as carelefsly fliv'd off the two Wings, which were infenfibly eat in a Trice; I alfo pick'd part of the Carcafe for Amufement, drank two or three brimmers of Wine, which was tolerable as it went down
without

without much Attention, and clos'd my Regale with some Fruit which I tasted, because it was there.

I felt my self much less afflicted after I had eat. A good Meal is an admirable thing in time of trouble; it's certain it lulls the Spirits into a Calm, and one cannot be very sorrowful whilst the Stomach digests.

I do not tell you that I lost sight of my Condition, I thought of it continually, but then it was in a tranquill manner; at last however my sorrow return'd. I omit the Account of every thing which passed after Mrs. *Haberd*'s Visit, to come to the Instant in which I appear'd before a Magistrate accompany'd by another Officer of Justice who seem'd to write, and of whom I neither know the Name nor the Employ, opposite to them was a Man extreamly pale, and of a dejected look, with some other Persons whose Depositions they seem'd to be taking.

They examin'd me; you must not expect an exact detail of this Examination, for I have entirely forgot what Order they observ'd in it; I shall only relate the essential Article, which was, that this Man who was so dejected, and who was the precise Man of the Alley, acknowledged he did not know me; I said the same by him. I told my Adventure, and told it with such pathetick Exclamations upon my Misfortune, that some of the Assistants were oblig'd to mask their Faces with their Hands, to conceal their Smiles.

When I had ended, I tell you again and again, cry'd the Prisoner, with Tears in his Eyes,

I had neither Confident nor Accomplice ; I do not know how far I might plead for my Life, but it's a burthen to me, and I deserve to lose it. I have kill'd my Mistress, I saw her expire, she dy'd with horror in seeing me, and calling me her Affassin ; I also kill'd my Friend, of whom I was become the Rival ; I stabb'd them both in a Transport of Rage, and now I am in Difpair, I look upon my felf as a Monster, I am a horror to my own thoughts, and should have stabb'd my felf had not I been feiz'd, I am unworthy of time to recollect or repent ; condemn me, revenge their Murders ; I ask for death as a Mercy ; fpare me the Pangs of delay which make me die a thoufand times over, and fend away this young Man, whom it's need-lefs to detain here, and whom I never faw except in that Paffage, where I would have kill'd him too for fear he fhould have known me, had not my Sword drop'd out of my Hand in attempting to make my efcape ; fet him at Li-berty, Sir, let him go, I reproach my felf for the trouble I have given him, and beg his Par-don for the Fright I fee him in, and of which I am the Occafion, he has nothing in com-mon with fuch an abominable Wretch as me.

I trembled at hearing him fay he defign'd to kill me, for that would have been worfe than a Jail However, notwithftanding this Acknow-ledgment, I could not help being forry for this unfortunate Criminal, his Difcourfe touch'd me, and in anfwer to his begging my Pardon ; Sir, faid I, I pray God to have Mercy upon you and your Soul.

But

But I fhall fay no more upon this Head.
Mrs. *Haberd* came again to fee me after the
Hurry of the Examination was over, attended
by the fame Secretary, who left us for fome
time alone. Imagine to your felf the Tendernefs with which our Hearts overflow'd, fo
chearful is the Mind, and fuch a Sweetnefs of
Satisfaction it feels when we have efcap'd any
great Danger! and really we had each in our
way efcap'd a very imminent one; for all things
confider'd, my Life was actually in Peril, and
Mrs *Haberd* had run the Rifk of lofing me;
which in her Turn fhe look'd upon as one of
the greateft Misfortunes in the World, efpecially if fhe had loft me on this Occafion

She gave me an Account of all fhe had done
for me, and of the new Obligations we had to
Mrs. *Ferval*, for the Pains fhe had taken to
ferve me, both with the Prefident and the
Magiftrate who examin'd me

We beftow'd a thoufand and a thoufand blef-
fings upon that Lady for her generous Favours
to us; my Intended was in an exftafy at her
Charity and Piety; oh the good Chriftian!
cry'd fhe, oh the the good Chriftian! and oh
the good Woman! cry'd I, for I durft not repeat
Mrs *Haberd's* Expreffions, nor employ the
fame Eulogium as fhe did; I thought my felf
obliged in Confcience to make ufe of others,
and indeed it would have been a burning fhame
in the very Face of my Intended, to extol the
Piety of a Woman who caft a hawk's Eye at
her Husband, and who only affifted me fo cordially, becaufe fhe was not fuch a good Chri-

ftian,

ftian. Befides was I in Prifon, which made me
fcrupulous; and I was afraid God fhould punifh
me if I exaggerated the Piety of thofe fervices of
which in all likelihood the Devil and the Flefh
had all the Honour.

I alfo blufh'd more than once whilft Mrs.
Haberd was magnifying Mrs. *Ferval* in this
manner, for I was not irreproachable my felf,
and I was afham'd to fee this good Woman fuch
a Dupe, fhe who fo little deferv'd to be one.

From our encomiums upon Mrs. *Ferval*, we
proceeded to what had paffed in my Prifon,
joy is very talkative, it allow'd us no interval,
I related to her all which the real Criminal had
faid, the Candour with which he juftify'd me,
and what Pity it was that he abandon'd himfelf fo unfortunately to his Paffion! and then
we returned to our felves, to our own Love and
Marriage. But perhaps you'll ask me who this
Criminal was; I will give you his Hiftory in
two Words.

About a Year ago his bofom Friend courted
a Lady who returned his Affection; but as he
was not of equal Fortune to her's, the Father
of the Lady not only refufed her to him in
Marriage, but forbid his Daughter from receiving any more of his Addreffes. In which
Dilemma, who fhould they make ufe of but this
very Perfon, who afterwards kill'd them, to write
and receive their Letters?

This Murderer, who was before acquainted
with the Family, but feldom vifited there, became now defperately in Love with the Lady
by often feeing her and hearing her figh for the
other

other. He was more wealthy than his Friend, and diſcloſed his Paſſion, which the Lady bantered for ſome time, as thinking it only a pleaſantry; but when ſhe found him in earneſt, ſhe was enrag'd, and ſent to acquaint her Lover with it, who reproach'd his Friend for his Treachery. At firſt he was aſhamed, ſeem'd to repent his Guilt, and promiſed to leave them in repoſe, but ſoon after renew'd his Suit, quarel'd with his Friend, and carry'd his infidelity ſo far as to propoſe him ſelf for a Son-in-law to the Father, who accepted him, and in vain endeavour'd to compell his Daughter to marry him

Our Lovers, grown deſperate, had recourſe to other means, both for writing and ſpeaking. An ancient Widow, who had been Chambermaid to the Lady's Mother, gave them the Liberty of her Houſe, where they ſometimes met, to conſult what Meaſures they ſhould reſolve upon The other having Notice of it, turn'd furious with Jealouſy; he was a Man of a violent Nature, apparently without Reflection, and one of thoſe Spirits which an exceſs of Paſſion corrupts and makes fit for any thing. He had them dog'd one day to their rendezvous at the Widow's, follow'd them in, ſurpriz'd them the Moment his Friend was kiſſing the Lady's Hand, and in his fury run him thro' the Body with his Sword, which he was going to ſecond with another Stroke, when the Lady threw her ſelf before her Lover, and receiv'd the Wound; the Murderer fled, and the reſt of the Story you know. To return to my ſelf.

Our

Our Secretary came back to us, and told us that I fhould be difcharged on the Morrow. Let us pafs to this Morrow, all the Particulars of this Prifon are melancholy.

Mrs. *Haberd* came to fetch me at eleven in the Morning; fhe would not go up, but fent me word fhe was there; accordingly I went down, and found a Coach waiting for me at the door; and what Coach? why Mrs. *Ferval's*, and Mrs. *Ferval* herfelf in it, which was on purpofe to give an *Eclat* to my Liberty, and the greater Luftre to my Innocence.

The Zeal of this Lady went ftill frather, before we take him home, faid fhe to Mrs. *Haberd*, I am of Opinion that we ought to carry him into that Quarter and over againft the Place where he was ftop'd; it's very proper that thofe who faw him hurry'd to Jail, and who may know him again elfewhere, fhould be acquainted with his Innocence. It's a Precaution which feems neceffary and perhaps, added fhe, addreffing herfelf to me, you may recollect fome of thofe who furrounded you when you was feiz'd.

Oh! as for that, yes, faid I, and if it was only the Surgeon, who lives oppofite to the Houfe, and who was call'd to drefs the Wounds of the Deceas'd; I fhould be glad to fee him again, to fhew him that I am an honefter Man than he imagines.

My God, what an incomparable thought this Lady has! cry'd Mrs. *Haberd* immediately, for it's to her you are indebted for every

Thing,

Thing, Mr. *de la Vallée*, and tho' fhe had only refpect to God in this Occafion.---- At the word God, which Mrs. *Ferval* was confcious was fupernumerary, let's drop all that, faid fhe interrupting her, when do you intend to be marry'd? To Night, if nothing prevents us, faid Mrs *Haberd*

Juft then we arriv'd at the Street which had been fo fatal to me, and which we had bid the Coachman drive to. We ftop'd juft before the Surgeon's Houfe, he was ftanding at his Door, and I obferv'd that he look'd wifhfully at me, Do you remember me, Sir? faid I, do you know me?

Yes, I think I do, anfwer'd he, pulling off his Hat very complaifantly, as to a Man whom he faw in a handfome Equipage with two Ladies, one of which appear'd of Diftinction. Yes, Sir, I remember you, I believe it was you who the day before yefterday was in yonder Houfe, (pointing to that where I was feiz'd) and who happen'd to--- he hefitated to bring out the reft, go on, go on Sir, faid I, yes it was me who was feiz'd there, and fent to Prifon; I was loath to fay fo, reply'd he, but I had taken fo much Notice of you that I *knew* you again at firft Sght Well, Sir, then you was no way concern'd in the affair in Queftion?

No more than you, anfwer'd I, and immediately explain'd to him how I came embroil'd in the Adventure Upon my Word, Sir, reply'd he, I'm heartily glad on't, and we'll tell it all hereabout, my Neighbours and my
Wife,

Wife, my Children, and I, and my Prentices, who the deuce would one truſt, if this
young Gentleman was guilty? Why! he has one
of the honeſteſt Countenances in the World;
oh! troth! they muſt all ſee you. Here,
Beſſy, (he call'd one of his Daughter's) Wife
come hither, and you too, ſpeaking to his
Prentices; here, look well at this Gentleman,
do you know who he is?

Oh! Father, cry'd Beſſy, he is very like
that Priſoner the other Day, yes, truly, ſaid
the Wife, he is ſo very like him that he is the
ſame, the very ſame at your Service, Madam,
reply'd I, ſo, ſo, cry'd Beſſey, why this is
comical enough, then you help'd to kill nobody,
Sir! Oh! no, anſwer'd I, I ſhould be very
ſorry to contribute to the Death of any Perſon, to bring them to Life is another Caſe.
Indeed, ſaid the Wife, we did not know what
to think, oh! as for that, ſaid Beſſey, if ever
any body had an innocent look, it was you to
be ſure.

The People began to gather about us, and I
was known by a great many of them. Mrs.
Ferval had the Complaiſance to continue this
Scene as long as it was neceſſary to re-eſtabliſh
my Reputation in the Quarter; after which I
took leave of the Surgeon and his Family, with
the Satisfaction of ſeeing my ſelf cordially bow'd
to by the People, and thoroughly acquitted
through the whole Street of the Crimes of
which they had ſuſpected me; without reckoning the Pleaſure I had to hear Elogies upon my
Countenance on all ſides me, which put Mrs.

Haberd into the beft Humour in the World,
and engag'd her to view me with more eager-
nefs than I had ever before perceiv'd in her.

I faw that fhe was penetrated with Pleafure as
fhe obferv'd at me, and that fhe congratulated
herfelf upon the Juftnefs of her Tafte in thinking me amiable.

I alfo won at the fame time upon Mrs. *Ferval,*
who gaz'd at me with more attention than ordinary, and I am perfuaded fhe faid within
herfelf, I have no fuch indifferent fancy neither, fince every body is of my Sentiment

But I only tell you that an *en paffant.* I
was very well contented too my felf, and perhaps fomething more.

We were drawing near Mrs. *Haberd's*
Lodgings, whither Mrs. *Ferval* would con-
duct us, when we faw at a Church Door, my
Intended's eldeft Sifter and Mr. *Doucin,* who
were talking together, and feem'd very earneft
in Difcourfe. A Coach which ftop'd the
Progrefs of our's, gave them all the time in the
World to obferve us.

Whenever I think of it, I cannot help
laughing ftill at the prodigious Aftonifhment
which they were both in at feeing us.

We turn'd them both into Statues ; they
were fo routed, fo thunder-ftruck, that they
had not fo much as prefence of Mind to give
us a wry Face, which we could not have fail'd,
had they been lefs furpriz'd ; but there are
fome things which ftupify ; and for an increafe
to their Confufion, we appear'd in a Moment,
which made our Apparition ftill more mortifying

and

and painful Chance join'd Accidents on purpofe to afflict them, it was triumphing over
them in a proud, and even an infolent manner,
had it been premeditated; and this was, and
pleafe you, that the very Moment they perceiv'd us, we burft out into a laugh, Mrs.
Ferval, Mrs *Haberd* and I, at fome pleafantry
or other of mine, which join'd to the pompous
Triumph in which Mrs *Ferval* feem'd to bear
us, was certainly enough to pierce them to the
Heart.

We bow'd to them very complaifantly, and
they return'd it as People who were aftonifh'd,
who did not know what they did, and who
funk under the weight of their adverfe Fortune.

You muft underftand that they were both of
them juft come from Mrs. *Haberd*'s the youngeft
(as we learn'd at our return) where they had
got intelligence of my being in Prifon; for
Mrs *d'Alain*, who was prefent at the Report of
the Jailor, could not help letting her Tongue
run, and it was in muttering all the while in
our Favour that fhe regal'd them with this good
News.

Imagine to yourfelf the Hopes which they
conceiv'd againft me. A Man in Prifon! what
has he done? It is not we who put him there,
nor is it the Prefident who refus'd to ferve us,
therefore it muft be for fomething foreign to our
Affair, how can I tell but they might go fo far
as even to fufpect me of fome Crime? they both
hated me enough to conceive that charitable
Opinion of me, and your Devotees take a
hatred

hatred againſt you as a proof of your Worth-leſsneſs Oh the cruel balk! to meet us on a ſudden in ſuch a ſplendid and proſperous Situation!

But let us leave them to their Confuſion, and arrive at the good Mrs. *Haberd*'s.

I will not go in with you, ſaid Mrs. *Ferval* to her, becauſe I have a little Buſineſs, adieu, take your meaſures ſo as to marry as ſoon as poſſible, loſe no time, and pray, let Mr. *de la Vallée* come and acquaint me with it when it is over, for I ſhall not be eaſy till then.

We will both of us come to inform you of it, anſwer'd Mrs. *Haberd*, that is the leaſt we can do, Madam. No, no, reply'd ſhe, giving me a little look of Intelligence which ſhe ſaw I underſtood, he is ſufficient, Madam, come your ſelf at your leiſure, and away ſhe went.

Oh! God pardon me, cry'd Mrs. *d'Alain*, as ſoon as ſhe ſet Eyes upon me, I believe it is Mr. *de la Vallée* that you have brought us again, my good Friend. You are right, Mrs. *d'Alain*, you are right, ſaid I, and God will pardon your believing it, for it is I, troth! good morrow Mrs. *Agatha*, (her Daughter was there.) oh! you are welcome home, Sir, anſwer'd ſhe, my Mother and I thought you was loſt.

How! loſt, cry'd the Widow, why if you had not come Home this Morning, I ſhould have went in the Afternoon and ſet all my Friends to work; your Siſter and Mr *Doucin* are juſt gone from hence, they came to ſee you, added ſhe to my Intended; go, go, I gave them but cold Comfort; you may ask what

Reception

Reception they had. The poor young Man is in Prifon, faid I to them, you know it well enough, it is you are the occafion of it, and it is very ill done of you let me tell you that In Prifon ! fince when ? oh ! fince when ? Why fince your Intrigues, fince your running all about to get him there, and away they march'd, I never fo much as ask'd them to fit down.

By this Difcourfe of Mrs. *d'Alain*'s which I have repeated, you may perceive that fhe was ignorant of the real Caufe of my Imprifonment; and indeed Mrs. *Haberd* had taken care to keep her in the dark in that Refpect, and let her believe that it was through fome Plot of her Sifter's. For if Mrs. *d'Alain* had been inftructed in the truth; what a good Fortune to her would fuch a Story have been ! the whole Quarter would have rung with my Adventure, and fhe would have told it from Door to Door, for the meer pleafure of faying how forry fhe was for me ; and it was fo much ill Fame well fav'd.

But, pray tell me this, pray tell me that, it was the particulars of my Imprifonment which fhe enquir'd into; and I invented her fome as faft as I could, concealing the true ones ; well, I have got a Parfon who would marry you this Moment, faid fhe, if it was not too late, but that fhall be after Midnight, if it is your Intention

Yes, Madam, anfwer'd Mrs. *Haberd*, and we fhall be very much oblig'd to you to give him notice ; I will go to him my felf by and by, faid fhe, it is Dinner time at prefent, come, come,

come, eat some of my Soup, I shall sup with you to Night; and as for Witnesses to your Marriage, I will furnish you with some who shall not be so proud as the others.

But I am weary my self of all these minute Circumstances, let us pass them by, and suppose the Evening come, that we have supp'd with our Witnesses, that it is two Hours after Midnight, and that we are setting out for Church.

In short we are there at once, [Mass is said, and we are marry'd in spight of this eldest Sister and the Director her Adherent, who shall have no more Coffee, nor no more Sugar-Loaves from Mrs. *de la Vallée.*

I have seen a great many forts of Love in my Life, and a great many Modes of saying and witnessing that one loves, but I never saw any which could equal the Love of my Wife.

Your worldly Wives, though the most lively and tender, old or young, none of them love in this Taste; I defy them even to imitate, or so much as resemble Mrs. *Haberd,* whom I must no longer call so; it will signify nothing that you are possess'd of the most sensible Heart in the World, join to that a violent Affection, you are never the nearer, in short put what you please into the Heart of a Woman, you will make of her something very lively and passionate, but you will not make a Mrs. *Haberd;* and all the Love which she will be capable of will not be sufficient to give you a just *Idea* of that of my Wife.

To

' To love like her, you muft have been thirty Years a Devotee, and for thirty Years have wanted the refolution to be one in carneft, for thirty Years you muft have refifted the temptation of thinking of Love, and for thirty Years have made a fcruple of hearing or looking upon Men, though at the fame time you had no a-verfion to them.

Oh ! marry after a Life of thirty Years in this reftraint, lie a whole Night by a Man, for there is a great deal in that ; let him be a Man whom you love through Inclination, which is ftill more, and then you will be another Mrs. *Haberd*, and I will anfwer for it whoever marries you will acknowledge I had reafon when I faid that her Love was different from that of any body elfe.

Give us the Character of this Love, may fome one fay, but foftly, for that is more than I can do ; all I can tell you, is, that fhe look'd upon me no otherwife than as if I had been an image ; and it was her continual habit of praying and of turning her Eyes affectionately whilft fhe pray'd, which gave her this Air when fhe look'd at me.

When a Wife loves you, it is with Love fhe tells you fhe does ; but it was with Devotion that mine told me fo, though with a Devotion incomparably delicious, you would have thought that her Heart had been treating amoroufly with me upon fome Cafe of Confcience, and that it had fignify'd God be thank'd who infpir'd me to love you ! and his holy Will be done ! and all her Tranfports took this turn ;

Love

Love only loft a little of its Air and Style, but nothing of its Sentiments Imagine now what muft be its Character.

It was ten o'Clock when we got up, it was three when we lay down, and we had need of repofe

Mr. *de la Vallée*, faid fhe, about a Quarter of an Hour before we rofe, we have between four and five thoufand Livres yearly Rent, which is a handfome Maintenance, but thou art young, thou muft apply thy felf to fome thing or other, what art moft inclin'd to ? To what you pleafe, Cofin faid I ; but I mightily like this Revenue, it bears fuch a charming report ! it is the common Nurfe of all thofe who have nothing ; indeed I have no occafion for any Nurfe but you, Cofin, you will let me want for neither good eating nor good drinking, but abundance hurts nobody, let us turn Financiers, and buy fome Place which will coft little and bring in a great deal, as the Cuftom is in fuch matters · the Lord of our Mannor enrich'd himfelf by that means, let us enrich ourfelves too

Yes, faid fhe, but thou art unfkil'd, and I am of Opinion that thou fhould'ft get Inftruction firft, I am acquainted with an Advocate who I believe would employ thee, art thou willing I fhould fpeak to him ?

I willing! cry'd I, what ! Cofin, have we two Wills then ? Is not your Will my Will ? Alas ! my darling, reply'd fhe, I would do every thing for thy Good ; but now I think on it, my dear Husband, our Troubles have made

me

me forget one thing; thou wanteſt a Suit of Clothes, and ſome Linnen; I'll go out this Afternoon, and buy thee both.

And *à propos* now you ſpeak of my Dreſs, my dear Wife, ſaid I; there is alſo another little Trifle which I have always had a fancy for, can't your Goodneſs gueſs what it is? In this world a little good Appearance hurts no Body.

Oh! what is it? my Jewel, reply'd ſhe
Nothing but a Sword and Belt, ſaid I, to be Mr. *de la Vallée* in good earneſt; there is no thing ſets a Man off ſo much: And, beſides, when you have that, all the better ſort of people are your equals.

Well, my Love, ſaid ſhe, thou art in the right; we'll buy them this Morning. There is a Sword cutler lives ſomewhere hereabout; it is only ſending for him. See, think, is there any thing elſe you deſire? No, ſaid I; for on this firſt Day of our Marriage the pious ſoul liv'd only for her young Spouſe: Had I told her that I had a mind to be a King, I believe ſhe would have promiſed to purchaſe a Crown for me.

Whilſt we were talking in this manner, the Clock ſtruck ten; our Coffee waited for us, and Mrs. *d'Alain*, who uſher'd it up, call'd at the Door, demanding to enter with her Equipage, which ſhe thought the moſt gallant thing in the world, as we were a new-married couple.

I would have got up, ſtay, Child, ſtay, ſaid Mrs. *de la Vallée*, you'll be too long in dreſſing you; ſee, this makes me remember that you want a Morning-gown too. Yes, indeed, I

want

want one, my dear, reply'd I; and with that I
ſhall have every thing.

Upon which, ſhe jump'd out of bed, ſlipp'd
on her Gown, and open'd the door to our impatient Landlady, who, as ſoon as ſhe came in,
Come, ſaid ſhe to her, and let me embrace you
with your dear languiſhing Eyes. Well, I hope
your Bed-fellow and you agreed. Ay, ay, you
ſmile; that's a ſign Yes, I never doubted it;
the merry Blade, I thought there would be
good living with him , is it not ſo? Turn out,
turn out, Spark, ſaid ſhe, coming to me, leave
your Pillow; your Wife is not there now, and
it will be night again preſently.

I don't know how, ſaid I, I am too man-
nerly to riſe before you; to morrow, as ſoon as
you will; for then I ſhall have a Morning-
gown. Oh! truly, ſaid ſhe, what fiddle faddle is here! If that's your only Want, I'll go
and fetch you one as good as new; my poor
deceas'd Huſband never put it upon his Back
above ten Times, and when you have it on,
I ſhall think I ſee him alive again.

Immediately, ſhe ſtepp'd into her own Apartment, brought the Morning-gown, and throwing it upon the Bed to me, Here, ſaid ſhe, it's
a thorough genteel one, keep it , you ſhall have
it a Pennyworth.

Will you have it? ſaid Mrs. *de la Vallée*.
With all my Heart, reply'd I; but what's the
price of it? I don't know how to chaffer.

Upon which, you ſhall have it for ſo much,
it's Dog-cheap; no, that's too dear; it's not
enough. In ſhort, they agreed, and the Morning

ing-gown was mine, which I paid for with that
refidue of Money which I had brought out of
Prifon with me.

We drank our Coffee, Mrs. *de la Vallè*
fupply'd my wants, as well of a fuit of Clothes,
as of Linnen, with our Landlady, and defir'd
her company in the Afternoon to affift her in
her Marketings, but as to the Suit, Chance
order'd it otherwife

A Taylor, to whom Mrs *d'Alain* let fome
Rooms upon the ground Floor, came about a
quarter of an hour afterwards, to bring her the
remainder of the rent he ow'd her. Oh! truly, Mr. *Simon*, you are come juft in the Nick,
faid fhe, pointing to me, fee, here's a Cuftomer
for you: We are going prefently to buy Cloth
for a fuit of Clothes for this Gentleman.

Mr. *Simon* made his bow to me, and, fur-
veying me, Why, faid he, I can fave you the
trouble of buying the Stuff: I have a fpick and
fpan new fuit by me, which I finifh'd but yefterday; the owner left it in my hands becaufe
he could not repay me the money I had advanc'd
for him: And yefterday Morning, and pleafe
you, he turn'd his back upon his Lodging,
without bidding farewel to any body. I believe
it will juft fit the Gentleman; it's an opportunity of furnifhing himfelf at once, and much
cheaper than he could at the Mercer's. There's
Coat, Waftecoat, and Breeches, of a fine firm
Cloth, the Trimming fuitable, lin'd through
with red Silk: There's nothing wanting.

That red filk flatter'd me; a filk lining,
what pleafure and magnificence for a Peafant!
What

What fay you, my Life? faid I to Mrs. *de la Vallée*. Oh! faid fhe, let us firft fee if it fits, my dear, that's all in all   It will fit as clofe as Wax, reply'd the Taylor, who run to fetch it; he brought it, I try'd it, it fitted me better than my own, and my heart beat under the filk Lining; we now proceeded to the Price.

This Bargain was longer in concluding than that of the Morning-gown, not on my Wife's part, for, faid Mrs *d'Alain* to her, pray don't you trouble yourfelf, this is my Affair. Come, Mr. *Simon*, perhaps you may keep this Frippery a year round before you can light of a Chapman to hit you fo again; for there muft be a Shape, and here's one for you   It's juft as if God had fent it you, perhaps there's never another in *Paris*.   Lower your Top-fail, don't over-ftand your Market   And thus, from offers to offers, our officious Haggler concluded the Agreement.

When the Habit was bought, an amorous impatience feiz'd my Wife, to fee me thoroughly equipp'd.   Child, faid fhe, let us fend directly and buy you a Sword, a pair of Stockings, a Hat, (and I'll have your Hat lac'd) a Shirt ready made, and all Accoutrements; fha'n't we?

Juft as you pleafe, anfwer'd I, with a gaiety which went to my very foul, and no fooner faid than done.   All the Tradefmen were call'd; Mrs. *d'Alain* was always bufy, always haggling, and before Dinner I had the pleafure to fee *Jacob* metamorphos'd into a Gentleman, with his filk Lining, his filver edg'd Hat, and

L   the

the Adornment of a Head of Hair which hung down to my Girdle, and on which the Barber had exhausted all his Skill.

I have already told you that I was a handsome Lad, but hitherto a person must have look'd attentively at me to have found it out; for what's a handsome Lad in an ordinary Dress? Why, he's bury'd alive; such Dupes are our Eyes in that respect: Or if one's observ'd to be handsome, what merit is there in that? They'll cry, ay, ay, the Man is well enough; there is but here and there a Woman less vain and coquetish than the rest, who has a more solid Taste than this, and who won't be deceiv'd. A few such I have met with, as you have already seen; but troth, under my new Garb, there needed nothing but eyes to see I was amiable, and the bare showing myself was enough; I was a personable Man, well made, had natural attractions, and all at the first Glance.

See what an Air he has! The dear Child, said Mrs. *de la Vallée*, when I walk'd out of the Closet where I had retir'd to dress myself: How! cry'd Mrs. *d'Alain*; why, he's perfectly charming And it was not in a talkative Strain that she spoke this. It seem'd to come from a Woman who thought so, and who, for some Moments, even forgot her Babble. By the astonish'd manner in which she gaz'd at me, I imagin'd that she coveted my Wife's Husband. I had pleas'd her at less charge before now.

What a delicate Shape he has! said she; whenever I marry, I'll take a Man who has

exact

exact such a one. Yes, Mother, said *Agatha*, coming in; but that's not all, he muft have a Mien too.

We din'd; Mrs. *d'Alain* was full of her Cajoleries, during the whole Repaft; *Agatha* only talk'd to me by her eyes, but faid a great deal more than her Mother, and my Wife neither faw, nor thought of any Body but me: And I, in my Turn, feem'd to fix all my Attention upon her.

Our witneffes, whom Mrs. *Haberd* had invited to Supper at our parting from them at Three o'Clock in the Morning, came about Five in the Evening.

Mr. *de la Valléc*, faid the Coufin, I think it will be very proper for you to ftep to Mrs. *Ferval's*; we fhall not fup till Eight, and you will have Time enough to go there: Make her a great many Compliments for me, and tell her that to morrow we will do ourfelves the honour of waiting upon her together.

Oh! right; that's well thought of, faid I, fhe gave us a particular Charge to come and inform her, and it is but good manners. Adieu, Ladies; adieu, Gentlemen · You'll excufe me for a little while.

My Wife thought fhe had made me recollect this Mrs. *Ferval*, but I fhould have put her in mind of her, had fhe forgot; for I died with Impatience to have her fee me as I was. Oh! how I go to pleafe her, faid I, to myfelf; it will be quite another thing than it has been. We fhall fee, in the Sequel, how it was.

The End of the Third Part.

THE

Fortunate PEASANT.

PART IV.

I WENT then to Mrs. *Ferval's*, where I met with no body in the Court before the House, but a Valet, who conducted me to her Apartment, by a little Stair-cafe, which I had not seen before.

One of her Waiting-maids, who came directly to us, told me, she would acquaint her Mistress. She returned a moment after, and showed me to that Lady's Chamber, where I found her reading, reclined upon a Sofa, with her Head leaning upon her Hand, and in a Dishabille, which was genteel, but negligent enough.

Imagine to yourself a Petticoat too short to reach entirely to the Feet, and which indulg'd

L 3   a little

a little view of one of the fineſt Legs in the World; (and that's a great beauty a fine Leg in a Woman)

The Slipper was fallen off from one of her pretty Feet, the barenefs of which had a particular grace in it.

I loſt none of the charms of this moving Poſture; it was the firſt time of my life wherein I was fenfible of the value of a Woman's leg and foot; till then I had only feen the faces and fhapes of Women, but in that inſtant I found they were Women all over. It's true I was but a Peafant ſtill; for what fignifies four or five Months refidence at *Paris?* but there needs neither refinement nor knowledge of the World to apprehend fome things at once; and efpecially when they prefent themfelves in their true point of light, there's nothing but Senfe requir'd, and that I had

Therefore this fine leg and this lovely little foot without it's flipper gave me a great deal of pleafure in beholding them.

I have feen many fights of this Nature fince, and they always pleas'd me, but never fo much as then; for as I've already told you it was the firſt time I was fenfible of them, which is faying all, there is no pleafure but lofes fomething by being known.

I made two or three bows to Mrs. *Ferval* as I came in, of which, I believe, fhe took no notice whether they were well or ill made; it was not acquired Graces fhe wanted, all her attention was fixed upon my natural ones, which

which were much more apparent to be observed as I was better dreſt.

By the air with which ſhe gaz'd at me, I imagin'd that ſhe did not expect to ſee me either ſo well made, or of ſo good a Mien.

How! cry'd ſhe in a ſurprize and raiſing her ſelf a little from her Sofa; what is it you *la Vallée?* why, I hardly knew you again; truly a handſome figure, a very handſome one; come here, Child, come here, reach a Chair, and ſit down; but that ſhape how admirable! that head and hair, how becoming! 'troth! he's too handſome for a Man, what a well-turned Leg too! you muſt learn to dance, *la Vallée,* be ſure don't fail, ſit down, nothing can look genteeler! added ſhe taking me by the hand to oblige me to ſit down.

Whilſt I heſitated thro' reſpect, ſit down then repeated ſhe with the accent of a Perſon who ſaid, forget who I am, and let's be ſociable.

Well, you great Boy, ſaid ſhe, I was muſing on you, for I love you, you know I do; and this ſhe accompany'd with a look which ſufficiently explain'd her manner of loving me; yes, I love you, and I'll have you attach your ſelf to me too; do you hear?

Alas! dear Madam, anſwer'd I, with a tranſport of Vanity and Acknowledgment; I ſhall love you too much perhaps, if you don't take Care.

And I had hardly pronounc'd theſe Words, when I ſeiz'd her Hand which ſhe abandon'd to me, and which I kiſs'd with all my Soul.

She remain'd ſilent for a Moment or two, and contented her ſelf with ſeeing my rapture;

ture; I only heard her breath in a very feeling Manner, and as a Perfon who fighs a little, fpeak then, do you love me too much, faid fhe, whilft I was fix'd in tranfport upon that hand; why are you afraid of loving me too much, explain thy felf, *la Vallée*, what is it you would fay?

It is, reply'd I, that you are fo amiable, and fo handfome, and I, who fee this, and am fenfible of it, am afraid of loving you otherwife than I ought.

Very well, faid fhe, you talk of love then, *la Vallée*; and I talk of nothing but what's true, reply'd I, it's impoffible I fhould help it.

Speak fofty, faid fhe; my Chamber-maid is there perhaps, (pointing to the anti-chamber:) Ah my dear Child! what have you been telling me? you love me then, fhall I who am fuch an inferior fellow, anfwer yes, reply'd I? Juft as you will, return'd fhe with a little Sigh: but thou art very young, I am afraid in my turn to confide in thee; draw nearer, that we may have a better opportunity of converfing, added fhe. I forgot to tell you that in the courfe of this Dialogue fhe had reaffum'd the pofture in which I firft found her; this flipper was always off, and the Legs were all the while expos'd, fometimes more, fometimes lefs, according to the different poftures fhe affected upon the Sofa.

None of the glances which I caft that way efcap'd her Notice; what a delicate little Foot, you have, Madam! cry'd I, advancing
my

my Chair clofer, for I infenfibly fell into the familiar: let my foot alone, faid fhe, and put on my flipper, you and I muft difcourfe a little upon what you have been faying, and confider what we muft do with this Love which you have for me.

Is it becaufe my Paffion is fo unfortunate as to offend you? faid I; ah! no, *la Vallée*, it does not offend me, anfwer'd fhe; on the contrary it touches me, you have only pleas'd me too much, thou art as handfome as the God of Love.

Alas! faid I, what is my handfomenefs in comparifon of your's? a little finger of you *is of more worth than my whole Body*; in you every thing is an object of admiration; behold that arm! that enchanting fhape. Thofe eyes of which I never faw the fellows! and inftanly mine greedily run her over from Head to Foot; did not you take Notice, added I, how I gaz'd at you the firft time I faw you? I thought you altogether charming, more fnowy than the down of a Swan. Oh Madam! if you knew with what pleafure I come hither, and how I continually imagined that I ftill held the dear Hand which I kiffed t'other day, when you gave me the Letter ---- ah! hold thy Tongue, faid fhe, clapping the fame Hand upon my Mouth to impofe me filence; hold thy Tongue, *la Vallée*, I can't hear thee with cold blood, after which, fhe threw herfelf again upon her Sofa with fuch an Air of emotion as gave me one my felf.

I look'd.

I look'd at her, fhe look'd at me, fhe blufh'd, my Heart went pit-a-pat, I believe her's kept the fame pace, and both our Heads were beginning to turn round, when harkee, *la Vallée*, faid fhe, you fee very well that we are liable to Intruders every Moment, and therefore fince you love me, you muft come no more here, for you are not fufficiently difcreet, a Sigh interrupted her going on.

Thou art marry'd, rejoin'd fhe directly after. Yes, I was this Morning, faid I. This Morning! anfwer'd fhe, well, give me fome Account of thy Love; haft thou a great deal? How doft like thy Wife? Doft thou like me as well as her? Oh! how I fhould doat upon thee in her Place. And oh! how happy I fhould think my felf by the Change, reply'd I. Do you fpeak true? faid fhe. But let us talk no more of it, *la Vallée*, we are too near one another, fit a little farther off, I am in perpetual fear of a Surprize. I had fomething to fay to thee, and this Marriage of thine has made me forget it; we fhould have been more at eafe in my Clofet, I am generally there, but did not imagine your coming this Evening. However, now I think on't, I have a great Fancy to take you there on purpofe to give you thofe Papers which I fpoke of t'other Day; are you willing to go with me?

She immediately got up, I willing! cry'd I, when paufing a Moment, No, faid fhe, we muft not go; if this Chambermaid fhould come and not find us here, who knows what fhe might think? We muft e'en ftay.

But

But I would fain have thefe Papers, reply'd I ; it is impoffible, faid fhe, there's no fuch thing as your having them to Day , and immediately fhe plac'd herfelf again upon her Sofa, but no longer in her former Pofture ; and thofe delicate little Feet, faid I, if you fit in this manner, I fhall fee them no more.

She fmil'd at this Difcourfe, and ftroaking me tenderly over the Face, let's talk of fomething elfe, anfwer'd fhe. You tell me you love me, and I forgive you ; but fuppofe, Child, I fhould alfo fall in love with thee, in which there is no Improbability, for how can one defend one's Heart againft fuch an amiable young Spark as thou art ! tell me, would'ft thou keep the Secret, *la Vallée* ?

Ah ! my dear Lady, faid I, to whom fhould I difclofe our Affairs ? I muft be a fine Rafcal indeed, don't I know the Indecency of fuch a a Behaviour, and efpecially to a great Lady like you, who is a Widow, and who does me a hundred Times more honour than I deferve, by returning my Affection ? Befides, don't I know that you are in a State of Devotion which won't permit fuch a Thing's being blaz'd in the World ? No ; anfwer'd fhe, with a little Blufh, thou art deceiv'd, I don't live fo devout as retir'd.

Oh troth ! reply'd I, devout or not devout, I love you as well one way as another ; can that hinder me from offering you my Heart, or you from receiving what I offer you ? One is what one is, and the World has no Bufinefs with it . After all, what is it which we do in this Life ?

A

A little good, a little harm; fometimes one, fometimes the other; we do as we may, we are neither Saints nor Saintefles, it is not for nothing that we run fo often to Confeffion, they are only the dead who never go there, but a-mongft the living find me one if you can.

What thou fay'ft is too true, we have all our foibles, anfwer'd fhe. Oh! there is nothing more certain, faid I; and therefore, my dear Lady, if by chance you fhould have a fmall Kindnefs for the meaneft of your humble Servants, there would be no fuch great Wonder in it, I am marry'd indeed, but tho' I was not I fhould love you neither more nor lefs, without reckoning that I was a Batchelor when you firft faw me, and if I have taken a Wife fince, it was not thro' your Fault, it was not you who oblig'd me to it; but it would be much worfe if we were both marry'd, whereas you are not; which is ftill an Abatement in our Misfortune, I take you as I find you, or rather I ought to let you alone, but I can't have Courage enough for that, fince my touching thofe enchanting Hands, which I held between mine, and fince the little Softnefles which you faid to me.

I fhould fay ftill moie to you, if I did not put a Reftraint upon my felf, anfwer'd fhe, for thou haft charm'd me, *la Vallée*, and thou art the moft dangerous little Spark that I know; but to return to what we were upon.

I have already told thee that we muft be dif-creet, and I am glad to find thou art fenfible of the neceffity of it, the manner in which I live, the Opinion People have of my Conduct, thy

own

own Gratitude both for the Services I have done, and defign thee, all require it, my dear Child , if the leaft Word efcapes thee, I am ruin'd, be fure remember that, and never forget it I befeech thee; at prefent let's confider of fome Method to fee one another now and then , if thou continueft to come here, it may occafion Reflections; for under what Pretence canft thou come? I hold fome rank in the World, and thou art not in a Situation to pay me frequent Vifits, they would not fail fufpecting I had a liking for thee; thy Youth and good Mein would eafily perfuade them to think fo, and that is what we muft avoid. You fhall hear my Contrivance.

In fuch a Suburb (I have forgot which it was) lives an ancient Woman whofe Husband had fome Obligations to me, and died about fix or feven Months ago; fhe lives in fuch a Place, and is call'd Mrs. *Remy* here, write down her Name and place of Abode directly, fee there is Pen, Ink, and Paper upon the Table.

Accordingly I wrote down the Name, and when I had fo done, fhe is a Woman implicitly at my Devotion, added Mrs. *Ferval*, continuing her Difcourfe, I will fend to her early to morrow Morning, to inform her that I want to fpeak with her Our Meetings fhall be at her Houfe, it's in a very remote Part, and where I am entirely unknown. She lives by herfelf, and her little Habitation is very commodious; there is alfo a pretty Garden that one may go through, the back Door of it opens into a bye unfrequented Street, and in that Street I'll alight from my
Coach,

Coach, I'll always go in at that Door, and you
shall go in at the fore one ; as to what my Servants may think, I am in no Pain about it ;
for they are us'd to wait on me to all forts of
Places, according to the different Charities which
we have to exercife, two or three Ladies of my
Acquaintance and my felf ; and I as often go
alone as in Company, either to vifit the Sick or
to relieve poor Families , my Servants know it,
and will readily believe it's for fome fuch Purpofe, when I go to Mrs. *Remy's*. Can you
meet me there to Morrow about five in the E-
vening, *la Vallée?* I fhall have feen Mrs. *Remy*
by then, and fhall have taken all my Meafures.

Oh! Madam, faid I, you may depend upon
my being punctual to the Appointment, I am
only forry it is not for this Moment: but tell
me, my dear Lady, we fhall have no Chambermaid then to over-hear us, and to hinder my
having the Papers.

No, no, reply'd fhe laughing, and we may
talk as loud as we pleafe too ; but I recollect one
thing, it's a long way from your Lodging to
this Suburb, you'll have occafion for a Hackney-
Coach every time to carry you, and that's an
Expence which will be inconvenient to you.

Oh! as for that Expence, faid I, my Legs
will defray it very well, don't you trouble your
felf about it : No, Child, faid fhe, rifing it is
too far, and would fatigue you too much, and
as fhe was fpeaking, fhe open'd a little Cheft,
out of which fhe drew a Purfe which was ordinary enough, but very well fill'd.

Here

Here, Child, added she, here is wherewithall to pay your Coach-hire; when this is gone, I'll give you more.

Oh! my dear Miftrefs, cry'd I, puff'd up with Self-love, and quite dazzel'd at my own Merit, oh! pray forbear, this Purfe makes me abfolutely afham'd.

And what is pleafant, I faid no more than the Truth; yes, in fpight of my Vanity, there was a little Confufion mix'd with the high efteem which I had for my felf. I was charm'd at having the Purfe offer'd me, but I blufh'd to accept it; the one flatter'd me, but the other I thought look'd mean.

However at laft notwithftanding my unwillingnefs, I yielded to her Sollicitations, and after having two or three times repeated; but Madam, but my dear Miftrefs, I coft you too much, there is no occafion to buy my Heart, it's already paid for, I have given it you for nothing; to what Purpofe this Money? At laft I fay I took it.

But you muft obferve, my dear Child, faid fhe, fhutting the Cheft; we only go to this Place, which I appoint to avoid Cenfure, you may fee me there with more liberty, but it muft be with as much Decorum as ever, do you hear *la Vallée?* I hope you won't make an ill ufe of what I do for you: I don't underftand Fineffe.

Alas! faid I, nor I neither, I only go for the meer pleafure of being with you, and to love your Perfon at my eafe, that's all: For as to any thing elfe, I affure you that I have no defign to difguft you in the leaft Article in the
World,

World, my Intention is to pleafe you; I love you here, I fhall love you there, and I fhall love you every where. Well, there's no harm in that, faid fhe, and I don't forbid thy loving me, *la Vallée*, but I would willingly have nothing to reproach my felf with; that's what I mean.

But whilft I remember, added fhe, I have another thing to tell thee of, and that's a Letter which I have wrote for thee to Mrs *Fecour*, you fhall carry it your felf. Her Brother-in-Law, Mr. *Fecour* is a Man of great intereft in the Finances, and refufes nothing to his Sifter's Recommendation; I have defir'd her either to prefent thee to him, or to write to him in thy Favour, that he may place the at *Paris*, and put thee in the Road to Preferment, it's the fureft way I can devife to make thy Fortune.

Immediately fhe took the Letter, which was lying upon the Table, and gave it to me; but I had fcarce received it, when a Footman brought Word of a Vifiter, and it prov'd Mrs. *Fecour* herfelf.

Directly I faw a pretty fat Woman enter the Room, of a moderate Stature, but with one of the moft furious Bofoms I had ever beheld; fhe feem'd otherwife a Woman without Ceremony, and at firft Sight a lover of Pleafure, but I'll give you her Picture fince I am got upon the Subject.

Mrs. *Fecour* was about three or four Years younger than Mrs *Ferval*, I believe fhe had been handfome in her Youth; but what was now moft obfervable in her Countenance, was

a

a frank Cordial Air, which made it very agreeable to look at

She had nothing of that Heaviness in her Carriage which is common to your over fat People, neither her good Plight nor her Bosom were Incumbrances to her, and she behaved with as much Sprightliness under her Mass of Flesh, as if she had been ever so lean ; to which you may add a hale robust Look, and a certain amiable Freshness of Complexion, such a Freshness I mean as proceeds from a good Constitution, and shows it's Professor an Enemy to inactivity.

There are few Women but what either have their favourite Affectations, or endeavour to persuade you that they have not, which is another Species of Coquetry ; but in this Respect Mrs. *Fecour* had nothing of the Woman in her, it was even one of her peculiar Qualities not so much as to know what Affectation meant.

She had a fine Hand, but she did not know it ; had it been an ugly one she would have been equally ignorant of the Matter, for tho' she was very susceptible of Love, yet she had no Thoughts of inspiring it ; but was always the Person pleas'd, without any design of pleasing. The Glances of other Women artfully say, Love me, that I may triumph in the Conquest ; but her's were pure Nature, and said without any Art at all, I love you, are you willing I should? Nor did they ask that Question out of Vanity, but for the mere Satisfaction of knowing your Mind.

From

From what I've been faying, the refult is this; that fhe was rather indecént, than coquettifh in her Behaviour.

For Example, if fhe lik'd you, this Bofom which I fpoke of, was difplay'd to you a thoufand different ways, not fo much with an Intention to tempt your Heart, as fo let you know that you had touch'd her's; it was her manner of declaring Love.

Mrs. *Fecour*, as a Companion, was rather merry than witty, was more free than bold, and more inclin'd to Libertinifm than Tendernefs; fhe lov'd all the World, and had a Friendfhip for nobody: carry'd her felf with the fame Air to all, to the Rich as to the Poor, to the Lord as to the Cit, neither efteeming the Quality of the one nor defpifing the moderate Eftate of the other. Her Attendants were not her Servants, they were Men and Women who liv'd with her; they ferved her and fhe was ferved; that was all fhe troubled her felf about.

What fhall I do, Sir, fhe'd ask you? and if *Bourguignon* came in, *Bourguignon*, how fhall I act in this Affair? *Jafmin* was her Counfellor if he was there; and you was the fame, if you happen'd to be with her; fhe call'd him *Jafmin*, and *You Sir*, that was all the Difference fhe was fenfible of, for fhe had neither pride nor good manners.

But one more ftroke at her Character, which fhall be a finifhing as well as a very fingular one.

Did you fay to her, I am uneafy or I am overjoy'd, I have fuch or fuch hopes, or I am in

fuch

fuch or fuch perplexities; fhe would only enter into your Situation becaufe of the Word, and not becaufe of the Thing; would only weep with you, becaufe you wept, and not becaufe you had Occafion to weep; fhe would laugh with you upon the fame Account, would intrigue for you without concerning her felf in your Affairs, or even fo much as reflecting that fhe had no intereft in them, and all becaufe you defir'd her to intrigue for you; in fhort, it was nothing but your Words and the Tone with which you pronounced them, that affected her; had you told her, Madam, your Friend or your Relation is dead, and had fpoke it with an Air of indifference, fhe would have anfwer'd in the fame manner, is it poffible? to which had you anfwer'd with an afflicted accent, Alas! its too true, fhe would have reply'd with an Air of Affliction, Oh! how forry I am!

In a Word, fhe was a Woman who had meerly Senfe without Sentiments, and yet fhe paffed for one of the beft Women in the World; for her Senfe upon a hundred Occafions ftood her exactly in the fame ftead as Sentiments, and did her as much Honour.

As particular as this Character may appear, yet it's more general than can eafily be imagin'd, it's the Portrait of an infinite Number of People, who are commonly call'd the genteel part of the World; I mean thofe genteel Folks, who only live for the Sake of Pleafure and Diverfion, who hate nothing but what you give them an Averfion for, are juft as you'd have them be, and never entertain any Opinion but what they receive at fecond Hand.

As

As to the reſt, it was not at once that I
diſcover'd Mrs. *Fecour* as I have deſcrib'd her,
our Acquaintance was but ſmall at that time;
but when I met with her ſome Years after, I
ſaw her often enough to know her thoroughly:
to return.

Oh! my God, Madam, cry'd ſhe to Mrs.
Ferval, how glad I am to find you at home!
I was afraid you was abroad, for it's a long time
ſince we ſaw one another; well, how do you
do?

And immediately, as I cut the Figure of a Gentleman there, ſhe drop'd me a Courteſy, gazing
at me very attentively all the while.

After the firſt Compliments were over, Mrs.
Ferval paid her one upon her looking ſo hearty.
Yes, anſwer'd ſhe, I am mighty well, thank
God! I enjoy an extraordinary ſhare of Health;
I wiſh my Siſter in-law was as happy, I muſt
go to ſee her preſently! poor Woman! ſhe
ſent me Word the day before yeſterday that ſhe
was very ill.

I never heard a Word of it, ſaid Mrs. *Ferval;* but perhaps according to Cuſtom it's rather
an Indiſpoſition than an Illneſs; ſhe's extreamly
delicate.

Oh! without doubt, reply'd the fat Goſſip,
I am of your Opinion, it's nothing but the
Vapours.

I was pretty much embaraſſed during this
Converſation, tho' leſs perhaps than another
would have been in my Place, for I began to
poliſh a little, and was only out of Countenance
thro' the Fear of being ſo.

As

As it happen'd, I had inadvertently brought away Mrs. *de la Vallée's* Snuff-Box ; I felt it in my Pocket, and to employ my felf, pull'd it out, and open'd it in order to take a Pinch of Snuff.

I had hardly open'd it, when Mrs *Fecour*, who often looked at me, as one looks at a Perfon one loves to fee , when Mrs. *Fecour*, I fay, cry'd ; oh' Sir, you have got fome Snuff, pray give me a Pinch, I forgot my Snuff-Box, and have not known what to do this Hour for want of it.

Immediately I rofe and prefented her ; I bow'd as I offer'd it, and as in that Pofture my Face approach'd her's, fhe took the Oopportunity to examine me at her eafe , and whilft fhe was taking her Snuff ftared at me without Ceremony, and fix'd her Eyes fo fteadily as to put me a little to the Blufh.

You are very young to accuftom your felf to Snuff, faid fhe; one time or other you'll repent it, Sir, there's nothing fo prejudical ; I tell all the World fo, and efpecially young *Gentlemen* of your Age when I fee them take it ; to be fure the Gentleman cannot be twenty yet.

I fhall be very foon, Madam, faid I, ftepping back to my Chair. Oh ! the charming Age, cry'd fhe. True, Madam, faid Mrs. *Ferval*, but he muft not lofe his time, for he has no Fortune , it is but five or fix Months fince he came from *Provence*, and we would fain procure him fome employ if we can.

Oh ! by all Means, reply'd fhe, it's the beft way imaginable ; the Gentleman will prepoffefs

all

all thofe who fee him in his Favour; I pro-
phefy him a happy Match. Alas! Madam,
faid Mrs. *Ferval,* he is already marry'd to one
Mrs. *Haberd,* a Gentlewoman of his own Country, who has between four and five thoufand
Livres a Year.

Aha! Mrs. *Haberd,* reply'd the other, I
heard talk of that Affair in the very laft Company I was in.

What fhe faid put us to the Blufh, Mrs. *Fer-*
val and I; why fhe blufh'd is what I cannot
tell you, unlefs it was that Mrs. *Fecour* had undoubtedly heard that I was an inferiour Fellow,
notwithftanding which fhe had furpriz'd her in
a regular Converfation with me; befides, fhe
lov'd this inferior Fellow; fhe was a Devotee,
or at leaft paffed for fuch; and all together was
enough to embarafs her Confcience a little.

For my part, it was very natural for me to
be out of Countenance; the Story which Mrs.
Fecour had learn'd of me, was that of a poor
Peafant, in plain terms a Footman, a little
Droll who was pick'd up upon the *New Bridge*;
and it was out of this Droll's Snuff-Box forfooth
that fhe had been very politely taking Snuff; it
was of him fhe had faid, to be fure the Gentleman cannot be twenty; was not this a fine
Farce for her to play a Part in? Had not fhe
fufficient Reafon to laugh at her having been
fuch a Dupe to my Mafquerade?

But my Apprehenfions were groundlefs, we
had to do with a Woman who paffed over every
thing, who only regarded the prefent, and never
troubled her Head with the paft. I was gen-
teely

teely dreſſed, and ſhe found me with Mrs. *Ferval*, which was enough for her, without reckoning my handſome Figure, for which ſee ſeem'd to have a ſingular Eſteem; ſo that continuing her Diſcourſe as unconcerned as ſhe had begun: O! this is the Gentleman then, ſaid ſhe, who marry'd Mrs. *Haberd*, ſhe was a great Devotee I am informed, it's ſomething pleaſant; but it cannot be above two or three Days, Sir, ſince you marry'd, for the news has but juſt took Air.

No, Madam, anſwer'd I, a little recovered from my Confuſion, ſince I ſaw it was all one to her, we were marry'd yeſterday.

So much the better, reply'd ſhe, I am mighty glad of it; the Woman is a little in Years, I am told, but ſhe has loſt nothing by ſtaying; truly, added ſhe, turning to Mrs. *Ferval*, I was inform'd he was a handſome Youth, and they did him no more than Juſtice; if I knew the Lady, I'd wiſh her Joy, ſhe has made a very good choice; pray, may I ask what her Name is at preſent?

Mrs. *de la Vallée*, reply'd Mrs. *Ferval* for me; and her Husband's Father is a very ſubſtantial Man, he is a great Farmer, who having ſeveral Children, ſent this to *Paris*, to endeavour to get into ſome employ or other: In a word, they are very ſubſtantial People.

Oh! undoubtedly, anſwer'd Mrs. *Fecour*: how do you ſay? People who live in the Country, Farmers! oh! I know what you mean: Yes, yes, they are very ſubſtantial People, very valuable to be ſure, there is nothing to be ſaid againſt that. It

It was I who brought the Match to bear, said Mrs. *Ferval*; ay, ay, was it you ? reply'd the other ; indeed the good Devotee is highly oblig'd to you , I have a mighty Opinion of the Gentleman only from his looks ; another Pinch of your Snuff, Mr. *de la Vallée* ; why, you have marry'd very young, my dear Child, you could not have fail'd matching your self advantageously some time or other, shap'd as you are, but you will be more at your ease at *Paris*, and at less Charge with your Family. You have Friends, Madam, added she, addressing herself to Mrs. *Ferval*, he is amiable, you must push him.

We are exceeding desirous of it, reply'd the other, and I must take the Liberty of telling you that the Moment you came in, I had just given him a Letter of Recommendation to yourself ; Mrs. *Fecour*, your Brother-in-Law is very capable of serving him , and I wrote it to beg the Favour of your Interest with him.

Oh! My God, with all my Heart, cry'd Mrs. *Fecour* , yes, Sir, Mr. *Fecour* must Place you, I protest I never thought of it, but he's at *Verfailles* for a few Days ; would you have me write to him in the mean time ? Hold ! it is not far from hence to my House, we have nothing to do but to step there for a Moment , I will even write, and Mr. *de la Vallée* shall carry my Letter to him to morrow. Indeed, Sir, said she, getting up, I am charm'd that the Lady has thought upon me on this occasion , let us go, I have some Visits to pay still , let us lose no time. Adieu, Madam, my Visit's short, but you see why I leave you. And

And immediately fhe embrac'd Mrs *Ferval*, who return'd her thanks; fhe thank'd her again, laid hold on my Arm in a familiar manner, took me down Stairs, made me get into her Coach; fometimes call'd me Sir, and fometimes my dear Child, talk'd to me as if we had been acquainted feven Years, ftill difplaying the bofom . in a Word, we arriv'd at her Houfe.

As foon as we came in, fhe introduc'd me into her Clofet ; fit down, faid fhe, I have but a Line or two to write to Mrs. *Fecour*, and they fhall be very preffing.

In fhort, her Letter was finifh'd in an Inftant · Here, faid fhe, giving it me, you will be well receiv'd upon my Account ; I have defir'd him to fix you at *Paris*, for it is neceffary you fhould ftay here to cultivate your Friends ; it would be a thoufand pities to fend you into the Country, where you would be bury'd alive, and befides we fhall be glad to fee you. I would not have our Acquaintance drop here however, Mr. *de la Vallée* , what fay you, is it a pleafure to you ?

And a great deal of Honour too, reply'd I ; fiddle faddle of Honour, faid fhe, we were not talking of that, I am a Woman without Ceremony, efpecially with Perfons whom I love, and who are amiable, Mr. *de la Vallée*, for you are extreamly fo ; oh extreamly ! the firft Man I ever had an Inclination for was exactly like you ; methinks I fee him, he is never out of my Heart ; I us'd to thou him, it is my Way, I defign to ufe you in the fame manner ; and if I fhould, would you be difgufted ? Are

M   not

not you willing I fhould treat you as I treated
him? added fhe, advancing the bofom, which by
chance I had my Eye already fix'd upon, it confus'd me a little and hinder'd my anfwering her;
fhe took notice of it, and ftood for fome time
obferving me.

Well, faid fhe, laughing, and what are you
thinking on? On you, Madam, reply'd I with
a low Voice, and my Eyes ftill rivetted as I told
you. On me! anfwer'd fhe, do you fpeak
truth, Mr. *de la Vallée*? Do you apprehend
that I have good Intentions for you? It is not
difficult to perceive, and if you queftion it, it
is not my Fault; you fee I am downright, and
I love that every one fhould be the fame with
me; do you hear, young handfome? What
Eyes he has! and yet for all that he is afraid to
fpeak, Harkee, Mr. *de la Vallée*, I have fome
Advice to give you; here you come from *Provence*, whence you have brought a bafhful Air,
which does not fit well upon one of your Age,
and particularly when they are made like you,
you muft embolden your felf a little, it is abfolutely neceffary in fuch a place as this; What
are you deficient in, that you fhould want affurance? Who does it belong to, if it does not
belong to you, my dear Child? You are fo
amiable! and this fhe fpoke with fuch a fincere
and fuch a careffing tone, that I began to relifh
her Compliments, when we heard a Coach drive
into the Court.

See! here is fomebody come to vifit me, faid
fhe, feal your Letter, Child, you will return
foon? As foon as I have deliver'd the Letter,
Madam, anfwer'd I,   Adieu

Adieu then, reply'd she, holding her Hand to me which I kifs'd at my eafe; well, well, another time be convinc'd that People love you; I am forry I did not give Orders for them to fay I was not at Home; perhaps I fhould not have went out any more, and we might have pafs'd the reft of the Day together, but we fhall fee one another again, I fhall expect you; do not fail.

The Hour you fhall be moft at Leifure, Madam, will you pleafe to tell it me? At what Hour you will, faid fhe; in the Morning, in the Evening, every Hour is alike, only the Morning is the fureft time to meet with me. Adieu, brown beauty, added fhe, ftroaking me under the Chin; learn to be freer with me for the future: Do you hear?

She had hardly done fpeaking, when a Servant came to tell her that three Vifitors waited for her in her Chamber; and whilft fhe went to them, I retir'd.

My affairs, as you fee, roll'd on at a *Jehu* rate: Adventures crowded fo thick upon me, that I was aftonifh'd at it myfelf.

Imagine how it muft be with a young Ruftick, like me, who, in the fpace of only two Days, was become the Husband of a wealthy Woman, and the Gallant of two Ladies of Quality. Befides, there was the alteration of my Drefs, which wrought a ftrange effect. The Title of Sir, with which I found myfelf honoured, who, but about a dozen days before, was call'd plain *Jacob*; the amorous flatteries of the two Ladies; and, particularly, that charming, tho'

M 2

impure

impure art, which Mrs. *Ferval* us'd to seduce
me; that lovely Leg, on which I could have
gaz'd for ever, those fine snow-white Hands,
which she so tenderly abandon'd to my Raptures, those Looks, so full of softness; in short,
the Air which breath'd through the whole, was
not all this enough to open my Heart? Was
not it a perfect School of Softness, Voluptuous-
ness, and Corruption, and consequently of Refinement too? For by the same Degrees as the
Mind taints, so it polishes. For my part, I
was wrapp'd in a Transport of Vanity, it was
something so novel. Till then, I had never
known the Delicacy of Living, and, from
that Day, I seem'd to be a different person, so
much Education and Experience had I acquir'd.

Therefore I return'd Home, quite lost in
Vanity, as I told you, but in a Vanity which
made me gay, not haughty and ridiculous;
my Self-love was always sociable, and I never
was more tractable and complaisant, than when
I had an opportunity of exercising my esteem
upon myself. Every one has his Character in
that respect, and this was mine. Mrs. *de la
Vallée* never saw me so caressing and amiable,
as she found me at my return.

It was late, and they were waiting for me
to sit down to Table; for you may remember
that we had invited our Landlady to Supper
with her Daughter, and the Persons who had
assisted as Witnesses at our Wedding

It's impossible to tell you the Compliments
which I made my Guests, and the Courtliness
with which I excited them to be merry. Our

two

two witneſſes were a little heavy, and they ſaw me ſo ſprightly in compariſon of themſelves, or rather ſo gallant in my manners, that they were quite dazzled at it, and, in ſpight of my exhortations to be familiar, they would not be acquainted with me but with diſcretion.

Mrs. *d'Alain* was alſo amaz'd, and, as much a Goſſip as ſhe was, I could diſcern that ſhe was more circumſpect, in regard to what ſhe ſaid, than uſual. My praiſe always fill'd up the intervals of the Diſcourſe, and they endeavour'd to give that praiſe the politeſt turn they could; ſo that I perceiv'd my behaviour had mightily increas'd their Conſideration for me.

Undoubtedly it was nothing but my Converſation with the two Ladies which had ſtamp'd this value upon me; I had brought from them I know not what air of diſtinction, which I never-had before.

The truth is, I conſider'd myſelf as entirely another Man, and could not help thinking when I look'd upon my Gueſts; theſe are good ſort of People enough, but beneath my Level: However, I muſt accommodate myſelf to them at preſent

I ſhall paſs over the Diſcourſe during our repaſt. *Javote* gave me a great many Glances, and I was the moſt pleaſant Companion at Table; but then my Pleaſantry was attended with Reſpect, and I appear'd ſo charming to Mrs. *de la Vallée*, that, in her Impatience to ſee me at her Eaſe, ſhe look'd at her Watch ſeveral Times, and told the Hour, as a handſome *Me-*

mento

mento to our Guefts, that it was time for them to withdraw.

At laft they got up, made their Congies, and left us alone, Mrs. *de la Vallée* and I.

And immediately, without any farther Ceremony, my pious Spoufe went to bed, under pretence of being fatigu'd. Come, Child, let's go to Bed, faid fhe, for it's very late; which was as much as to fay, Come, becaufe I love you; at leaft I underftood her fo, and follow'd her with a hearty good will, for I really lov'd her, and fhe was very comely and defireable, as yet; I have already told you fo in the beginning of this Hiftory. Befides, my Breaft was fo full of tender Images, my Heart had been fir'd fo many different ways, and I had had fo much Love made to me that Day, that it fet me upon the amorous Pin in my turn, to which you may add the convenience of having fuch a Woman as Mrs. *de la Vallée* with me, who requir'd nothing more than to liften to my Tranfports, which is another very prevailing Motive.

Whilft I was undreffing myfelf, I would have given her an account of my Vifit. I talk'd to her of the generous intentions which Mrs. *Ferval* had to ferve me, of Mrs. *Fecour*'s arrival there, of the Letter which fhe had given me, and of the Journey which I was to take the next morning to *Verfailles* to deliver it: But I chofe a wrong time; for whatever intereft Mrs. *de la Vallée* took in my Affairs, I could fay nothing to merit her attention; all I could get from her was a few monofyllables. Ay, ay, ay, fay you fo? That's well; and directly, come, come, we'll talk of that here.

Accordingly, I went, and farewel the Story; I forgot to purfue it, and my dear Wife never once put me in mind of it.

How charming and fervent were the tenderneffes fhe faid to me! I have already given you her Character, and can only add this, that no Devotee ever made a more paffionate ufe of the privilege of fhewing her chafte Affection. I have feen the moment when fhe has cry'd, Oh! the pleafure of fruftrating the attempts of the Devil, and of being able, without fin, to be as happy as finners!

At laft we both fell faft a-fleep, and it was at Eight o'Clock the next Morning, when I refum'd the account of my Vifit.

She highly prais'd the good Intentions of Mrs. *Ferval*, and begg'd God to be her recompence, as well as Mrs. *Fecour's* ; after which, we got up, and went out both together, I for *Verfailles*, and fhe to hear Mafs, and pray for the good fuccefs of my Journey.

I went ftrait to the Inn where the Stage-coaches put up ; I met with one for four People, three of the places were already taken, and I took the fourth.

The Companions of my Journey were an old Officer, a Man of good Senfe, who to a venerable Afpect join'd a plain and uniform Appearance.

A tall meagre Creature, with little, black, fiery Eyes, and a very difturb'd Countenance, we difcover'd foon after that he was a Lawyer;

M 4

and

and his Bufinefs, to judge by his Looks, was the moft fuitab'e for him of any in the World.

After thefe came a young Gentleman of a pretty good Figure; the Officer and he gaz'd at each other as Perfons who had met before, but did not know where. At laft they recollected themfelves, and remember'd that they had din'd together.

As I was neither with your Mrs. *d'Alain's*, nor with Ladies who were in Love with me, I plac'd a guard upon my Expreffions, and endeavour'd to fay nothing which might betray the Farmer's Son; fo that I fpoke but little, and contented myfelf with liftening to what the others faid.

One hardly perceives that a Man fays nothing, when he liftens with Attention, at leaft one continually imagines that he is going to fpeak; and to hear attentively, is almoft the fame thing as to anfwer.

Every now and then I dropp'd a Yes without doubt, no truly, you are in the right; and all conformable to that opinion which I faw the moft prevailing.

The Officer, a Knight of St. *Lewis*, was he who engrofs'd moft of the Converfation. His honeft military air, his age, and frank open behaviour, won infenfibly upon our Lawyer, who was very filent, and more inclin'd to mufe than to fpeak.

I don't know how it was introduc'd, but our Officer happen'd to talk to the young Gentleman about a Woman who was at Law with her Husband, and fued for a feparate Maintenance.

The

The Story touch'd our Lawyer to the quick, and having look'd two or three times upon the Officer, and seemingly taken a friendship for him, he join'd in the Discourse, and join'd in it so heartily, that, from one Harangue to another, and from Invective to Invective against Women, he insensibly own'd that he was in the same case as the person they talk'd of, and that he was also in Law with his Wife.

Upon this acknowledgment, they dropp'd the Adventure in question, to come to his, and they were in the right, for the one was more interesting than the other, and, if I may use the Comparison, exactly the same as preferring an original to a meer copy.

Ay, ay, Sir, are you in Law with your Wife, then? said the young Gentleman to him. That's a bad story; it's a melancholy situation for a gallant Man. Well, but pray what might be the subject of your Quarrel?

What! reply'd the other, that's pleasant, as if it was a Wonder for a Man to have a quarrel with his Wife, is not it enough to be her Husband, to have an establish'd Suit against her? Every Husband is in Law, Sir, and is either Plaintiff or Defendant. Sometimes the Suit is never carried out of his own House, and sometimes it is remov'd higher, mine is removed.

For my part, I never would marry, interrupted the Officer, I don't know whether I have done right or wrong, but hitherto I have not seen any occasion to repent. How happy you are! reply'd the other, I envy you, and wish

wifh myfelf in your place. I alfo made a refolution of living a Batchelor, and even refifted
a great many temptations, which better deferv'd to damn me, than that which I funk under. It's paft my Apprehenfion; faith I can't
tell how it came about. I was in Love, indeed, but very little, and not half fo much as
I had been elfewhere; yet, for all that, I
married.

Undoubtedly, then, the perfon was rich, faid
the young Gentleman No, reply'd the other,
fhe was no richer than her Neighbours, and
not fo young neither. She was a great Girl,
of between two and three and thirty Years of
Age, and I was forty. I had a fuit at Law
with a Nephew of mine, a great wrangler,
and I have not done with him yet, but will ruin
him, like a Rafcal as he is, was I to fpend to
the uttermoft Farthing. But that's a ftory by
itfelf, which I will alfo tell you, if we have
time.

My Devil (it is my Wife I fpeak of) was a
Relation of one of my Judges; I was acquainted with her, and went to intreat her to follicit
for me. And as one Vifit draws on another, I
repeated mine fo frequently, that I went to fee
her every Day, tho' without knowing why, or
wherefore, except through Habit. Our Families
being equal, and her Fortune tolerable, the
Report run, that I was to marry her. We
laugh'd at the News; however, we muft fee
one another lefs often, to ceafe this Noife, faid
fhe to me, laughing, or at laft they'll talk ten
times worfe. And why fo? reply'd I; I have
a great

a great mind to fall in Love with you, what say you, are you willing I fhou'd? She neither anfwer'd me yes, nor no.

The next Day I return'd, ftill bantering about this Love which I told her was to feize me, and which, I believe, had already laid hold on me, or rather had ftolen upon me unawares; for I felt nothing of it, nor ever once faid to her, I love you. I never faw any thing like this wretched habitual Love which gives a Man no notice; I am in a paffion whenever I think on't, and the bare remembrance of my Adventure choaks me. Would you imagine it? About five Days after, a wealthy Widower, who was fomething older than me, took it in his Head to court my *Belle*; I call her my *Belle*, through Pleafantry, for one may fee a hundred thoufand fuch Faces as her's without taking Notice of them; and except two great Eyes, which the Prude had, and which were not fo handfome neither, as they appear'd to be, her Face was a very ordinary one, and had nothing to recommend it but its whitenefs.

This Suitor I fpeak of, chagrin'd me: Whenever I went, I found him there; which put me out of humour. He and I could never be of an opinion, and I took all opportunities to affront him. There are fome People for whom we conceive an Antipathy at firft fight; and to that it was I attributed my Averfion to him. I underftood no better, but I was deceiv'd, as you'll find; for, in reality, I was jealous. This man, undoubtedly, was weary of living a Widower; he talk'd of Love, and then

then of Marriage; I heard of it, and encreas'd my hatred to him, which was always the moſt cordial in the World.

Are you determin'd to marry this Man? ſaid I to my fair one. My relations and friends adviſe me to't, ſaid ſhe; on his ſide he preſſes me, and I don't know what to do, I'm not reſolv'd upon any thing as yet. What would you adviſe me to? Me! to nothing, anſwer'd I, muttering, you're your own Mi-ſtreſs; marry, Madam, marry, ſince you have a fancy for't. Oh! my God, Sir, cry'd ſhe leaving me. at what a rate you talk! truly, if you don't care for People, you might be ſo civil as not to tell them ſo: Troth! Madam, it's you that do not care for them, anſwer'd I. This was a pleaſant declaration of Love, as you ſee; but it was the plaineſt I ever made her, and even that eſcap'd me without reflection. After this I return'd home very thoughtful. In the evening one of my friends call'd upon me. Do you hear, ſaid he, that a contract of marriage is to be ſigned to morrow Morning between Mrs. ſuch a one and Mr. ----- I juſt came from thence, the relations are actually met; but ſhe herſelf does not ſeem very forward in it; I thought ſhe look'd a little melancholy, tell me are not you the occaſion on't?

How! cry'd I, without anſwering his Que-ſtion, do they talk of a contract then? Alas! my dear friend, I believe I'm in love with her, why mayn't I as well marry her as another?

ther ? I wifh with all my heart I could hinder this contract.

Well, faid he, if fo, you've no time to lofe; run directly to her, and hear what fhe'll fay to you. Perhaps things are gone too far, reply'd I, quite ftruck to the Heart. And if you'll be fo good as to go your felf and fpeak to her for me, you'll do me a fingular Pleafure, added I with a filly confufed Air

Very willingly, faid he; ftay here for me, I'll go immediately; and bring you her anfwer in a Moment.

Accordingly he went, told her I lov'd her, and that I defir'd the preference before the other He love me! faid fhe, why this is pleafant enough! he always made a fecret of it to me, tell him to come here, we'll fee what's to be done.

Upon this anfwer which my friend brought me, I run to her; fhe ftep'd into a room apart, where I fpoke to her.

What is this which your friend has been telling me? faid fhe, with her great eyes full of tendernefs; have you any thoughts of me then? yes, truly, reply'd I, out of countenance. And why would not you tell me of it before? faid fhe I proteft I don't know how to act at prefent, you perplex me.

Upon which I took hold of her Hand, you are a ftrange Man, added fhe. Why, troth! faid I, an't I as good as the other ? As it luckily happens he's juft gone, faid fhe, and befides, there's a little difficulty arifen about the contract, which we muft endeavour to improve.

prove to our Advantage; there's none but my relations within, let's go to them.

I follow'd her, and talk'd to the relations, whom I gain'd over to my intereſt; the Lady was in good earneſt, and to make a ſpeedy end of the affair, one of them propos'd the ſending for a Notary.

I could not ſay no; ay, ay, quick, quick; away they went, the Notary came; and my head turn'd round with the rapidity of their proceedings; they treated me juſt as they pleaſ'd, I was trap'd; I ſign'd, they ſign'd, and immediately the Licence was ſent for The devil a word of love was there in the midſt of all this, in ſhort we were marry'd; and the next morning after the wedding, I was aſtoniſhed to find my ſelf nooz'd; but to whom? why at leaſt it's to a very ſenſible Woman, ſaid I to my ſelf.

Yes, faith! to a very ſenſible one, it was a ſign I was thoroughly acquainted with her; would you think what ſhe became at the end of three Months, this Woman whoſe ſenſe I was ſo fond of? why, an ill-humour'd, ſerious bigot, tho' at the ſame time a very talkative one, for ſhe made it her buſineſs to criticiſe my words and actions; in ſhort ſhe was a grave Fool who ſhow'd me nothing but a long auſtere Viſage, and piqu'd herſelf upon the melancholy vanity of living retir'd; not for the profit of her Family, for that ſhe abandon'd, ſhe thought it a diſgrace to her to take care of her Houſe, and was above giving in to ſuch a vulgar piety: no, no, ſhe ſtay'd at home

for

for nothing but to pafs her Life in a contem-plative idlenefs, and to read holy Lectures in her Clofet; from whence fhe would come with a devout, affected crabbednefs upon her coun-tenance, as if the having fuch a Face was a merit in the fight of God Almighty.

Soon after Madam began to reafon upon Religion; fhe had her opinions forfooth, could difpute about Doctrines, and was an errant Theologian in petticoats.

I could have difpens'd with this pretty well, had fhe ftop'd here, but our female Theo-logift grew refractory and troublefome.

If I kept a friend to dine with me, Ma-dam would not eat with the profane Man; fhe was indifpos'd, and muft dine apart in her Chamber, where fhe begg'd God's pardon for the libertinifm of my conduct.

Nothing but a Monk, or at leaft a Prieft, or a Bigot like herfelf, could go down with her, and I was never without a Capuchin or a Caffock at my table. I don't fay but they are very good fort of People; but then thefe good fort of People are not made to be the Comrades of good Companions like us; and my houfe was neither a Convent, nor a Church, nor my table a Refectory.

But what put me the moft out of Patience, nothing was too nice, nor too delicate for thefe fervants of the Lord, whilft I was for-ced to take up with more ordinary Fare for my worldly friends and finners; you fee there was neither good fenfe, nor morality in that.

Well,

Well, Gentlemen, I have engrofs'd a great deal of your Attention, but I fhould have ended here, I am a lover of Peace, and had not it been for a Clerk that I had ---

A Clerk! cry'd the young Gentleman interrupting him; fure that muft be fomething remarkable.

Yes, faid he, I became jealous of him, and as God would have it I was in the wrong. My Wife's Friends treated my Jealoufy as Malice and Calumny, and look'd upon me as a meer reprobate to fufpect fuch a virtuous Woman, who only vifited the Churches, and who thought nothing amiable but Sermons, Offices and holy Water, all this was mighty well, they faid juft what they pleas'd.

All that I know of the Matter is, that this Clerk for whom I had frequent Occafion on Account of my Bufinefs, and who was fon to her deceas'd Mother's Chambermaid; a great numfcul Rafcal, whom I kept out of Complaifance, a handfome Cur enough, and one who had a predeftinated look, as fhe faid.

This Lad, I fay, was ufually fent by her on her Meffages, to inquire after the Healths of Father fuch a one, and Mother fuch one, this Mr. and that Mr. firft to the Vicar's, and then to the Curate's; after which he would come and bring back their Anfwers, go into her Clofet, fit down and chat with her, place her Table, *Agnus* and Reliquary before her, reach down her Books, and fometimes read to her.

I grew uneafy at it, and fwore moft heartily; what do you mean by this heteroclitical Piety?

faid

said I, what the Devil of a Saint are you to rob me of my Clerk? our Union was not very edifying.

Madam call'd me her Crofs, her Tribulation; and I call'd her by he firft Name which came upper-moft, I was not nice in my Choice. This Clerk ftuck in my Stomach, I could not down with him. If I fent him any confiderable way, I fatigu'd him. In truth! faid fhe, with a Charity, which I believe could not advantage her Soul much, in truth! he will quite kill this poor Boy.

At laft the Animal fell fick, and a fever feiz'd me the next Morning.

I had a very violent one, but it was my Servants who waited upon me, and it was Madam hei felf who waited upon the Booby.

My Husband's the Mafter, faid fhe upon that Occafion, he has nothing to do but to order what he'd have; but as for this poor Boy, who'll take Care of him, if I fhould abandon him therefore it was meerly out of Charity, that fhe left me to fhift for my felf.

Her Impertinence probably fav'd my Life. I was fo exafperated that I got well out of fpight; and as foon as I was upon my Legs again, the firft fign of Amendment I fhow'd, was the kicking the Object of her Charity out of Doors. My Saint was ready to burft with Indignation, and came like a fury to ask the Reafon of it.

I know well enough Sir, what your Motives are, cry'd fhe, your unworthy Sufpicions are but too vifible, and God will revenge me upon you, God will revenge me!

I

I could not relifh her Predictions; fhe deliver'd them in the Tone of a Fury, and I anfwer'd her as much like a Brute; what the Plague! faid I, do you think my kicking your Rafcal out of Doors will fet me at odds with God Almighty? go, get you gone with your equivocal Piety; do not make my Head ach, but leave me in Repofe.

What did fhe do? we had a little Chambermaid in the Houfe, who was a very genteel, handy Girl, and who was an Eye-fore to her Miftrefs, I fuppofe, becaufe fhe was younger and handfomer than her felf, and becaufe I approv'd of her. I fhould have dy'd perhaps in my Illnefs had not it been for her.

The poor little Girl would fometimes comfort me for my Wife's ill-humours, and appeafe me when I was in a Paffion; which made me on my fide uphold her, and take a liking to her. I alfo kept her becaufe fhe was an underftanding Girl, and a very notable one.

My Wife, I fay, after Dinner, called her up into her Chamber, took I do not know what Pretence of quarreling with her, box'd her upon fome anfwer fhe gave her, reproach'd her with my Kindnefs for her, and turned her off.

Nancy (for that was the Girl's Name) came in Tears to take her leave of me; telling me her Adventure, and her Box on the ear.

As I faw there was nothing in the Affair, but a vindictive Malice on my Wife's part' go, go, faid I, do not afflict thy felf, do you ftay, *Nancy*, I will take care of the reft.

My

My Wife flew in a Rage, and would fee her no more : But I was immoveable in my Refoluti-on, a Man ought to be Mafter in his own Houfe, and efpecially when there's a Reafon for't.

My Obftinacy did not at all mollify the Ri-gour of our Correfpondence ; we talk'd toge-ther fometimes, but then it was purely to quarrel.

You are to obferve, if you pleafe, that I had entertained another Clerk who was my Wife's Averfion, fhe could not endure him ; and there-fore harraffed him about for nothing, and all to fpight me ; but the Lad did not value it, I had bid him not mind her, and he follow'd my Or-dres to a little ; he paid her no manner of Re-gard.

I was inform'd a few Days after, that my Wife had a Mind to pufh things to Extremi-ty.

Would to God of his mercy the Brute would once ftrike me ! faid fhe, fpeaking of me ; I heard of it ; no, no, faid I, hold you there ! be convinced that I will never do you that Pleafure ; as for Mortifications you fhall have enough of them, your Patience fhall never want Exercife, fo far I vow, but no farther.

My vow prov'd unfortunate, one fhould fwear for nothing. In fpight of my laudable Refolves, fhe fo far exceeded me one Day, and was fo devoutly provoking with her Tongue ; that at laft the Devil tempted me fo effectually, that recollecting her former Impertinences and the box on the Ear which fhe had given *Nancy* upon my Account, I could not forbear giving

her

her one, in Prefence of fome Witneffes who were her Friends.

 It efcaped me as quick as lightning; fhe flew in an Inftant to demand Juftice, and ever fince we have been at law together to my great Regret. for this Saint of mine, in fpight of the Clerk which I've thrown in her Difh, may Chance to caft me, if I cannot find fome powerful Friends, whom I go to feek at *Verfailles*.

This box on the Ear makes me uneafy for you, cry'd our young Gentleman, when he had ended, I am afraid it will prejudice your Caufe. It's true that Clerk is an Article of which I have no better Opinion than you; you have certainly I believe been very ill-ufed in that Particular, but then it's a cafe of Confcience, which you are at a lofs how to prove; and this unlucky box on the Ear had its Witneffes.

Softly, Sir, reply'd the other with a chagrin'd Air, we'll drop thefe Reflections upon the Clerk, if you pleafe; I can think of thofe things without a Prompter, do not difturb your felf, as to the box of the Ear it muft pafs as it may, I am only forry at prefent that I gave her no more than one; as to the reft, let us fupprefs the Commentary. There was not fo much harm perhaps in the Affair of the Clerk as you imagine, I have my Reafons to produce. This Clerk was a Coxcomb; my Wife might love him without knowing fhe did, and offend God fecretly without any formal Injury to me. In a Word, was there harm or was there none? If I fay there was, the beft way is to let me fay it.

Without

Without doubt, cry'd the Officer, to pacify him; ought one to believe an angry Husband, who is so liable to be deceiv'd? For my Part, I can see nothing in the Story you have been telling us, but an insociable and misantrope Woman; that is all.

But let us change the Discourse, and inquire a little what our two young Fellow-Travellers are going to *Versailles* for, added he, addressing him self to the young Gentleman and me. As for you, Sir, who have hardly left the College yet, said he to me, to be sure you only go to divert yourself, or out of Curiosity.

Neither for the one, nor the other, answer'd I, I am going to sollicit a Post from a Gentleman in the Ministry. If the men refuse you, appeal to the Women, reply'd he bantering.

And you, Sir, (it was to the young Gentleman he spoke) what may be your call to *Versailles?*

I am going to wait upon a Nobleman, said he, to whom, the last time I had the Honour of seeing him, I presented a Book of which I'm the Author. Oh! yes, reply'd the Officer; it's the same Book of which we were talking the other Day, when we din'd together. The very same, answer'd the young Gentleman. Have you read it, Sir? added he.

Yes, I return'd it yesterday to one of my Acquaintance who lent it me, said the Officer. Well Sir, and pray, tell me what you think of it? answer'd the young Gentleman. What signifies my Opinion? said the Officer, that can decide nothing, Sir, but pray, let me know how you like it, cry'd the other pressing him.

Truly,

Truly, Sir, reply'd the Soldier, I cannot tell what to anfwer you, it's paft my time of Day to judge of fuch things, it is not a Book which is calculated for fuch as me, I am too old.

How, too old! cry'd the young Gentleman. Yes, faid the other, I believe a very young Perfon might take a great deal of Pleafure in reading it, for nothing comes amifs to an Age which only défires to laugh, and which is fo greedy of joy that it takes it upon Content wherever it finds it; but we grey-beards are a little more difficult; we refemble in this Refpect your pall'd Epicures, who won't be tempted with ordinary Diet, and whom nothing can excite to eat but fomething exceeding nice and delicate. Befides I have not been able to penetrate into the defign of your Book, I neither know where it tends, nor what it aims at. One may venture to fay that you have not given your felf the trouble of felecting your Ideas, but have indifferently receiv'd all that came, which is quite another thing; in the firft Cafe, you affemble, reject and chufe; but in the fecond, you take the firft which prefents itfelf, be it never fo foreign, and fomething always prefents itfelf; for I am of Opinion that the Mind continually furnifhes either good or bad.

As to the reft, if things meerly extraordinary can be call'd curious, or an unlimited Licence agreeable, your Book ought to pleafe; if not the Mind, at leaft the Senfes; but I believe it's nothing but want of Experience which has deceiv'd you, and without reckoning the little Merit there is in this laft way of Writing, and

the

the Capacity you appear to have of fucceeding in the other; it's forming a wrong Notion of your Readers in general to hope to pleafe them by fuch Methods, it's true, Sir, we are naturally deprav'd and Libertin; but in Compofures of Wit, this Maxim muft not be taken literally, nor are we to be ftorm'd Sword in Hand upon that footing. A Reader will be manag'd; and if you have a Mind to engage his depravity in your Intereft, you muft go gently to Work, you muft lead foftly, not drive.

This Reader however loves Freedoms in an Author, but not exceffive and exorbitant ones; fuch as thofe are only fupportable where the reality foftens the indecency of them; they are then, if ever, in their proper Places; and we pafs them by, becaufe we are more Men at that time than another; but we cannot fo eafily excufe them in a Book where they become dull, fcurrilous and fhocking, becaufe of the little Agreement they have with the compos'd State of a Reader.

It is true this Reader is alfo a Man, but then he is a Man in tranquillity, has tafte and delicacy, is one who expects his Mind to be diverted; and though he is willing enough you fhould tickle his depravity, yet it muft be with decency and good Manners.

Notwithftanding what I have faid, there are feveral good Things in your Book; I affure you I remark'd a great many of that kind my felf.

As to your Style, I have no fault to find with it, except it is that your Periods are fometimes
too

too loofe and tedious, and by that means confus'd and perplex'd ; which undoubtedly proceeds from your not having fufficiently digefted
your *Ideas*, or from your not having rang'd
them into any certain order; but you are only
a beginner yet, Sir, and this is a fmall Fault,
which you will correct in writing, as well as
that of criticizing others ; and efpecially of criticizing them in that familiar waggifh tone, with
which you feem to be affected, and which you
will laugh at, and blame in your felf when you
are a little more of the Philofopher, and when
you have acquir'd a more folid and worthy way
of thinking ; for you will have a good deal more
Wit than you have, at leaft I have feen things
in you which promife it ; you will not make
much account of what you have hitherto been
Mafter of, and hardly any of what you may
attain to hereafter At leaft this is the manner
in which I have heard fome of our greateft
Writers talk.

What I obferv'd of your Criticifms was occafion'd by that which I faw in your Book, and
which is level'd at----(he nam'd him,) who was
in Company with us that Day we din'd together. I muft frankly acknowledge to you, that
I was furpriz'd to find fifty or fixty Pages of
your Work heavily employ'd againft him ; I
could heartily wifh for your fake they had been
left out.

But fee we are arriv'd at our Journey's end !
you ask'd my Opinion, and I have told it you as
a Man who loves your Talents, and who wifhes
to fee you one Day the Object of as many
Criticifms

Criticifms as the Perfon we are fpeaking of ;
perhaps for all that you may not be a more
capable Man than him, but at leaft you will bear
the part of a Man who appears to be fomething.

Here our Officer ceas'd, and I have repeated
his Difcourfe almoft the fame as I then appre-
hended it.

Juft then our Coach ftop'd, we got out, and
every one feparated to go about his particular
Bufinefs.

It was not yet Noon, and I made the beft of
my way to deliver my Letter to Mr. *Fecour*, I
had no difficulty in finding him out , for he was
a Man in great truft, and extreamly well known
in the Miniftry.

I had feveral Courts to traverfe before I came
to him, but at laft I was introduc'd into a great
Clofet, where I found him in a pretty numerous Company.

Mr. *Fecour* appeared to be between five and
fifty and fixty Years of Age ; he was tall but
not fat, fwarthy in his Countenance, and of
a gravity not cold and damping, for that is natural, and proceeds from the Character of the
Mind. Whereas his was rather humiliating than
damping : It was a proud imperious Air which
fhow'd that he was confcious of his Importance, and would be refpected.

Thofe who approach us are fenfible of thefe
differences more or lefs confufedly ; we all
know one another fo well in the Article of
Pride, that it is impoffible for any one to conceal

N

-ceal himfelf in that particular . It is fometimes, though inadvertently, the very firft thing which a Perfon obferves when he addreffes a Stranger.

But be that as it will, this was the Impref-fion which Mr. *Fecour* made upon me. I ad-vanc'd towards him in a very fuppliant manner ; he was writing, I believe a Letter, whilft his Company was talking

I made him my Compliment with that Emotion which is unavoidable, when one is a little Fellow, and goes to ask a Favour of a great Man, who neither aids, encourages, nor looks at you ; for Mr. *Fecour* heard all I faid to him without once cafting his Eyes on me.

I ftill held out my Letter which I prefented him , but he never offer'd to take it, and his little attention for me left me in a pofture which was altogether ridiculous, and from which I did not know how to recover my felf.

Befides, there was the Company I fpoke of ftaring at me , it was compos'd of three or four Gentlemen, not one of which had a Mien ca-pable of comforting me in my Perplexity.

They were rather opulent than magnificent in their Appearance, fo that I made but a con-temptible Figure before them, notwithftanding my little Silk lining.

Befides they were People advanc'd in Years, and I was no more than eighteen, which is not an Article of fo much indifference as any one may imagine ; for had you feen with what an Air they obferv'd me, you would have judg'd that my Youth was ftill another motive of Confufion for me.   What

What can this Fop want with his Letter? seem'd they to say by their liberal bold looks, which were full of unceremonious Curiosity.

So that I was nothing better than a meer Jack-pudding amongst them, who furnish'd them with a Moment's Amusement, and serv'd them to despise an *en passant*.

One examin'd me haughtily on one side; whilst another who was walking up and down this vast Closet, with his Hands behind him; stop'd sometimes by Mr. *Fecour* who continu'd writing; and there set himself to consider me conveniently at his ease.

Imagine to yourself the Countenance I must have.

Another with a pensive and abstracted Air, fix'd his Eyes upon me as if I had been a Chair or a Wall, and as a Man who was not sensible that he saw any thing.

And as this Person to whom I was nothing, embarass'd me to the full as much as he to whom I was so inconsiderable, I plainly perceiv'd that I was never the better off with one than the other.

In short I was struck with an inward Confusion. I shall never forget the Scene I am also gotten rich myself, and at least as wealthy as any of the Gentlemen I speak of but I am yet to comprehend how any Mens Tempers can become so cavalier in respect to their Fellow-Creatures, let the others be who they will.

At last however Mr. *Fecour* finished his Letter, and holding out his Hand to receive

that

that which I prefented him ; let's fee, faid he·
and immediatcly, What's a clock, Gentlemen ? Almoft Noon, reply'd negligently he
who was walking about ; whilft Mr. *Fecour*
broke open the Letter, which he read over
very haftily.

Mighty well, faid he, after he had read it.
fee' here's the fifth Man within thefe eighteen
Months that my Sifter-in-law has either wrote
or fpoke to me, to provide for, I can't devife where fhe picks up all fhe fends me ;
but there's no end with her : and this is more
recommended than any of the reft. The original Woman ' Here, you'll judge of her by
what fhe writes, added he, giving the Letter
to one of the Gentlemen.

And directly, Well, I'll take care of you,
faid he to me : I fhall return to *Paris* to-
morrow, come to me the next Morning.

Upon which I was going to take my leave
of him, when he ftopp'd me.

You are very young, faid he. What are
vou fit for ? Nothing at all, I'll venture a
Wager.

I have never yet been in any Employ, Sir,
anfwer'd I. Oh ! I don't doubt it, reply'd
he ; fhe never fends me any others and it
will be a great Happinefs if you know how
to write.

Yes, Sir, faid I, blufhing ; I alfo underftand a little Arithmetick. How now ! cry'd
he, bantering, why you do us too much Honour. Go till after to morrow.

Upon

Upon which, I retir'd, with the satisfaction of leaving these Gentlemen ready to burst with laughing at my Writing, and Arithmetick; when a Footman came to tell Mr *Fecour* that Mrs. such a one (it was so he explain'd himself) desir'd to speak to him.

Ha, ha! answer'd he, I know who she is, she comes very *à propos*, let her enter. And do you stay (it was to me he spoke).

Accordingly, I stay'd, and immediately two Ladies came in, very modestly dress'd, one of them was a young Person of about twenty Years of Age, accompanied by a Woman of about fifty.

Both of them had a melancholy suppliant air.

I never in my Life saw any thing so distinguish'd and affecting as the Face of the youngest; one could not call her a handsome Woman neither, there are other sort of features requir'd to the Composition of a Beauty.

Imagine to yourself a Countenance which has nothing in it glaring or regular enough to surprize the Eyes, but which, at the same time, wants nothing which can surprize the Heart, nothing which can inspire Respect, Tenderness, or Love, for what one felt for this young Lady, was a mixture of all I mention

There was, if I may use the Expression, a Soul upon her Countenance; but a Soul which was noble, virtuous, and tender, and consequently most charming to look at

I shall say nothing of the ancient Woman who accompanied her, and who only interested

herself

herself in the Affair by her Modefty and Sorrow.

Mr. *Fecour* had rifen from his Seat when he difmifs'd me, and was ftanding in the middle of the Clofet talking to thofe Gentlemen. He made a flight Bow to the young Lady, as fhe came towards him.

I know what brings you here, Madam, faid he, I have revok'd your Husband, but it's not my Fault if he's always ill, and incapable of attending his Employ. What would you have me do? Thefe are continual abfences.

What! Sir, faid fhe, with an Accent which was made to obtain every thing, is there no Hope, then? It's true, my Husband is in a bad State of Health, but hitherto you have had the Goodnefs to compaffionate our Condition, continue us the fame Favour, Sir; don't treat us with fo much Rigour! (and this word Rigour in her Mouth pierc'd to the very Soul) you'll throw us into a Perplexity which would touch you if you knew the whole of it. I beg you would not leave me in the Affliction which I am in, and to which I muft return, if you are inexorable: (Inexorable! was there any appearance he could be fo?) My Husband will recover; you are not ignorant who we are, nor of the extream want we have of your Protection, Sir

Don't fancy to yourfelf that fhe cry'd whilft fhe talk'd in this manner; had fhe wept, I think her Sorrow would have had lefs Dignity in it, and would have appear'd lefs folemn and affecting.

But

But the Perfon who accompanied her, and who kept a little behind her, had her Eyes bath'd in Tears

I never queftion'd a Moment but Mr. *Fecour* would yield, I thought it was impoffible he fhould hold out Alas! what a Novice I was! he was not fo much as once mov'd.

Mr *Fecour* enjoy'd an abundance, he had liv'd for thirty Years together in an uninterrupted plenty; and to talk to him of Perplexities, or Wants, or even of Poverty itfelf, was talking of Things which he had no Notion of, the bare Words excepted.

But without doubt his Heart muft have been naturally hard, for I can't believe that Profperity confirms any but your natural Obdurities.

It's no longer in my Power to oblige you, Madam, faid he, I can't forfeit my Word, I have already difpos'd of the Employ · Here's the young Man to whom I have given it, he'll tell you the fame.

At this Apoftrophe, which put me to the Blufh, fhe caft a Look at me, but a Look which feem'd to addrefs this tender Reproach. What then! will you alfo contribute to my Misfortunes?

No, Madam, reply'd I, in the fame Language, if fhe underftood me; and immediately, It's then the Poft of this Lady's Husband which you defign for me, Sir, faid I to Mr *Fecour* Yes, anfwer'd he, it's the fame. I am your Servant, Madam.

Hold, Sir, cry'd I, ftopping him, I had much rather wait till it fuits your Convenience

N 1

to give me some other   I am not press'd, permit me, if you please, to leave that honest
Gentleman in the Possession of this.   If I was
in his place, and sick as he is, I should be very
glad that any one should use the same Behaviour
to me, as I use to him.

The young Lady never once offer'd to back
my Discourse, which was an excellent Proceeding, but remain'd silent, and with her
Eyes fix'd upon the Ground, expecting Mr. *Fecour*'s Resolution, without abusing, by any Im-
portunity of her own, the generosity which I
shew'd, and which might serve as an Example
to our Patron.

As for his part, I saw that he was astonish'd
at the Example, without being pleas'd with it,
and that he did not approve of my giving my
self the air of being more compassionate than
him.

You rather chuse to wait, then, said he to
me, this is novel enough! Well, Madam,
you may return; we'll see at *Paris* what may
be done, I shall be there after to Morrow.
Go, added he to me, I'll talk to Mrs. *Fecour*.

The young Lady made him a very low
Curtsey, but no Reply; the other Woman follow'd her, and I her, and away we went out,
all three   But by the Tone with which our
Gentleman dismiss'd us, I despair'd that my
Action could any way serve the young Lady's
Husband; and I plainly perceiv'd by her Looks
that she drew no better Omen from it than my
self.

But

But I am going to tell you fomething which will furprize you, one of thofe Gentlemen who were with Mr. *Fecour*, went out a Moment after us.

We had ftopp'd at the top of the Stair cafe, the young Lady and I, where fhe return'd me Thanks for my Endeavour to ferve her, and fhew'd a gratitude with which I faw fhe was really penetrated.

The other Lady, whom fhe call'd her Mother, alfo join'd her Thanks, and I had prefented my Hand to the Daughter to affift her down Stairs, (for I had already learnt that little Politenefs) when we faw the Gentleman I fpoke of coming towards us, who approaching the young Lady, Don't you dine at *Verfailles* before you return, Madam ? faid he, ftammering, and with a blunt Tone

Yes, Sir, anfwer'd fhe. Well, reply'd he, after you have din'd, come to me to fuch an Inn, I am going there, and fhall be glad to fpeak with you; pray don't fail ¹ And you alfo, faid he to me, do you come at the fame time, you fhall not repent your Trouble; do you hear ? Adieu, a good Day, and away he pafs'd on.

Now this fat little Man, for he was both one and the other, as well as a Stammerer, was he with whom I had been the leaft diffatisfied at Mr. *Fecour*'s, and who had appear'd the leaft difcouraging to me It's good to remark that *en paffant*.

Can you guefs what he wants with us ? faid the young Lady to me. No, Madam, anfwer'd fwer'd I; I don't fo much as know who he is, I never faw him before in my Life.

We were got to the Bottom of the Stairs during this Difcourfe, and I was juft going to take my Leave of her with a great deal of Regret, when, at the firft Offer I made to that Purpofe, Since you and my Daughter are both to go to the fame Place prefently, don't leave us, Sir, faid the Mother, but do us the Honour to dine with us, for after the generous Attempt which you have made to ferve us, we fhould be very forry to have only a momentary Knowledge of fuch a worthy Gentleman as you are.

To invite me there, was to divine my Wifh. This young Lady had a fecret Charm which attach'd me to her, but I imagin'd that I only efteem'd her, was forry for her, and therefore interefted myfelf in what concern'd her.

Befides, I had acted the handfome part by her, and we are pleas'd with the Company of thofe whofe Acknowledgment we merit, at leaft this was all I comprehended by the Delight which I took in feeing her For as for Love, or any fentiment approaching it, they were entirely out of the Queftion; they never enter'd my Thoughts

I alfo applauded my Affection for her, as a laudable Tendernefs, and a Virtue, and there's an infinite Sweetnefs in believing one's felf virtuous, fo that I follow'd thefe Ladies with the moft innocent Satisfaction in the World, faying inwardly to myfelf, Go, thou art an honourable Fellow.

I ob-

I obferv'd that the Mother fpoke two or three Words a-part to the Landlady, which, without doubt, was to order fomething or other extraordinary ; but I durft not difcover that I fufpected her Intention, nor oppofe it, for fear it fhould look as if I had never known what good Living was.

About a quarter of an Hour after, Dinner was ferv'd, and we fat down to Table

The more I look at the Gentleman, faid the Mother, the more I find his Countenance anfwerable to his Behaviour at Mr. *Fecour's*. Oh my God ! Madam, reply'd I, who would not have done the fame at feeing your Daughter in the Affliction fhe was in ? Who would not have endeavour'd to refcue her from her Uneafinefs? It's very melancholy to meet with People in Trouble, and not to be able to aflift them, and efpecially when they are Perfons fo deferving as fhe I never was fo much affected in my Life as I was this Morning , I could have cry'd with all my Heart, and it was with difficulty I refrain'd from it.

This Difcourfe, tho' artlefs enough, yet was not the Language of a Peafant, as you fee ; the young Man of the Village was no longer difcernable, it was only the frank and benevolent young Man which appear'd.

What you fay, Sir, adds a new Obligation to that which we have to you already, faid the young Lady, blufhing, and perhaps without knowing why fhe blufh'd, unlefs it was that I had exprefs'd myfelf in a very tender manner, and that fhe was afraid of being too much touch'd touch'd by it; for it's certain, her Looks were more complaisant than her Words. She said what she wou'd with her Tongue, and stopp'd when she pleas'd, but when she look'd at me, the Case was alter'd, at least it seem'd so to me. And these are Remarks which are obvious to any one, and especially in the Disposition I was in.

For my part, I had nothing of that Gaiety and Vivacity which I usually had, and yet I was charm'd with being there, I only aim'd at a genteel and respectful Behaviour, that was all that amiable Countenance would allow in me; and one can't be what one will before some Faces, they have too much Awe in them.

I should never end, if I was to repeat all the obliging things which these Ladies said to me, and the great esteem they shew'd for me.

I ask'd them where they liv'd at *Paris*; and they told me, as also their Name, and that with a Franknefs which witnefs'd the fincere defire they had to see me there.

It was always the Mother who answer'd firft, after which, came the Daughter, who modeftly confirm'd what the other had said; and always, at the conclufion of her Difcourfe, I had a look which feem'd to fay more than her words.

At laft, Dinner being over, we talk'd of our Appointment, which we could not help thinking a very fingular one.

The Clock ftruck Two, and away we went. We were told that our Gentleman had juft din'd, and as he had inform'd his Servants that he expected us, we were had into a little

Room,

Room, where we waited for him, and where
he came to us a few moments after, with a
Tooth-pick in his Hand. I speak of the
Tooth-pick, because it serves to characterize
the Reception which he gave us.

I must give you his Picture. He was a fat
Man, as I have already told you, of a Stature
under the moderate Size, a heavy Gait, and a
scolding Mien, and of such a rapid Speech, that
in speaking four Words he murder'd, at least,
two.

We receiv'd him with a great many Reverences, which he let us continue as long as we
pleas'd, without being so much as once tempted
to return them, except by a little Nod of the
Head, and I don't believe his Carriage proceeded from Pride, but rather from a Forget-
fulness of all Ceremony. It was a Method
which he found commodious for him, and into
which he was insensibly fallen, by daily seeing
so many who were his Subalterns.

He advanced towards the young Lady with
the Tooth-pick, which, as you see, was very
suitable to the Simplicity of his Manners.

Oh! it's very well, said he, you are come,
then; and you, also, added he, looking upon
me. Well, and what's the Matter that you
look so melancholy? Poor young Woman! (I
need not tell you who this was address'd to)
who is this Gentlewoman that you are with?
Is she your Mother, or your Relation?

I am her daughter, Sir, answer'd the young
Lady. Oh! you are her daughter, it's mighty well, she has the Air of a good Woman,

and you too, for my part I love good people.
And this Husband of your's, what fort of
a Man is he? whence comes it that he's fo
often ill? is he old? has not he a little of the
Debauchee in him? all queftions which were
very grating, and yet ask'd with the beft in-
intention in the World, as you'll fee in the
Sequel, but which had nothing of the mollify-
ing in them, they were in a Manner fo many
little Affronts to one's felf-efteem.

We fay of fome people that they have a
heavy Hand, and it's certain this honeft Gentleman had not a very light one.

But to return it was the Husband he in-
quir'd after; he's neither Old, nor a Debauchee, reply'd the young Lady, he's a Man
of exceeding good Morals, and no more than
five and thirty Years of Age; but it's his
Misfortunes which have over-whelm'd him,
it's his troubles which have ruin'd his Health

Ay, ay, faid he, I believe it, poor Man!
that's pity; you mov'd me, when I faw you,
and your Mother too, I took notice that fhe
cry'd, but tell me, you find it hard to live
then, how old are you?

Twenty, Sir, reply'd fhe blufhing. Twenty! faid he, and why would you marry fo
young? you fee the effects of it, Children
and Croffes will come, you have but little, then
you fuffer, and farewell Oeconomy, but no
Matter! fhe's genteel, your Daughters, very
genteel, added he fpeaking to the Mother,
I like her figure much, but it's not for that
I defir'd to fee her, on the contrary, fince
                                                    fhe's

she's so prudent, I'll serve and assist her. I make great account of a young Woman who has conduct, when she's handsome and in necessity, I hardly ever saw her fellow; indeed we don't fly from those who are otherwise, but then we don't esteem them. Continue, Madam, always continue the same; and I am also mightily satisfy'd with this young Man here, yes, mightily edify'd; he must be an honourable youth by the Manner in which he talk'd just now, go, you are a good Heart, you have pleas'd me, and I have a friendship for you, his behaviour at Mr *Fecour's* was very handsome, it astonish'd me. As to the rest, if he does not give you another employ (it was to me and of Mr. *Fecour* he was speaking,) I'll take care of you, I promise you I will, come to see me at *Paris*, and you also (it was to the young Lady those Words were address'd,) we must see what Mr *Fecour* will determine for your Husband; if he replaces him, well and good, but independent of all that, I'll serve you, I have some views which will suit you, and be advantageous. But pray sit down, are you in haste? it is but half an hour after two, tell me a little of your Affairs, I should be glad to be acquainted with them; whence comes it that your Husband has had misfortunes? was he rich? of what Country are you?

Of *Orleans*, Sir, said she. Oh! of *Orleans*; that's a very fine City! reply'd he. Do your Relations live there? What's your Story? I have a quarter of an Hour to spare, and as I

intereſt myſelf in what concerns you, it's natural I ſhould deſire to know who you are,
you'll do me a pleaſure, let's hear.

Sir, ſaid, ſhe, the ſtory won't be long.

My Family is of *Orleans*, but I was not
brought up there. I am the Daughter of a
Gentleman of ſmall Fortune, and who liv'd
with my Mother about two leagues from that
City upon a little Eſtate which remain'd to
him from the ruins of his Family; and there
he dy'd.

Aha! ſaid Mr. *Bono*, (which was the Name
of our Patron) the Daughter of a Gentleman!
in good time, but what ſignifies that when
one's poor? go on.

It's now three Years ſince my Husband made
his Addreſſes to me, reply'd ſhe He was a
Gentleman of our Neighbourhood; good! cry'd
he immediately, ſee! we advance a-pace with
our Gentility. proceed.

As I was then thought agreeable; yes, ſaid
he, very right, you are ſo ſtill; Oh! you was
a little toaſt, you was the prettieſt Laſs in the
hundred, I am ſure on't: well!

I was alſo courted at the ſame time, continu'd ſhe, by a wealthy Citizen of *Orleans*.

Oh! that was ſomething, interrupted he
again, there was a Foundation, it was that Citizen you ſhould have marry'd.

I am going to tell you, Sir, why I rejected
him. He was a well-made Man, and one I had
no Averſion for, tho' I cannot ſay I lov'd him;
I only endur'd him rather than the Gentleman,
who notwithſtanding had as much Merit as he,
and

and as my Mother who was the only Perfon I depended upon after my Father's Death.

As my Mother, I fay, had left me the Choice of both, I do not doubt but that flight Sentiment of Preference which I had for the Citizen, would at leaft have determin'd me in his Favour, had not it been for an Accident, which all at once inclined me to his Rival.

It was about the beginning of Winter, and we were walking one day by the fide of a Foreft, my Mother and I and thefe two Gentlemen ; I had feparated my felf a little way from them, for I do not know what trifle which amufed me, when on a fudden a monftrous Wolf leap'd out of the Foreft, and run towards me.

You may imagine the Confternation I was in ; I flew towards my Company fcreaming with all my Power. My Mother being frighted, endeavour'd to fave her felf, and fell thro' too much Precipitation ; the Citizen alfo fled, tho' he had a Sword by his Side.

The Gentleman ftop'd, tho' alone, drew his Sword, run to me, fac'd the Wolf, and attack'd him in the very Moment that he was going to jump upon me and devour me

He kill'd him, tho' not without running the rifque of his Life, for he was wounded in feveral Places, and alfo thrown down by the Wolf with which he roll'd upon the Ground for a long time without quitting his Sword . At laft he difpatch'd that furious Animal.

Some peafants whofe Cottages border'd upon the Place, and who had been alarm'd by our

Cries,

Cries, came running to us, but not before the
Wolf was dead ; however they took up the Gentleman, who had no Power to rife himfelf, and
who ftood in extream need of fpeedy Affiftance,
having loft a great quantity of Blood.

For my part, I lay about fix Paces from him
in a Swoon, nor was my Mother in a much
better Condition ; fo that they were forc'd to
carry us all three to our Houfe, from whence we
had wander'd a confiderable way in walking

The bites which the Gentleman had receiv'd
from the Wolf, were curable enough ; but
fince worfe Confequences were to be dreaded
from the fury of that Animal, as wounded as the
Gentleman was, it was thought neceffary that
he fhould fet out the next Morning for the Sea.

I own to you, Sir, that I was touch'd by the
contempt which he had fhow'd for his Life to
fave mine (for he might have efcap'd as well as
his Rival) and ftill more touch'd to fee that he
was not at all vain upon the Action, that he fet
no Value on it, and that his Love affum'd no
Confidence upon that account.

I am not belov'd, Madam, faid he, juft as
he parted ; I have not the Happinefs to pleafe
you, but I am not fo unfortunate neither, fince
I have had that of teftifying to you that nothing
is fo dear to me as you are.

Nor ought any Perfon at prefent to be fo dear
to me as you, reply'd I without any Evafion,
and before my Mother, who appov'd my Anfwer.

Yes, yes, cry'd Mr. *Bono* directly, all this
is wonderful ! there's nothing fo fine as fuch

Senti-

Sentiments as thefe, when it's for a Romance,
I forefee that you'll marry him becaufe of his
Wounds, but hold, I had rather this Wolf had
not come in your way. it would have been luck-
ier for you to have mifs'd him, he did you a deal
of injury. But *à-propos*, this Citizen does he
run ftill? did not he return?

He had the Affurance to appear the fame evening, faid the young Lady He return'd to
our Houfe, and bore the Prefence of his wounded Rival for at leaft an Hour; which made him
ftill more defpicable than the Cowardice with
which he had abandon'd me in my Danger.

Oh! troth, cry'd Mr. *Bono*, I do not know
what to fay to that, your Servant as to love in
fuch a Cafe; as for the Vifit, let it pafs, I blame
him, but as for his Flight, it's quite a different
thing; I cannot think he was fo much in the
wrong on't, not I, this Wolf was a very vil-
lainous Animal, it muft be allow'd, and your
Husband was no better than a rafh hot-head at
the Bottom. But conclude, the Gentleman
came again, and you marry'd him, was not it fo?

Yes, Sir, reply'd the young Lady; I thought
my felf oblig'd to it.

O! as you pleafed for that, anfwer'd he, but
I regret the run-away, he would have been the
beft Match for you, becaufe he was rich; your
Husband was excellent at killing of Wolves, but
we do not always meet with Wolves in our
Way, and we have always Occafion for wherewithall to live.

My Husband, faid fhe, when I marry'd him,
had an eftate, he enjoy'd a fufficient Competence.

tence. Good! reply'd he, fufficient! what muft I underftand by that? What is fufficient does not always fuffice, but let us hear, how did he lofe this Competence?

By a law-fuit, anfwer'd fhe, which we had with a Nobleman in our Neighbourhood for certain Rights; the Suit at firft was a thing of nothing, but at laft it became fo confiderable, that upon his cafting us, which he did by the Dint of intereft, we were entirely ruin'd. My Hufband was oblig'd to come to *Paris* to endeavour to procure an employ, and being recommended to Mr. *Fecour*, he gave him one; the fame wh'ch he took away a few days ago, and for which you heard me entreat him. I do not know whether he'll reftore it, he faid nothing to me which feem'd to promife it; but I fhall go back with a great deal of Comfort, Sir, fince I have had the Happinefs to meet with fuch a generous Gentleman as you are, and one who has the Goodnefs to intereft himfelf in our Situation.

Yes, yes, faid he, do not afflict your felf, you may depend upon me; we ought to affift People who are in trouble; I would have nobody in Pain if I could help it, that's my way of thinking, but that's impoffible. And you, my Lad, of whence are you? Of *Champagne*, Sir, anfwer'd I.

Oh! that's an excellent Country for Wine, reply'd he, I am glad on't, have you a Father living there? Yes, Sir; fo much the better, faid he, you may bring him to me then, for one's often deceiv'd: well, who are you?

The

The Son of an honeſt Man who lives in the Country, anſwer'd I; which was true enough, and at the ſame time ſhunning the Word Peaſant, which appear'd harſh to me; your Synonima's are not forbidden, and as often as I have occaſionally found them for my purpoſe, I have taken the Liberty to uſe them; but my vanity never exceeded thoſe bounds, and I ſhould have ſaid plainly, I am the Son of a Peaſant, had not the other Expreſſion pop'd into my Mind.

The Clock ſtruck three; Mr. *Bono* pull'd out his Watch, and immediately riſing. Aha! ſaid he, I muſt leave you, we ſhall ſee one another again at *Paris*, I ſhall expect you there, and will be as good as my Word Good morrow, I am your Servant. But *à propos*, I ſuppoſe you return preſently, I ſhall ſend my Equipage to *Paris* in a Moment; you may as well go in my Coach, your Stage ones are chargeable, and that will be ſo much Expence better ſav'd.

Upon which he call'd to one of his Footmen is *Picard* almoſt ready to ſet out? ſaid he. Yes, Sir, he is putting his Horſes to the Coach, anſwer'd the Servant. Well then, tell him to take theſe Ladies and this young Man with him, reply'd he. Adieu.

We would have return'd him thanks, but he was already too far off. We went out, the Equipage was ready in an Inſtant, and away we went very well ſatisfy'd with our Gentleman and his blunt Humour.

I will ſay nothing to you of our Converſation upon the Road, let us make haſte to *Paris*, where

where we arriv'd in very good time for my Appointment, for you may remember that I had one with Mrs. *Ferval*, at Mrs. *Remy's* in the Suburb.

Mr. *Bono's* Coachman drove our two Ladies to their own House, where I left them after a great many Compliments, and new Invitations on their side for me to come to see them.

After which I sent back the Coachman, took a Hack, and went for my Suburb.

BOOKS *Printed for* Charles Corbet, *at* Addison's Head, *and* Richard Wellington, *at the* Dolphin and Crown, *without* Temple-Bar.

1. THE Vocal Miscellany, a neat Pocket Volume, dedicated to the Ladies of Great-Britain. Being a Collection of above four hundred celebrated Songs (which is near one hundred and fifty more than any Book of the Price extant) and many of them never before printed; with the names of the Tunes prefix'd to each Song, neatly bound in 2 Vols. and adorn'd with Frontifpieces. Price 6 s

N. B. Thefe 2 Vols. contain not only a good Collection of the moft elegant among the old Songs, but alfo above two hundred new ones, wrote by celebrated Hands, and never before printed. And befides the particular Care taken in the Choice of the Compofitions, in which the Opinion of the beft Judges has been confulted, the Tunes are likewife mentioned; which muft be allow'd a very great addition to the Work, as it enables the Reader to fing what might otherwife have been poffibly pafs'd over only as a Copy of Verfes.

2. Love Letters between a Nobleman and his Sifter, *viz.* F---rd Lord Gr---y of Werk, and the Lady Henrietta B---rkl---y, under the borrow'd Names of Philander and Sylvia. Done into Verfe by the Author of the Letters, from a Nun to a Cavalier. Adorn'd with a Frontifpiece, reprefenting Philander aud Sylvia. Printed in a neat Pocket Volume, on a fine Paper, and a good Letter. The Second Edition. Price Bound, only 1 s. 6 d.

3. The Hiftory of the Devil. Containing a State of the Devil's Circumftances, and the

various

various Turns of his Affairs, from his Expulfion out of Heaven to the Creation of Man, his Proceedings with Mankind ever fince Adam, and his more private Conduct, down to the prefent Times His Government, his Appearances, his Manner of Working, and the Tools he works with.

> *Bad as he is, the Devil may be abus'd,*
> *Be falfly charg'd, and cau'elefly accus'd,*
> *When Men, unwilling to be blam'd alone,*
> *Shift off thofe Crimes on Him which are their*
> *Own.*

The Second Edition.   Adorn'd with a Frontifpiece.   Price 5 s.

4. The Motto's of the Spectators, Tatlers, and Guardians, tranflated into Englifh.   Price Bound, 2 s. 6 d.

5 The Complaint of Job, a Poem. Price 1 s.

6. Apollo and Daphne, an Opera. Price 1 s.

7. The Stage Mutineers, or a Play-Houfe to be Let: A Tragi-Comi-Farcical-Ballad Opera.   As it is acted at the Theatre Royal in Covent Garden. By Mr. Phillips.   Price 1 s.

> *Bella !-----Horrida Bella.*   Virg.

8. *Alma Mater*, a Satyrical Poem on the Univerfity of Oxford.   Price 1 s.

9. The Fair Suicide, being an Epiftle from a young Lady to the Perfon who was the Caufe of her Death. Price 6 d.

10. A New and Eafy Method to underftand the Roman Hiftory, with an exact Chronology of the Reign of the Emperors; an Account of the moft eminent Authors, when they flourifh'd, and an Abridgment of the Roman Antiquities and Cuftoms; by way of Dialogue.   Price 2 s.

The Fortunate Peasant

Puff and Sell   28

Transfer of Stock   29

The Logic of Honour 31

Good appetite is worth
        Keeping   34

Repudiates the bargain "

The director of the Ladies 70

The direction of the
Director limited   71

The Director directed   86

A Goddess of 50 Years 181

CPSIA information can be obtained at www.ICGtesting.com
Printed in the USA
LVOW050247010212

266474LV00004B/75/P